Praise for *WWOOFing 1*

I recommend the book *WWOOFing Nor*
is considering joining or are part of the WWOOF community. From
the first chapter when Margaret Halliday arrives in New Zealand you
will be intrigued. She takes you on her journey travelling through New
Zealand and then her home country, Scotland. Margaret explains the
different activities that can be experienced while WWOOFing, from
feeding lambs to picking strawberries. She recounts the physical
experience of helping on the land and explains in perceptive,
intelligent detail what meeting, living and working beside new people
can be like. She informs that you may be out of your comfort zone and
have to cope with difficult or tragic situations but there are also
wonderful times that bring lifelong friendships. You will experience
different personalities, beliefs, cultures and attitudes and that it is up
to you to make the most of them.

I genuinely had a smile on my face when Margaret was welcomed
into people's homes and lives. These were her favourite WWOOFs –
they had a good balance of varied work, stimulating conversation,
tasty food and interesting social events. This book is full of beautifully
descriptive narratives which involve you with the people, places and
activities that Margaret experienced, as if you were with her on her
journey.

I believe this book is not necessarily country specific, it shows the
similarities and connections between us no matter where we are in the
world.   Jane Bryan-Stange *WWOOF New Zealand*

WWOOFing North and South is a travelogue, offering glimpses of the
feelings of a seasoned traveller amidst the more mundane details of
the daily experience of a WWOOFer. There are a lot of WWOOF
exchanges detailed in this book, with more than half the forty-seven
chapters telling about a new place and host.

Margaret does get homesick, she does suffer physical ills, but
usually she finds starry skies, beautiful swimming spots, good friends,
and the constant lure of the land. She is a great proponent of
WWOOFing who approaches it as much as a lifestyle choice as a
cheap way of seeing the world.   *WWOOF UK*

BY THE SAME AUTHOR

Prana Soup: An Indian Odyssey

Good Vibrations: A Story of a Single 60s Mum

WWOOFing North and South

Margaret Halliday

To all WWOOFers, past, present and future,
WWOOF hosts and the WWOOF organisation.

Contents

PART THREE: Scotland

PART ONE

NEW ZEALAND

ONE

Kiwi Starter

A one-and-a-half-metre-long forked hazel stick was my questionable companion on a round-the-world trip, which commenced just before 9/11, 2001. My poor stick was x-rayed, wrapped with security tape and sometimes removed from my grasp, to languish in some dark corner of the plane's hold. When I was allowed to keep it my fellow passengers regarded me uneasily, subtly moving away, or making jokes. 'You'll be needing that to catch snakes,' one cheery lad remarked, while the rest of the English-speaking queue for Bangkok sniggered nervously.

They allowed me to keep my stick on the flight from Singapore to Auckland. I stood in the aisle, trying to find it in the overhead locker. A helpful young man located it, gave it to me and said, 'You'll not be allowed in with that. Biosecurity are very strict, you know.'

I waited in one of the long, slow queues for customs, received my six-month tourist visa and went to the baggage carousel, where a hound sniffed my stick suspiciously and a biosecurity official examined it minutely. 'It's been varnished so no worries,' he said, handing it over with a smile. I headed for the exit, shouldering my backpack, my trusty companion held tightly in my hand. At last I was outside breathing in the balmy midday Auckland air, my pulse racing with excitement and no sign of jet lag. I easily found the airport bus and looked avidly out of the window as the suburbs passed by. Everything reminded me of home – the neat gardens full of colourful flowers, the tidiness, traffic on the left and English speech. But it was also different. It was summer instead of winter, green instead of grey, relaxed and warm instead of rigid cold.

This trip to New Zealand would be different from the other places I'd visited. I was going to work my way round the country, volunteering on organic farms and smallholdings. In return I'd receive food and lodging. This is known as 'WWOOFing' – worldwide opportunities on organic farms, a wonderfully cheap way to get to

1

know a country and its culture.

The bus quickly reached the centre where the highest landmark, the Sky Tower, rose 328 metres into the blue sky. I'd reserved a bed at the central youth hostel, a large modern building a short walk from the bus terminus. I was keen to escape the city and start WWOOFing as soon as possible, so I phoned my chosen host from the *WWOOF* booklet, which gave details of location and the type of work. Unfortunately, they were full. I tried others and was getting desperate when one of the hosts gave me a friend's number, who wasn't in the booklet, but I trusted that it would be all right. A man's voice answered the phone, with a trace of a German accent, 'Sure, I've got plenty work and can give you a room in my house,' he said. It was arranged that he'd meet me off the bus at Whangarei, north-east of the capital, the following afternoon.

In the morning I walked to the bus station where I boarded a north-bound coach. It sped through beautifully green countryside dotted with tree ferns in areas of bush. Further north long sandy beaches between high cliffs came into view. Then I saw mangroves in muddy swamps. Now it was reminding me less of home. I felt myself falling in love with this verdant land.

Three hours later, after a lunch stop, I got off the coach and was instantly hailed by a fit-looking, fair-haired man. 'You must be the WWOOFer,' he stated, shaking my hand. 'I'm Franz.' This was an easy guess as I'd been the only single female to leave the bus. I followed him to his mud-spattered truck. In it, to my relief, was a young woman and a small girl, sitting in the back.

'Hi, I'm Jenny and this is Rosie,' she said with a smile. I immediately relaxed. *This is going to be fine,* I thought. As we drove along the narrow, winding roads I discovered that Franz was forty-two and German. He had lived in New Zealand half of his life and had travelled widely in Africa and South America. Jenny, his girlfriend, was a local Kiwi, with her own place just down the road from his. Rosie, her daughter, was seven.

After about half-an-hour we arrived at Franz's home. It was a huge, wooden octagonal house which he had built himself, surrounded by seven acres of ground. There were bananas, plum and pear trees, mandarin bushes, vegetables and flowers. He had also built an African hut, incongruously complete with pizza oven. Like many Kiwi houses it had a rainwater supply tank, with an electric pump. The space inside

2

the house was enormous. Downstairs there were three bedrooms, a huge bathroom with a massive, multi-coloured mosaic bath and a spacious kitchen-cum-lounge/dining room. I was delighted to find that my room was upstairs in the dome, which was accessed by a winding wooden staircase and had eight windows looking out on the sky all around. From it I was able to peer down through the carved banister to the lounge below.

Jenny made a delicious seafood pasta with mussels they'd snorkelled for that morning and served it with salad and sweet corn from the garden. I felt completely at home and happily did the washing-up. Afterwards, in the evening calm, I walked along the drive and across the road. There was a vast expanse of sand, the tide being way out from the estuary; in the distance there were small islands. There was no-one around – it was so peaceful. I returned to the house and went to bed, the jet lag catching up with me but before I went to sleep I gazed out of all the eight windows at the starlit sky and the moon. Never had I seen so many stars and the moon seemed to be the wrong way round. Then, to the strident song of the cicadas, I fell asleep.

*

The next few days passed peacefully. It was hot in the middle of the day so I worked early morning and then again before dinner, around five hours in total, which was what most Kiwi hosts expected. I weeded, raked, spread mulch around plants, planted bananas and cleaned the huge house windows. In the afternoons I went swimming or kayaking with Franz, Jenny and Rosie. The sea's waves knocked me over, but once past them it was calm and perfect for swimming. Rosie was learning to surf on her small board, fearless.

I was keen to see some of the many beaches in the area and on the fifth day at breakfast Franz said, 'We're going out to collect seaweed today. It's great for mulching the bananas and enriches the soil.' He threw the wheelbarrow into the back of the truck and we set off. He drove like a whirlwind and I clung onto the window ledge, the wind tearing through my curly, brown hair. I soon lost count of the number of beaches. At each one we ran along the sand, piling seaweed into the barrow. There was hardly time to pause for breath. At one beach, the waves were so high I was scared to swim but Franz raced

3

in, diving under them, laughing with delight. I watched, astonished at his fearlessness. Finally, we came to a beach with a wonderfully blue, calm sea. *Now I can swim.* But Franz said, 'Only for three minutes. There's no time.'

Why the hurry? Later I would understand his haste. I rushed into the sea, the joy of it dampened by the time restriction. Then we were off again, gathering seaweed in one last desperate dash.

At the last place there was a little shop with a bench outside. 'Do you fancy an ice lolly?' he asked.

'Yes, thanks Franz. I'm parched.' I sat down on the bench, ready to fully enjoy it but once again he was in such a hurry: he had an appointment to keep.

'Come on, we have to go.' He was already heading for the truck, frantically licking his lolly. I clambered in, clutching mine. He drove with one hand, the other holding his ice. He ate it so fast, I wondered if he'd tasted it at all. Once home, he grabbed a sandwich. I watched him, munching slowly. He had hardly swallowed his last mouthful. 'Do you want to come out in the catamaran?'

'No thanks. I'll just rest, if that's OK?'

'Yes, that's fine,' he responded. And with that he was off.

*

I heaved a sigh of relief. The morning had been frantic, exhausting even, almost surreal. All I wanted now was to wind down and relax with a cool shower. I entered the big bathroom and stepped into the shower cubicle. Turned on the water. None came. *Damn.* I pulled on my sweaty, grimy clothes and climbed up to my room, hot and a little irritated. I lay down on the bed and tossed and turned in the sticky heat until, finally, I sank into a deep sleep.

I was awakened by voices, men's voices, coming from downstairs. There seemed to be a lot of them. *Franz must be back with some friends,* I thought. Slowly I slid off the bed and looked through the banister. *What a shock.* There were three large policemen talking to another guy. No Franz. As if in a dream, I glided down the stairs. Four pairs of eyes turned in my direction. 'What's happened?' I stammered.

'What's your relationship to Mr Schmidt?' one asked.

'I'm the WWOOFer,' I replied.

The policemen looked warily at each other until one asked,

'What's that?' I hesitantly explained my presence in the house.

'Sit down,' another one said, who seemed to be in charge. 'Mr Schmidt is dead. He was electrocuted dragging his catamaran onto the sand. The mast touched the electric wires above. He was found by the electricity men who were investigating the power cut.'

He paused, watching me closely. I sat stunned, unable to grasp what had happened. He looked at me more kindly. 'I'm going to have to ask you some questions.' He extracted from me every detail of that hectic day, for I must have been the last person to see him alive. I felt as if I were a suspect and wanted to cry, *why are you interrogating me?*

Finally, he stopped, placing his notebook and pen in his top pocket. 'Would you like us to provide victim counselling?'

'Oh, I don't need that. I hardly knew him,' I muttered, still feeling as if I were in a dream.

After they'd gone I felt the African hut calling me. The wind had got up and there was a strange atmosphere. I lit some candles and sat inside in the quiet stillness thinking of Franz and his last, hurried day, rushing toward his appointment with death. Jenny appeared at the entrance, her suntanned face pale and drawn. She sat down next to me. 'Please tell me everything about today, Margaret.' Once more I related all the details of that strange, hectic day. Then we sat silently gazing at the flickering flames of the candles.

*

We came out of our reverie with the arrival of Douglas, a neighbour. He had been there for a meal a couple of evenings before. Jenny got up saying she had to make some phone calls. When she'd gone Douglas said, 'Jenny needs some space. She'll have to phone his family in Germany and his ex-wife.' He went on, 'We're having a memorial dinner tonight and you're welcome to come.' I gratefully accepted and went to freshen up and change. By then the electricity was back on. I walked up the hill behind the house to Douglas's place. It had a superb view of the beach, distant hills and islands. He had a lovely golden Labrador. 'She was acting funny all afternoon,' he remarked. 'Barking and running to and fro looking down at the beach.'

Gradually other neighbours came. When we were all gathered together, I joined in the group hug and prayer for Franz. Then I gazed down at the beach where he had died. It seemed unreal. Tomorrow I'd move on and soon it would become just a distant memory.

TWO

Hokianga Heaven

The day I left Franz's place was Waitangi Day, a national holiday, and I was going there. Waitangi is where the treaty between the Maori people and representatives of Queen Victoria's government was signed on 6 February, 1840. With this momentous treaty the Maori tribes accepted British governorship, but also they were granted Maori citizenship and land rights.

One of Franz's neighbours gave me a lift to Whangerai where I got a bus north to Paihia, a tourist hub for the beautiful Bay of Islands. After booking myself into a hostel and consuming a Chinese carry-out lunch, I walked across the bridge to Waitangi, where dozens of Maori children were jumping into the sea, screaming and laughing, their coffee-coloured bodies glinting in the hot sunshine.

I saw the Treaty House, where the treaty was signed, and wandered down its splendid sweep of lawn to the bay where I rested in the shade marvelling at the views all around of the Bay of Islands. Across the lawn was the Maori *Whare Runanga* (meeting house), completed in 1940 to mark the centenary of the treaty. It was covered with magnificent wooden carvings of the major Maori tribes.

The next day I went on a cruise of the Bay of Islands. Swimming with dolphins was promised, but only if they were adults, so when we sighted a group of about fifty bottle-nosed dolphins with their babies, we could only watch, entranced, as they swam under the hull and leapt out of the sea all around us – a superb, unforgettable sight. Later shoals of skipjack tuna glided past, while gannets dive bombed into the water with their yellow, pointed beaks. We stopped at the town of Russell, a quaint place with late nineteenth century wooden houses and a hotel. I walked across the peninsula and swam in the sea on the other side. There was a bench at the top with lovely views of blue sea dotted with green islands where I sat and wondered about Franz, his sudden exit from the world, and was glad to be alive.

*

Fortunately, when I phoned my second WWOOF choice, they had a vacancy. It was in the Hokianga, a wild, unspoilt region around the convoluted Hokianga Harbour over on the north-west side of Northland. I'd been instructed to get off the bus at Rawene, a tiny settlement where the ferry made a short trip across the harbour to Kohu Kohu, a delightful place in a quiet backwater on the north side of the harbour. I strode onto the small ferry and sat down on the only bench, next to a young man, also with a backpack.

'Hi, I'm John,' he said. 'Where are you heading?'

There weren't that many places to choose from. 'I'm going to WWOOF at a community in the hills above Kohu Kohu,' I replied.

'I guess we're going to the same place,' he laughed. 'It's a small country, New Zealand, especially if you're WWOOFing. I keep bumping into folk that I've met before.' He had been travelling around for several months WWOOFing and so was able to give me recommendations, as well as some warnings about unsuitable places which made you work too hard or didn't feed you enough. 'The great thing about being a WWOOFer is that if you don't like somewhere, you can just up and leave, although that doesn't often happen,' he said, smiling at me reassuringly.

We were met off the ferry by Wally, one of the community members, with his muddy truck; WWOOFing hosts never had clean vehicles. 'Welcome to Kohu Kohu, the best place in New Zealand,' he said, and I was soon to agree with him. There was no sign of any habitation at the ferry terminal as the village was further along the road, in the opposite direction from where we were going. Wally, who was a Kiwi, chatted easily as he drove up a steep, unsurfaced road with few dwellings visible. Rolling green hills stretched for miles, cattle and sheep grazing in fields interspersed with areas of thick bush.

After about twenty minutes he turned off the road down a steep track and stopped outside a wooden shack. We clambered out, keen to explore our new abode. Wally led the way into the shack. 'This is where the WWOOFers stay,' he said. 'There are two rooms, one with bunk beds, the other with a double bed.'

'I'll take the bunk room, if you'd like, Margaret,' offered John.

'That's kind of you,' I replied, taking off my pack and depositing it in the front double room.

Wally explained the bathroom situation. 'There's a bathroom in here, but please go easy on the water. We haven't had much rain this summer and are running low. You can always freshen up with a swim in the pond, plus we've built a small sauna there, which is a great way to relax after a hard day's graft.' He passed a hand over his shiny, balding head, smiling at us through his glasses.

'What a wonderful idea,' John responded, 'I'll start one tonight, if that's OK?'

'Sure, no worries,' was Wally's reply.

There was something missing, something important, I'd noted. 'Where's the loo, Wally?'

'Oh, I thought I'd forgotten something!' he chuckled, 'follow me.' We trailed behind him down a narrow path to where a small, timber shed was situated beneath the shade of some trees. He pulled aside the multi-coloured bead curtain in the doorway. 'This is our pride and joy, our compost loo,' he stated and proceeded to explain its workings. 'You notice there are two seats, one of which is covered up. That one's full and it's left to break down, after which we go round the back, where there's a drop, and dig out all the great, sweet-smelling compost.'

'Where do you use it?' I wanted to know.

'We spread it round our fruit trees in the orchard,' he answered. 'It's probably OK to use it on the vegetables, but we don't like to risk it.' We stepped outside the loo. 'Please pee around the place and only use the loo for solid stuff,' he explained. 'It's not good for it to get too wet – that's when it can become smelly. After you've been cover it up with brown vegetation, like wood chippings or dried grass, which we keep in the big bowls inside. If you notice them becoming empty feel free to forage for some more – there's plenty stuff around.'

Wally looked at us. 'Any questions?' Neither of us had any, but I was thinking, *when's lunchtime?*

'Right, I guess it's time for lunch,' he said, reading my mind. He led the way past our WWOOFing shack to another larger timber building, accessed by a flight of wooden steps, with pots of geraniums on either side. 'This is the main communal area,' he said, sitting down on one of the worn settees on the veranda to take off his boots. We did likewise and followed him into a large, airy room, with a wood-burning stove on one side, surrounded by old, comfy chairs, and a spacious kitchen on the other.

We helped set the long table, while Wally produced a large bowl of garden salad, decorated with nasturtium flowers, a leaf beet and

9

cheese quiche and a loaf of home-made brown seeded bread. 'There's only the three of us for lunch today. Angela, the owner and another woman and her daughter will be here for dinner,' we were told. 'Before each meal, except breakfast, when we help ourselves, we have a sharing circle,' he said, stretching out his hands. We stood around the table laden with wholesome food and shut our eyes. 'Blessings on the food, the land from which it came and welcome to our new WWOOFers, Margaret and John,' Wally intoned melodically.

Over our meal he explained that we were expected to work around four to five hours a day, with about one day a week on cooking and kitchen cleaning duty, although everyone helped with clearing the dishes and washing-up. He told us that most people worked mornings, resting in the heat of the afternoon and possibly doing a little more work before dinner, especially watering the vegetable gardens with water pumped from the pond.

In the afternoon Wally showed us the rest of the place. Across a wide expanse of lawn there was a large wooden building, with an outside deck. 'We call this the Whale Lodge,' he said, sliding open the glass door. The reason for the name was immediately apparent. The far wall was covered in a striking mural: two large greyish-blue whales swam in a turquoise sea, waves breaking on its surface, hilly islands rising on either side. Above was a white sky in which black and white clouds were suspended, strange, serpent-like creatures sliding out of them. Against this wall was a drum kit and various other musical instruments, including a piano. It was a charming, spacious room, with sunlight flooding through the French windows which overlooked the bush-covered land, totalling around sixty acres. We wandered around, taking in the calm atmosphere. 'We use this space for yoga, meditation, music and meetings. A lot of WWOOFers come in the early morning to meditate or practise yoga,' Wally said. I decided to do this before breakfast each day. I'd found it hard to keep doing the yoga and meditation I'd studied in India on this round-the-world trip. The Whale Lodge was the perfect place to reconnect.

Wally lived in a caravan on the edge of the bush, while the others inhabited caravans tucked away in the vegetation. There were also two small wooden cabins where WWOOFers could stay. We were shown the vegetable gardens, bursting with produce: lettuce, spinach and leaf beet, tomatoes, courgettes, squashes, carrots and kumara (sweet potatoes), onions and herbs: basil, parsley, mint, oregano and marjoram, all grew abundantly in the warm, semi-tropical climate. Banana trees flourished on the slopes above the garden, their huge leaves pointing out horizontally to catch the light, a profusion of flowers, nasturtiums and marigolds, surrounding them. In the orchard were apple, pear, plum, peach, nectarine and avocado trees. There were also orange, lemon and mandarin bushes, while other more exotic fruits were feijoa, passion fruit, tamarillo and persimmon; their sweet fragrance filled the air. These didn't mature until the autumn, when I would taste their delights.

Later John and I were put to work sieving earth into barrows, which he wheeled down to the vegetable garden, where it would be used for sowing seeds in the small greenhouse. By early evening we were ready for a swim and sauna. John took kindling and little logs inside and lit the pot-belly stove, which soon heated up the small space. We stripped off and sat sweating, melting in the heat. Then we dived into the pond, squealing with the shock of the cold water. I pushed through the pond weed's silky tendrils which caressed my body. Then I rolled over and gazed at the darkening sky, the Milky Way hazily close amongst a myriad of stars. I wished that I could stay like that forever, suspended in time. Clambering out I sat on a wooden bench, wrapped in a towel. John went back in the sauna. I took a deep breath of the air, laden with the scents and smells of vegetation. Eerie cries from the possums echoed around the place while the croaking of frogs in the pond provided a melodious accompaniment.

Suddenly, in the moonlight, I spotted a woman walking slowly barefoot along the narrow path, which wound its way around the pond, overhung by large willow trees. As she approached I saw that she was beautiful, curvaceous, with long, wavy dark-blonde hair, hazel eyes and golden skin. She was not so much walking as gliding along on her broad feet, her shapely legs just glimpsed beneath her long, flowing skirt. She seemed calm, almost detached from reality but at the same time like Mother Earth, totally at one with her environment. She paused for a moment, threw her arms up wide towards the sky, and took a deep breath of warm air, sighing with contentment.

'Oh – I didn't see you there,' she exclaimed, coming out of her reverie.

'Sorry to disturb you,' I replied, watching as she sat down slowly on the bench beside me.

'You must be Margaret, the new WWOOFer.'

'Yes, that's right and I guess you're Angela?'

Angela turned out to be another German but she'd lived so long in New Zealand that she'd become more like a Kiwi – relaxed in her own skin, open to whatever the universe flung at her, and it had flung a lot. 'I'm going for a swim,' she said, slipping out of her clothes, wading into the water as it gradually enveloped her. Then with a small cry she started to swim strongly towards the far side.

While we'd been at the pond Lillavarti, the other female member of the community, had been busy preparing a delicious vegetable curry with rice, naan and salad. We stood in a circle, Kaishalah, Lillavarti's ten-year-old daughter, joining us. John felt moved to say, 'Thanks to the universe for bringing me to this wonderful place,' with which we all agreed. The food tasted especially good after our swim and sauna and not long after we'd done the dishes we went to bed, already feeling as if we were home.

*

Sundays were rest days. It felt good to lie in bed, listening to the rain pattering on the roof. It rained frequently, but there was also plenty of sunshine. We had a sharing circle in the Whale Lodge and John showed us his Osho Zen Tarot cards, each with an exquisitely coloured image depicting conditions and states of mind. The goal of the deck is not to foretell the future, but to develop awareness, an understanding of the here and now. In that setting, with the whales looking on, it was easy to be present in the moment. Lunch was eaten in almost total companionable silence, the mood produced by the cards lasting until the table was cleared.

Then Angela announced, 'There's a music party at our neighbour's house later today, if you fancy going?' We certainly did. The nearest neighbour lived a good fifteen-minute walk up the road, and as we drew near sounds of lively jazz and blues music filled the air.

We were welcomed in true Kiwi style by Bruce, the owner. 'Come on in out of the rain,' he urged us, pushing through the throng inside. 'There's nibbles in the kitchen and plenty of punch. Just help yourselves,' he said, disappearing outside to join the smokers, who were lounging around on the large deck. Marijuana grew well in the hot, humid conditions and I smelt whiffs of it entering the room. A

12

jovial, plump man with a bushy white beard was playing a piano, while a tall, striking-looking woman whose long black hair was tied back with a rainbow-coloured scarf, accompanied him, singing into a microphone, her strong voice easily reaching the high notes. After a few glasses of punch they let me sing. Gripping the mike I warbled, *'But now that your lips are burning mine, I'm beginning to see the light.'* Emery, the pianist, an amiable American, had handed me the lyrics. At the end there were claps and cries of, 'Good on ya, gal!' I knew I'd been a little flat, a little off key, but it didn't matter. These folk were uncritical, simply enjoying themselves after a hard week's work on the land; I felt as if I were one of a great, big happy family – a wonderful sensation.

Wally gave us all a lift back in his truck through the pouring rain. It was dark and difficult to see out of the windows. Suddenly we saw two bright eyes peering at us and he swerved, just missing the possum. 'Damn! I should've got him,' he swore. Kiwi drivers deliberately run over possums, who stand stupidly in the centre of the road, blinded by the headlights. They are a major introduced pest, destroying vast acres of native bush, inflicting terrible damage to trees such as rata, totara and the pohutukawa, called the 'Christmas tree', with its magnificent crimson flowers in December.

*

One day after lunch Mick, who I'd met at the music party, turned up to use the computer. He was an intriguing character and lived in a house bus on Bruce's land. When he'd finished he came and sat next to me on the sofa outside the communal area. 'I'm going down to Kohu Kohu, if you'd like to come,' he said. As I still hadn't been there I accepted. It was a fine day after all the rain, but Mick was still wearing wellies, in which he seemed comfortable driving his jeep. I'd noticed that Kiwis who lived in the country either drove barefoot or with their welly boots on.

Kohu Kohu was a lovely little place with a few one-hundred-year-old kauri wooden villas, a masonic lodge, an Anglican church, an old police station and a disused primary school – a new one had been built in the village. Mick told me that there were about one hundred and fifty inhabitants, whose houses were scattered widely around. 'Come and I'll show you the main tourist attraction,' he chuckled as we walked along the road by the harbour. He stopped and pointed to a broken timber jetty, on the end of which was resting an ancient rusting lorry. 'That's it! Every tourist that comes here takes a photo of it. We've even got postcards in the post office.' To prove his point we went into the tiny post office, which had restricted opening times, and, of course, I bought a postcard of the famous site.

As Mick showed me round he told me about himself. 'I was recruited from England twenty-three years ago as a maths and science secondary teacher. Then I took early retirement to look after my wife. She died of motor neurone disease seven years ago.' We'd sat down on a bench outside the church and he looked so sad, I didn't know what to say. Then he suddenly said, 'Let's go to the shop for ice cream.'

'Good idea,' I replied, glad that his mood had changed.

While we sat enjoying our ice creams he told me a strange story. 'When I was eleven years old I saw a newsreel about the famous Opononi dolphin and I said, "I'll live there some day." Then I forgot all about it, until I landed up here.' Opononi is a small settlement on the southern shore of the Hokianga Harbour. A friendly dolphin came to visit so many times back in 1955, he was called 'Opo'. He played with children and learned tricks with beach balls, becoming a national attraction. He was found dead, possibly killed accidentally by illegal dynamite fishermen. Outside the pub there is a sculpture of Opo, which marks his grave.

Another afternoon Mick took us on a jaunt west to the wild and rugged coast around the isolated settlement of Mitimiti. He liked to test Susie (his Suzuki jeep) to the limit, which we were soon to discover. The empty sandy beach stretched for miles, wild waves pounding at its edge as the tide went out. 'We're going to drive along the beach to go back,' he announced with a gleam in his eyes.

John encouraged him, 'Sounds great, mate.' Alarm bells were ringing in my head, but I kept silent not wishing to spoil their fun. We drove south for miles, heading towards the mouth of the Hokianga Harbour, with no sign of habitation. The sand was firm and flat. But then we reached a steep gully, with rocks on the other side. There was no way round it.

'Right, we'll have to go down and then up and over the rocks,' Mick said gleefully, revelling in the challenge to come.

'I'm getting out,' I said, opening the door.

'No worries, Margaret. Susie can do it.' I got out and watched in dreaded fascination as Susie went down into the gully. Mick accelerated hard up the other side, sand flying in all directions. Then he negotiated his way across the rocks, slowly, carefully, the jeep balancing at such crazy angles, I thought that it must topple over. It didn't. I scrambled up to join them on the flat sand on the far side. Mick looked at me, laughing loudly. 'You see, she did it!' I congratulated him on his driving skills and got in once more. There were a few trickier bits where John had to get out and direct him over the rocks and gullies. Finally, we almost got stuck in the sand, but Susie conquered this last obstacle and was rewarded by mad dashes through a freshwater stream to rinse the sea water from her body. I swam in the sea at the harbour mouth, watched by the guys, who said it was too cold.

On my last Saturday John went surfing with Wally while Mick took me to the Broadwood Agricultural Show, further along the road from the community. Many Maori lived there. They cooked meaty lunches wrapped in tin foil, in pits lined with hot stones (*hangi*). The show was a lively affair, with sheep shearing and wood cutting competitions, accompanied by frantic commentaries and frenzied cheering from the onlookers. There was also horse-jumping, prizes for champion goats, bulls, rams and so on, as well as for floral displays and home produce like vegetables, fruit and jams.

Afterwards we went back to Kohu Kohu to visit the singer from the music party. She lived in a beautiful, old wooden house, which had an aviary in the garden. She also had two cats, one of which was three-legged. He proved that he could get around by catching a baby kingfisher, which she rescued. We decided to take it to the Tree House Backpackers, where it flew away easily. They kept many exotic birds there and I was given a guided tour around the attractively designed accommodation. It is one of the best backpackers in the country.

I had been in the Hokianga for ten days. It was time to head south but I promised that I would return towards the end of my trip, as I gave everybody a big hug. 'Well, no-one's died while you've been here, so I guess you're not cursed,' Angela joked. 'We'll be happy to have you back.'

THREE

Old Man in a Caravan

The drive down the west coast wove its way through Waipoua Kauri Forest, sanctuary to several huge kauri trees, the oldest of which precedes Jesus Christ at around four-thousand years old, with a girth of 5 metres. The tallest kauri, *Tane Mahuta* (The Lord of the Forest) towers to 51 metres. The bus stops to give passengers the opportunity of viewing it up close as it is a short walk from the road. I stood staring up at this giant, on whose distinctive, blotchy mosaic bark grew numerous epiphytic plants. These massive trees have a spiritual significance to the Maori and I understood this as I felt dwarfed by and yet at one with its splendour.

The small town of Thames is the starting point for exploring the beautiful Coromandel Peninsula and I took a bus there the following day. I found a cheap backpackers not listed in the *Lonely Planet* guide book and was given a room to myself, followed by a delicious Devonshire tea in their café. I had to find somewhere to WWOOF but after about twenty phone calls I had to give up – they were either full or out. Thames had a history of gold-mining and I visited the mine the next morning. A strange-looking man with a long, straggly grey beard and hair to match showed me round, rather reluctantly. Somehow we touched on the subject of ghosts. He fixed me with a spooky stare. 'Ghosts aren't spirits. They are demons of past people which vaporise when you say, "Jesus".' I must have looked unconvinced. 'I've experienced this, you know,' he insisted, making me feel uneasy.

I was glad to get out of there and board the bus bound for Coromandel town. I stayed in another backpackers and managed to arrange a WWOOF. It was with an old-sounding man, which I wasn't too happy about, having previously decided not to go to places with lone males, but there were no other options. *He sounds harmless,* I told myself and he had said that another female WWOOFer would also be there. The area around Tauranga, where I wanted to go, was intensely agricultural and the farmers tended to use temporary paid labour at peak times like fruit picking.

Since I had moved on to Whitianga, on the north-east coast of the Coromandel Peninsula, I took an early morning bus back to Thames. As it sped along there were stunning views of the Alderman Isles to the east where silvery streams of sun stabbed through puffy clouds, while to the west showers of rain swept across the green bush-covered hills of the Coromandel range. Thames was reached in a couple of hours and soon I was on another bus bound for my destination of Kati Kati, just north of Tauranga in the Bay of Plenty region.

John, my WWOOFing host, was there to meet me. He was accompanied by the female WWOOFer, Erica. John was a fit and wiry character in his early seventies. Erica was a large and solid thirty-year-old Austrian. She seemed already to be at ease with John I noted as I climbed into the back of the muddy van with her. We had been travelling for around half-an-hour, mainly in silence, as I was feeling drowsy after my early start. Suddenly Erica muttered, 'We're nearly there. Be prepared for a shock. See, it's over there.'

'Where?' I was anxiously looking in the direction she was pointing but could only see a large, dilapidated shed, with a corrugated iron roof. 'Where's the house?'

'There's no house. Just the shed.' She laughed at my worried face. 'Don't worry. It's not that bad.'

John drew up before the shed's big metal door. 'Welcome to my humble abode,' he solemnly said. Drawing a large key out of his pocket, he unlocked the heavy door and slid it open. I gaped in astonishment. 'I just can't bear to throw them away. They're like my children and one of these days I'm gonna fix 'em up.'

We carefully navigated our way through a variety of ancient cars, in varying states of disrepair. Car parts, tools and other stuff I labelled as 'junk' filled the spaces in between. Erica pointed at one, a mini with what looked like a metal tent on its roof, complete with a ladder leading up to it. 'That's my place,' she said, smiling. *Thank God,* I thought. *There's no way I could get up there. But where will I stay in this dump?* My unspoken question was soon answered as a caravan came into view at the far end, behind some more car wrecks.

Opening the caravan door John remarked, 'This is where you'll sleep. You've got privacy from me at the other end, so no worries.' He went in and pulled across a faded curtain. *Some privacy!* I was not impressed, but tried hard not to let it show. He must have guessed my thoughts, though. 'I know it's a bit different. That's why I didn't give much of a description in the *WWOOF* booklet. Give it a couple of days and you'll feel fine. Most of the folk who come here are like that.'

What could I say? I was stranded in the middle of the countryside with no transport. The least I could do was to stick it out for one night. John had more thrilling information to impart. 'The only thing is, I share with my four cats. They're sweeties but they do love to hunt at night and bring their trophies in the early hours.' I shuddered, surveying the filthy bedding in disgust.

'Well, I'll stay for tonight and then we'll see,' I said regretfully.

'Great!' he exclaimed. 'Let me give you a tour to the most important bits.'

I followed him along a winding path through the clutter. A toilet, complete with seat, was hidden in a corner behind some cars. 'A very clever Aussie guy plumbed that in a couple of weeks ago,' he enthused. I tried not to imagine how it was before that. Next we went outside where the 'shower' was. It was simply a hose, supplying only cold water and in full view of the neighbour's kiwi fruit orchard, alongside of which was a narrow track. 'No worries. It's a nice, refreshing shower in this heat and you hardly ever see anyone over there. Just tell me when you're going to have one and I'll make myself scarce,' he chortled. Then he showed me a small outside sink which was connected up to a rainwater tank. 'We get plenty rain here, so it never runs dry and it's good, clean water, so no worries.' *No worries, no worries,* I repeated to myself in an effort to relax.

We wandered through his garden, which was very overgrown. Some WWOOFers had made raised beds and had carved their names into the wooden surrounds. 'Made by Sean and Lorna from Ireland. January 2001.' Others had painted colourful signs with their names and origins. Still more were thanking John for their wonderful stay. It was all most surprising.

On the other side of the garden was a field. John pointed out his four sheep, some chickens and ducks, all of which had names which he lovingly recited. He certainly did seem a lovely guy and I wondered why he was alone. Later he told me he had never married because the ones he had liked had not wanted him and vice versa. It was obvious that he took in WWOOFers for company rather than anything else.

For lunch I picked salad from the garden – lettuce, leaf beet, herbs and tomatoes, while Erica cooked up a pot of noodles – very simple and cheap food indeed. Afterwards John drove us about five miles away to a sandy beach. He left us there to explore: there was no plan to collect us. I swam in the warm sea while Erica traipsed around beachcombing; she was not keen on getting wet. We walked right round the cove until we found a back road. There was no traffic until eventually we got a lift from a man in a truck who was gnawing on a chicken leg while driving. His terrier, perched on the seat beside him, kept trying to snatch it. At the same time he was turning round to chat with us. We could not understand him – his accent was too coarse and his mouth too full. He had long, matted hair and was unshaven. Despite all this, he seemed to know where we lived and took us right up to the door. He drove away, waving the remains of the chicken bone out of the window.

We were famished after our adventure. The three of us foraged in the garden and found potatoes, carrots, kumara, leaf beet and more salad leaves. We prepared a big pot of vegetables and had them with omelettes, courtesy of the chooks (chickens). We chatted a while, then went to bed. I was exhausted after my long and eventful day and fell asleep immediately, all my worries evaporating into dreams.

The next morning dawned bright and sunny. I washed in the outside sink and things did not seem so bad. A good night's sleep does wonders for the spirits. John had not snored and no cats had disturbed me with their offerings. When I went back to the caravan my host was busy stirring a large saucepan of thick porridge. He ate no dairy, partly due to the lack of a fridge, but also because he claimed it was bad for the health.

After downing large bowlfuls of porridge Erica and I did some clearing and weeding in the garden. We discovered more vegetables, including potatoes, beetroot and onions, which we harvested for later. John called us in for a lunch of baked beans on toast plus salad. After clearing up he announced that we were free that afternoon. He certainly did not overwork us, unlike some of the other hosts. I took the opportunity to do some clothes washing in the sink (there was no washing machine). Then I washed myself with the hose, keeping a watchful eye on the kiwi orchard track. Not a soul was around. The large bushes were laden with the green fruit, which was almost ready to harvest. My whole being glowed after the exhilarating coldness of

19

the shower.

We had vegetable curry with rice for dinner over which we had an interesting discussion about genetically engineered crops, which our host knew a good deal about. Like most folk in the organic movement he was against their introduction. Then John switched on his small, portable TV. As there was nothing on that interested me I went for a wander outside and then caught up with my diary and read some of the fascinating comments by WWOOFers in his *WWOOF* book. Most of them were young, from Europe, Australia or Japan and camped in their own tents in a field next to the sheep.

A second night passed peacefully. The following day John said that he did not want to work. He included us in this. Erica, however, decided to clean the caravan. I helped her and soon it was transformed. Our host appeared muttering that he wouldn't be able to find anything. 'No worries. I've put everything back in exactly the same place,' she said soothingly.

After lunch he was going to the city of Tauranga on business. He offered us a lift so I decided to take this opportunity to leave as I was bored and had planned to move on to Tauranga anyway. Erica was going to stay a while longer. She got on well with John and seemed to enjoy bossing him around. He dropped me at the youth hostel. ''Bye Margaret, thanks for all your hard work,' he said as he drove off happily, Erica at his side. He was taking her out to dinner that evening. Lucky Erica!

FOUR

Tauranga to Taupo

Tauranga, situated on the Bay of Plenty, is New Zealand's fastest growing city. Its favourable climate and position has attracted many businesses, as well as retirees, and the expanding suburbs are full of newly-built brick bungalows with neat gardens. I spent two nights there and walked round Mt Maunganui, a town just across the inlet from Tauranga, which is at the foot of the mountain. There were lovely sea views all around, the water a clear blue and I swam and picnicked at a couple of fine beaches. I was walking barefoot up a small hill at the walkway's end when I felt a sudden stab of pain. It must have been a bee sting and my big toe swelled up painfully but had gone down by evening. Many folk go barefoot in New Zealand as it's so clean underfoot and I found it easier to walk like this.

Next I travelled south to Rotorua, the most thermally active area in the country and the most popular tourist spot on the North Island, despite the stench of sulphurous air. I stayed there three nights, visiting the tourist sites. Traversing the walkway round Lake Rotorua I noticed many signs asking people not to stray from the path as the ground was unsafe. It certainly looked unsafe, with numerous bubbling mud pools and sulphur encrusted beaches. A school party were doing a geology project on the precarious land so I joined them to take a closer look at the steamy ground which was hot to touch.

A major plus for the residents of the city is a free supply of geothermal water and I had a super-hot bath at my hostel. I also visited the famous spa on the lake shore, luxuriating in the small pools at different temperatures. Another spectacular sight was the Lady Knox Geyser; they put a bag of pure soap down into it to make it go off at the same time each day. It shot into the air on cue to our gasps of excitement. Certain algae thrive in volcanic soil and near the geyser was a large 'champagne' pool, fizzing just like a glass of bubbly. The Waimangu volcanic valley had superb scenery, including hot, steaming lakes, streams and springs, vividly coloured bottle green, orange and yellow from the algae. A bright turquoise inferno crater lake gleamed in the sunshine.

There is a strong Maori presence around Rotorua and on my last day I visited Ohinemutu, a Maori village on Lake Rotorua. I entered St Faith's Anglican Church and was immediately affected by its peaceful atmosphere. I sat down on one of the wooden pews, admiring the beautiful Maori carvings, woven panels and stained-glass windows. My favourite window had a large, silvery-white etching of Christ in a Maori cloak with the lake behind giving the illusion that he was walking on water.

*

On the way to Taupo my bus got stuck in a jam for an hour because it was the Ironman Triathlon that day and they were running round the lake after a gruelling bike ride and swim. I was heading to my next WWOOF, the Tauhara Centre, situated 8 kilometres outside Taupo, high on a hill overlooking the lake. Lake Taupo is the largest lake in New Zealand, right in the centre of the North Island. It was formed by one of the biggest volcanic eruptions the world has ever known, about 25,000 years ago.

I took a taxi to the centre where I was met by Andrew, the manager and his wife, Moira, who lived there. 'Welcome to Tauhara,' they said, leading the way to the WWOOFers' lodge. 'The WWOOFers feed themselves when we're not running courses,' Andrew informed me, 'but we supply the food. There are no courses today and no other WWOOFers, so you've got the place to yourself. A couple are arriving on Monday. There's no work today so you can settle in and enjoy the peace and quiet while you can. You'll have to work tomorrow afternoon, even though it's Sunday, as forty guests are coming to celebrate a fiftieth birthday.'

'OK, that's fine,' I replied, content to have the rest of the day to myself. There was an octagonal meditation sanctuary in the grounds with wonderful views of the lake and mountains beyond. It felt good to meditate, especially in such a lovely space. Afterwards I found the library which had a wide selection of books, including ones on spirituality and the organic movement.

At WWOOFing places the work was usually on the land but at Tauhara it was mostly domestic, apart from one day a week which was spent in the garden. Catering for forty people involved a lot of preparation and I spent all afternoon scrubbing potatoes, washing salad and cleaning dishes, while Rose, a paid worker, produced an incredible amount of food – vegetable loaf, roast vegetables, dips, roast meats and two large cheesecakes for dessert. She was good company and the time sped by until dinnertime when I was allocated the roast vegetables to dish out to the guests, who formed an orderly but lively queue. There were many Maori amongst them, who liked meat, otherwise the food would have been vegetarian. While all this was going on a WWOOFer arrived earlier than expected and joined in the serving as if she'd been working there for ages. When all the guests had been served we sat down and ate the delicious food. Rose was definitely a great cook. The new WWOOFer introduced herself, 'I'm Sky from East Germany,' she said looking happily at us. She was in her early thirties with long, fair hair, blue eyes, fine features and an easy-going manner. Most of the WWOOFers I met were similarly relaxed; probably they wouldn't have been travelling in this manner if they were of an uptight disposition.

The following morning was spent clearing up and cleaning the dining hall, lounge and two guest bungalows, which I did together with Sky. She was a fast and efficient worker, but it still took us until early afternoon, with a break for lunch. Sky had a car and we went into Taupo to check our emails. When we were parking an old lady got knocked down, who we'd just beckoned across the road. She lay on the road, her head bleeding copiously. The female driver who'd done it stood, distraught, repeatedly saying, 'I didn't see her, I didn't see her.' We managed to stop her moving the old lady until a doctor came and then an ambulance. They quickly assessed the damage and in no time she was sitting up while they cleaned away the blood. Then the police came and questioned us, but we hadn't actually seen what happened. *Oh dear, not another encounter with the police,* I thought, remembering poor Franz.

My sister, Jean and her husband, Ken, were coincidently motor homing around New Zealand at that time and our paths crossed in Taupo. They arrived at the centre after dinner and I showed them round the place then sat in their spacious rented motorhome and caught up with all our news. They planned to stop by the lake that night and stay at the centre the following night to have a shower and use the campers' kitchen, for which there was a small charge.

The other WWOOFer, a young Korean lad, arrived that evening and we spent the next morning cleaning guest houses, before helping to prepare the staff lunch, a weekly event when we all ate together. Jean and Ken arrived and took me to the Huka Falls, just outside Taupo. The clear, turquoise water plunges through a narrow cleft in the rock, a giant torrent spraying everywhere. Later we found a hot stream entering the river where people were bathing. We joined them, staying in the hot water because the river was too cold for swimming. We had sardines, bread and salad in the motorhome at their idyllic camp site by the lake. Black swans and mallard ducks swam around a small jetty, hoping for crusts of bread. The Tongariro National Park's volcanic mountains were clear in the evening light, a marvellous view to accompany our meal. We said our goodbyes in the morning at the centre. They were heading north to Auckland and their flight home. 'Lucky you getting to stay here another four months,' they said enviously.

FIVE

The Twilight Zone

My fifth WWOOF was described in the booklet as being on the edge of 'the twilight zone'. It was also a 'high energy' area. I was intrigued. Then 'by chance' I found a book at the Tauhara Centre which recounted that the twilight zone was, *'The plane of desolation between our world of human images and thoughts and the pure spiritual world that lies beyond'*. Well, that did it! I just had to go, even though it was with another lone male.

We had had a couple of long chats on the phone and he sounded interesting. The guy who had written the wacky description had gone off in his house truck with a woman. His friend, Angus, was leasing the farm from him. 'Ian's a right dope head,' he remarked, 'that's why the entry in the *WWOOF* book about the farm's so far out. It's sure attracted a lot of crazy folk. Still, you sound sane enough and you come from my home country. One of these days I'll get back to dear old Scotland.'

Andrew ran me into Taupo to get the bus to Turangi, at the southern end of the huge lake. Angus was to meet me there as his farm was way out west, where buses didn't venture. I spotted his van from the bus window. He was leaning on it and did not look like a hippy. He looked like a farmer, which indeed he was, in his brown, open-necked check shirt and faded jeans. He was stocky, with a short, sandy beard and hair. I went over and introduced myself. 'OK, hop in. We've got a long way to go,' he said driving off.

Although I had looked at the map I did not realise quite how far it was, or how rough the roads were. We set off around midday and arrived about six hours later, stopping twice on the way. The first was to visit a farmer friend of his who had a couple of fine jet boats. I played with his five-year-old son while the two men chatted. Then after a while we arrived at the tiny village of Ohura, where Angus downed two pints of beer in the pub, catching up on the gossip with three of his pals. From there it was a further 20 kilometres along an unmetalled road, through a lot of native bush and incredible jaggy hills. Finally, we came to his place, a three bedroomed wooden bungalow.

The farmland stretched up behind, the hills cleared of bush for sheep and cattle to graze. At the edges the bush grew green and dense.

While my host fed the three large pigs and chooks with their chicks, I made pasta with a fresh tomato sauce. When you are a WWOOFer you get used to making yourself at home very quickly, especially navigating your way around new kitchens. 'Ah, that looks good. It's great to have someone to cook for me.' We both ate ravenously after the long drive. 'Just leave the dishes 'til morning. You must be tired.' He showed me my room at the end of a long corridor. It was in a reasonable state, if rather bare, with clean sheets on the bed. We said goodnight and I unpacked my things quickly and went to bed, where I soon fell asleep, relieved that my new place was habitable and my new host amiable.

The following day was Sunday, a 'no work' day according to Angus. I was just out the shower when the doorbell rang. Being clad only in a towel I didn't answer it. Eventually I heard my host grumbling his way to the door. I heard the sound of male voices in the kitchen. Once dressed I joined them. 'This is my neighbour, Derek. He's a lone farmer too and lives about a kilometre down the road.'

Derek was, like us, in his early fifties. He had a round face and ruddy complexion. 'Hi there. How long you planning to stay?'

'Oh, about a week, I think.'

'You oughta stay much longer. Keep Angus company. It's a lonesome life stuck out here. I drop by every morning to check he's still alive and kicking.' They both guffawed loudly at this, until Angus had a coughing fit. 'See, he's not well. It's that pipe he smokes.'

'Well, I hope he doesn't die while I'm here. I've already had one host drop dead on me. The police'll get suspicious.'

'What's that?' They both looked aghast. I told them the tale of my first WWOOF and they laughed some more.

We drank mugs of strong tea, then they went outside to smoke. I foraged around and found some breakfast cereal. Then I gave the kitchen a good scrub and cleaned out the fridge. When Angus came back in, the kitchen was gleaming. 'What've you been up to? This place looks great, but it's Sunday, I told you – you don't need to work.'

'That's OK. I'll stop now.'

'I'm going out this afternoon with Derek to shoot wild pigs in the bush. We go on quad bikes. It's great fun. Fancy coming?'

'Oh, no thanks,' I hastily replied. This was not my idea of fun.

26

Instead I went exploring the hilly land. I climbed to the highest point, called 'energy peak'. There were spectacular views all round, with no sign of habitation, except Derek's farmhouse a bit further down the road. Craggy hills, dotted with sheep and cattle, were interspersed with areas of dark green bush, studded with tree ferns, cabbage trees, nikau palms and the 'tea trees', manuka and kanuka. In the far distance the volcanic cone of Mt Taranaki (2518 metres) could be faintly seen. It certainly had high energy. I gazed and gazed, lost in the magical beauty all around.

Energised I sped back down to the house. Angus had said to use some of the red snapper he had caught. I made cauliflower cheese and potatoes, then fried up some of the snapper to go with it. On his return from hunting Angus had a shower. Then we sat down to eat. It was delicious, especially after our exertions. Over dinner he told me about his communications with extra-terrestrial beings. Seemingly they were attracted to the area by the high energy. He had seen their spaceships landing on top of the hills. I listened sympathetically, quietly thinking that living in isolation did strange things to the mind. Still, he seemed normal enough apart from this, and who knows? He may have been right.

Next morning I was up bright and early for work. Derek popped in again for a chat and some tea. I cleared the weeds in the polytunnel and mulched round the tomato plants with them. After that I helped Angus with the sheep. This was thrilling. I perched on the back of his ATV (all-terrain vehicle) with Scope, his lovely black and white sheepdog. I hung on tightly, screaming now and then, as we careered up and down the steep hills, Scope herding the sheep to his commands and curses. They were brought into the pens. Then I helped move them, counting the ewes and then the lambs. After each count I shouted out the number to Angus. When we had finished he asked, 'How many's that then?'

'I told you before.'

'Yes, but I can't remember. I thought you were keeping count.'

'Ditto,' I responded, laughing nervously. Luckily he could see the funny side.

'Let's have some lunch, then we'll do it all again.' With that we went off very fast on the ATV, Scope running alongside, barking furiously with excitement. He received a well-earned dish of dog biscuits and a huge bowl of water on our return. We had sandwiches and buns. The freezer was well stocked with them as once a week he made a trip to a supermarket in New Plymouth. They sold him out of date loaves, cakes and buns, which were for the pigs. However, much of it was still edible and this was frozen for our use.

We both had a short rest after lunch. It was hot in the middle of the day, so a brief siesta was necessary. Then we went back to the pens to recount the sheep. This time I made sure to remember the numbers. So did he. We were both relieved when the totals tallied.

For dinner I cooked omelettes with vegetables from the small garden. Afterwards I looked at the *WWOOF* book. In it was a photo of the owner, Ian, who definitely resembled a hippy, with long, greying hair. He was rather handsome and the book was also full of young and pretty female WWOOFers' photos. They had written glowing accounts of their stay. When I pointed this out Angus said, 'Oh, Ian regularly fell in love with the WWOOFers, in fact he's away with one right now! Can't be bothered with that sort of thing meself,' he observed.

The following day dawned bright and sunny again. I was left alone while my host went to New Plymouth for the pig food, the bank and other business. Meanwhile I finished clearing the polytunnel and vegetable garden of weeds. After lunch I went with Spoke, who'd broken his chain, to clear ragwort flowers in one of the fields. Ragwort is poisonous to livestock and by removing the flowers before they seeded I was preventing it from spreading. By mid-afternoon I had run out of bags to put them in, so I stopped and returned to the bungalow for a drink. It was boiling hot.

Angus arrived soon after this. Then thirty cows came with their farmer. They needed more grass than he could provide so he paid Angus seven and a half dollars (about £3.50) per cow per week for the grazing. Easy money, I guessed.

There was more snapper so I made a mild creamy coconut curry as I was unsure of what he liked. 'Delicious, but it could be a lot spicier,' was his verdict. Later we went up 'energy peak' on the ATV to see the sunset. The sky westwards over Mt Taranaki was streaked with all shades of orange, crimson, pink and yellow in a turquoise sky. We sat and watched in companionable silence as it slowly faded into the darkening night. 'No sign of my pals tonight,' he said wistfully.

'Maybe tomorrow,' I answered. With that we sped homewards, disturbing the silence with the engine's noise.

Next morning after breakfast we went to the ragwort patch with plenty of bags. Angus went off to do other jobs. I cut off all the remaining flower heads with shears and stuffed them in the bags. It was scorching hot and after two-and-a-half hours of this my head and back were aching. Then he came to the rescue on the ATV. The bags were piled on, along with me.

After lunch and a rest we went up the hills again on the vehicle. I stayed by a field's gate to stop the sheep from following as Angus and Spoke separated twenty heifers from them into the field, where there was more grass. This was a tricky business and poor Spoke got shouted at a lot. My position by the gate was rather precarious as the heifers charged into the field in a panic. The sheep were not far behind and I had to run at them, screaming and waving my arms, to prevent them chasing after the heifers into the sweet grass. Sheep are not as stupid as people believe.

Once the heifers were safely in the field, we went down the hills on the ATV towards the bush. To my surprise there were narrow tracks through it. Scope was following us. Then he disappeared. A few minutes later he came bounding along holding something carefully in his mouth. We stopped to look. Scope dropped the small, furry brown bundle: it was a wild cat, hissing and fighting. Scope got his nose scratched. Angus shouted, 'Leave it!' The cat took advantage of the dog's distraction and made its escape. We came to an opening in the trees. Angus switched off the engine. It was very peaceful after all the noise, cool and magical, with the sunlight barely penetrating the huge trees' leafy canopy. 'This is Fairy Dell, Ian's name. He used to come here to get stoned. He grew cannabis somewhere around. The climate's just right for it, warm and damp. I don't go for it meself. Like to keep a clear head. God knows what I'd see if I took that stuff. See plenty without it!'

Both laughing, the engine spluttered into life, shattering the tranquillity. Soon we were home, where I had a much needed bath to scrub off the dirt and relax. I made another snapper curry, spicier this time.

'Wow! This is blow your head off spicy!' Angus gulped down his beer, his face going red.

'Well the last time you complained it wasn't spicy enough.' Despite his moaning he ate it all up, as did I.

He went to bed early, saying he had not slept well the previous night, 'Because of the ETs.' Then I remembered that I had had a strange dream about them too. I went outside for some air and to watch the stars for the first time there. The night was warm and clear. The stars seemed to be all falling, going fast in different directions, but still staying in the sky. It was mind blowing and I began to understand how Angus might see spaceships and their occupants.

We both had a good night's sleep and woke to a change in the weather. It was cloudy and heavy with a spattering of rain. A strange day to build a bonfire, but that's what he wanted to do. We made it round an old tree stump in one of the empty fields. We piled on dead branches, the ragwort flowers and lots of rubbish, there being no collections in these isolated parts of the country. 'You'll need some kerosene to get this going,' Angus stated. I prided myself with being able to start a bonfire with only some paper and matches.

'No. I'll get it going. Just you wait and see.' It needed a few tries, but eventually smoke began billowing out and then the flames leapt high, catching the drier stuff, until the whole thing blazed fiercely. We stood back away from the searing heat and acrid fumes. 'What did I tell you?' I crowed.

'I reckon you're an arsonist,' he dryly retorted. We both laughed until our sides ached. I was due to leave the next day for my next WWOOF. I suddenly felt sad, realising that I did not really want to go. Despite the isolation I hadn't felt bored or lonely. My host was good company and I loved working with the animals, which was a new experience for me. Nevertheless, I would need to leave as Angus was going to New Plymouth to visit his son for a few days. Derek was going to look after the farm and animals. I could have stayed but felt it would not be the same without him. That evening he went to Ohura for tobacco and some beers with his pals. I ate alone and he made himself mince and tatties on his return. He joined me in the lounge afterwards, cradling a mug of tea. As he sat rolling a cigarette he suddenly asked, 'Would you like a healing back massage, Margaret?'

It was the first time that he'd ever mentioned anything like this. 'That would be nice, Angus, if you're not too tired. Have you done any massage training?'

'Yes, I did a course a couple of years back,' he said, inhaling deeply

30

on his roll-up. 'Just sit in that chair with your back to me and try to relax,' he ordered.

I did as I was told and he began to slowly massage my aching muscles through my clothes. His movements were somehow light but simultaneously deeply moving and I felt myself begin to relax, slipping into a kind of meditative state. After what seemed like a long time, he stopped. 'That was lovely, Angus. Thank you,' I said, coming out of my trance.

'I'm glad you liked it. It helps me relax too, you know. Something to do with energy transfer, I guess.'

The sun reappeared next morning. It was eleven by the time we departed. It was a huge wrench to leave the place and I gave Scope a big hug, trying not to cry.

It was a lovely, scenic drive to New Plymouth and my traveller's heart soon lifted at being on the road again. I briefly met Angus's son, who was a tall, skinny twenty-four-year-old, with a sweet smile. They went with me to the bus station. I bought a ticket going south to Wanganui, where I was to WWOOF at a Quaker settlement. Angus waved goodbye to me from the van so there was no time for sentimental farewells. I watched them drive away with a lurch of my heart.

*

When I went back to New Zealand the following year I wanted to return to Angus's, but when I phoned a strange man's voice answered. 'Never heard of an Angus. I live here now with my family.' He sounded almost hostile and I was unable to ask any more questions. It was unsettling. New Zealand is a small place and it was odd that he had never heard of him. Maybe the extra-terrestrials had spirited him away in their spaceship after all?

SIX

Quakers and Yogis

The Quakers of Wanganui were mainly an amiable, elderly and peace-loving bunch who only expected three hours work a day from their WWOOFers. It was a small community, with fourteen separate houses for the members. When I arrived in the early evening they were all busily preparing the WWOOF sleep out place for painting and had ordered in fish and chips. 'Come into the dining room,' a tall, lean man with white hair and striking, bushy black eyebrows told me. 'We all congregate here once a week – the other days we do our own thing.' The fish and chips, wrapped in newspaper, was unceremoniously dumped in the centre of the table and we all tucked in, eating with our fingers. It was delicious and was followed by a large dish of plums from their orchard and chocolate cake with ice-cream. My offer to help clear away was brushed aside. 'Go and explore the place,' the white-haired man, who came from Holland and was called Henrick, suggested.

I felt in need of solitude after the noisy dinner and followed a sign which pointed the way to their peace garden. It was a tranquil spot tucked away in a corner of their land, full of the scent of herbs – lemon balm, mint and sage, while a tiny fountain trickled into a small pond in which swam some large goldfish. I sat down on a wooden bench and listened to the bedtime birdsong, amongst which I could hear the bellbird's liquid cry. In the distance there was the sound of traffic and I missed the total peace of Angus's farm, and indeed of Angus himself; we had become close in my short time there.

My accommodation was in one of the smaller houses and I went for meals to Henrick's place which he shared with his young, blonde German wife, Ingrid. She had originally been a WWOOFer there but had fallen for Henrick and was happily integrated into the community. I spent the morning putting masking tape around the rooms in the sleep out and explored the twenty-acre land in the afternoon, still feeling unsettled. I made a vegetable curry with their home-grown produce for dinner and met the other WWOOFer – a young woman from the South Island who was heading up to the Hokianga to look for land. 'Oh, I loved it there,' I enthused, 'you'll need to check out Angela's place near Kohu Kohu – it's quite special.'

The next day, Sunday, was a rest day and I attended a Quaker meeting in town. We sat on chairs for an hour in companionable silence, after which three people got up to speak about the continuing Palestinian/Israeli conflict. Then we had tea and cake to celebrate a lady's eighty-ninth birthday. Afterwards one of the kind ladies gave me a lift to the *Waimarie* side-paddle steamer. I was in luck – it was just leaving for a trip on the river. This vessel was brought over from Britain in 1900 and reassembled in Wanganui, where it sailed on the river for fifty years. It sank in 1952 and remained submerged for forty years. It was raised and re-launched, fully restored on the first of January, 2000. After the boat ride I spent some time in the interesting Riverboat Museum and then walked back to the Quaker settlement along the river bank. It was a long way and I was glad of a rest on my return. Dinner was the remains of my curry with garden salad and roast pumpkin. Henrick had made a delicious lemon drizzle cake which we had with stewed fruit and cream for dessert. I was moving on the next day and felt rather guilty at my small work contribution in return for their generous hospitality. I voiced my concern to Henrick. 'No worries! We've enjoyed your company. May your travels bring you peace and joy,' was his splendid reply.

*

The clocks had gone back and the weather had a distinct autumnal feel – cold with driving wind and rain. I had arranged to WWOOF further down the coast at Paraparaumu, just to the north of Wellington, where there was a yoga centre surrounded by ten acres of bush and organic gardens. It was run by a couple – Eric and Kathryn, who had a twenty-month-old son, Ananda. Another WWOOFer, Lynn, from Devon, had arrived just before me. She was about my age and cared for Ananda after a lunch of soup and salad, while I did some housework. The house was cold and uncomfortable and my room, an outside sleep out, was freezing. However, Kathryn gave me a hottie (hot water bottle) and lots of blankets which kept me warm all night.

A big plus of being there was that the WWOOFers were allowed to attend their excellent yoga classes free of charge and sample some of their alternative medical methods. Eric gave me an iridology test.

He peered into my eyes and announced, 'Margaret, your system is far too acidic – you should cut out wheat and dairy from your diet.' I had encountered many folks in the WWOOFing community with this viewpoint, so it came as no surprise. They ate millet for breakfast and were strict vegetarians and dairy-free. It was doubtless a healthy diet but I was hungry, especially in the damp and cold environment.

The sun made an appearance in the morning and Lynn and I were put to work for four hours clearing bindweed and brambles from around the edge of the property. It was a horrid job and my arms were scratched to bits, my hands stuck with prickles, despite wearing gloves. We took a short tea break, moaning to each other about the demanding work.

'I think I'll move on tomorrow, especially if it's raining,' I said. It was and I did, leaving Lynn baby minding. One of the yoga class participants gave me a lift to the station where I took a train the short distance to Wellington, the capital.

SEVEN

Onward to the South Island

Wellington lived up to its name – 'Windy Wellington', accompanied by squally showers of freezing rain. All the hostels I phoned were full with rugby supporters: there was an All Blacks game the following day. I was offered floor space in a backpackers' lounge, already occupied by five people but sharing with five drunken rugby supporters and sleeping on the hard floor was an unattractive prospect. Instead I booked the 5.30pm ferry to Picton on the South Island.

The three-hour crossing was calm, with wonderful views of mountains and the numerous islands and inlets of the Marlborough Sounds. Claire, a likeable Kiwi lass, met me as arranged from the ferry and took me to the Jugglers Rest Hostel. As we drove along she enthused about the hostel. 'It's run by jugglers and fire-eaters and our guests always end up juggling, or even fire-eating!'

It was a beautiful backpackers surrounded by gardens and after breakfast I received my first free juggling lesson inside; it was pouring with rain outside. In the afternoon it cleared up and I walked the short distance into the pretty little port to buy some food. I cooked up a huge vegetable stew and shared it with Claire, a young Belgian lad and two Israeli girls. Afterwards we chatted, drank wine and listened to some great folk and jazz music, lounging around the cosy wood-burning stove.

After two nights I went to WWOOF with a lovely family in the Marlborough Sounds for four nights, mainly weeding their flower and vegetable beds. Next I took the mail van to Havelock Youth Hostel, a converted school-house which boasted Lord Ernest Rutherford, who discovered the atomic nucleus, as a former pupil.

From Havelock taxi boats ply the Sounds, taking people to and from their homes, many of which can only be reached by boat. I took one which was transporting an elderly couple and their luggage to their holiday home. The scenery was stunning and as we returned in the late afternoon, on one side the hills were bright green in the sunshine, while on the other black clouds gathered over the dark and mysterious mountains. I sat outside singing loudly, my voice drowned by the engine's noise.

Over dinner at the hostel I met a well-built, tall Englishman with a shaved head. 'I'm Paul,' he said, 'and I'm working as a cook in one of the cafés. I love it here and I've just put a deposit on a block of land.'

'That's great! I wouldn't mind settling in New Zealand myself,' I replied.

When we'd finished eating and clearing up he asked, 'Would you like to go up to Cullen Point? There's a great view of Havelock and its surroundings.'

'What a good idea,' I said. He drove me there and we sat on a rock gazing at the full moon shining on the sea, the lights of Havelock glittering far below. He hadn't struck me as being a spiritual type but we had a surprisingly deep conversation about destiny, both feeling that everything happens for a reason in our lives and we can learn from our experiences, no matter how good or bad they may be.

*

On leaving Havelock I travelled west by minibus on twisty, narrow roads through the mountains to Nelson, then straight on to Motueka, where my driver got done for speeding. After Motueka there was no public transport to Takaka so I hitched, first with a Kiwi man, then to the top of Takaka Hill with a young guy from Oxford who had a kayaking business and a Kiwi wife. A family with two small girls on the back seat ran me down the hill to Pohara in Golden Bay where I was met by Vera, my new WWOOF host from the Sans Souci Inn. She owned it with her Swiss husband, Keto and they had two young children. My accommodation was a caravan in the garden, equipped with a comfy bed and plenty of bedding for the cold nights.

This hard-working Swiss couple had built the whole wonderful place, made of mud bricks, or adobe, with a turf roof. There was a restaurant and several guest rooms, while they lived in a separate house. The dry compost toilets were quite palatial and sweet smelling. I worked in the kitchen evenings cleaning dishes before loading them into the dishwasher. Keto was the chef and during a lull he said, 'It's fun to watch the guests when they come back from the loo. They always start whispering and then there are lots of giggles. One by one the others go to experience them and we get lots of comments, usually positive, in the guest book specifically about the toilets.' I also worked in the mornings washing the breakfast dishes and then helped clean the guest rooms. The food was delicious, especially their home-made ice-cream and mousse. After lunch I explored the beach which was a two-minute walk away or cycled around the area on one of their bikes.

One afternoon I hitched to the Pupu Springs, a sacred Maori place. The Springs were perfectly clear with lovely colours – the waters seeming to dance over bright green plants and greyish-cream sand. I was waiting at the roadside, my thumb outstretched, when a fawn-coloured Mercedes slowed to a stop. The driver leant across his passenger. 'Hop in. Where yer heading?' His handsome, tanned face had a cheeky grin. I stood uncertainly assessing the situation – two, cool, hippy-looking characters, both male, were offering me a lift. Was it safe? 'Well, are you getting in? We won't eat you,' the driver assured me. I got in.

'Hi, my name's Mel,' the guy in the passenger seat drawled in an American accent, turning round and flashing me a smile, his blue eyes squinting through his wispy fair fringe. His long hair was tied back in a ponytail. He handed me a business card. 'I make my living painting stones called 'chak-roks',' he informed me.

'Oh! Can you make enough money doing that?'

'Sure can. Famous folk buy my chak-roks. Sting's got one.'

'Is that right?' I was impressed but sceptical.

'So what are you doing here?' the driver asked.

'I'm travelling around and doing some WWOOFing,' I said.

'Right – so you're another one of these weird dogs,' he joked. I got a bit fed up with people making this type of comment, but I smiled politely, not wanting to upset him and soon we were in Pohara where they dropped me off, inviting me to visit the jewellers in Takaka which the driver owned. In total I had six lifts and two of them had visited the Findhorn community in Scotland. The Golden Bay area is full of hippies and alternative life stylers.

On my day off I took a bus to Totaranui. The driver was the same one who had been done for speeding in Motueka and as I was the only passenger we had a good chat. He listened to my ravings about the beauty of New Zealand. 'I'd love to live here but the entry requirements are quite strict,' I sighed sadly.

'No worries! You might find a good Kiwi bloke to marry on your walk today – plenty of folk do it for a backhander,' he said.

'You must be joking! It can't be that easy,' I responded.

'I'd marry you myself if I weren't already taken,' he quipped, chuckling loudly as he drew up beside the shuttle bus to Bark Bay in the Abel Tasman Park. I was going to walk part of the Abel Tasman Coastal Track which is 51 kilometres long and takes three to four days to complete. It was a perfect day the sun shining in a cloudless sky, a cool sea breeze blowing as I set off through superb scenery. The track wound its way through bush-covered hills and over bridges spanning gurgling streams and waterfalls, with tantalising glimpses of turquoise bays fringed by white, sandy beaches through the trees. I walked the 7.8 kilometres in just under three hours, with plenty of rest and snack stops. Most people managed it in two hours but I was pleased with my progress, apart from tripping and nearly falling down a steep slope to the sea at the start, and hardly being able to stand at the end. I reached Sandfly Bay, with no sign of the pesky beasts, finally finishing at Torrent Bay in time for the shuttle boat to Kaiteriteri, from where I got two lifts back to the Sans Souci Inn.

*

From Pohara I headed north-west towards Collingwood where I stayed at the friendly hostel, the Inn-let. They took WWOOFers but already had one and I was content to simply stay there and relax. I hitched all the way, the last one with three girls who were also staying at the hostel. It was a twelve-bedded, cosy place near the sea, surrounded by lovely gardens and bush. The rain began and the three girls, myself, a Japanese couple and a Swiss woman and her daughter, settled down after dinner to read and chat beside the wood-burning stove. Katie and Jonathon, the owners, were a likeable Kiwi couple who arranged kayaking, caving and walking trips.

It poured with rain the next day and in the evening I went with the three girls to the nearby Mussel Inn to hear a great Kiwi rock band. Their songs had funny and unusual lyrics, which included topics such as sandwiches, blood on the floor and Goldilocks and the Three Bears. There was dancing and I joined in as much as my arthritic knees would permit. The guys who had given me a lift in the Mercedes were there, complete with a couple of pretty women.

The sun shone in the morning and the girls drove me to Farewell Spit – the northernmost tip of the South Island. We staggered along the beach, sand blowing everywhere in the strong wind, so we drove on to the Puponga Visitor Centre where we sat outside drinking cappuccinos and munching muffins while enjoying panoramic views of the Spit. The girls were leaving and I walked along the Spit to Fossil Point on the west side, where the Tasman Sea pounds onto deserted, wild beaches. The shrill cries of oyster catchers filled the air while many white-winged black swans bobbed on the choppy waves. Whales often get beached up in this area, unable to swim against the strong currents and enormous waves.

I hitched back with a big, red-bearded Canadian farmer. 'I come here every year for their summer and go home in April when the snow has melted to farm.'

'That sounds like a great lifestyle,' I enthused.

'Yep – it's pretty damn good. I've got a VW caravanette as well as this four-wheel Suzuki jeep and I store them in Takaka for just one dollar a day,' he explained, gripping the steering wheel with both his meaty hands as he swung round a tight bend.

The city of Nelson was my last stop before travelling down the West Coast. When I checked my email I was concerned to see one from the Whangarei police requesting a statement in connection with Franz's death. I found the police station, full of trepidation that I might be arrested, but they simply wanted to close the case and needed me to go over my account. The two months since his death had been so full of travelling that I'd forgotten all about my first tragic WWOOF; as I gave my statement it all came flooding back as I relived that final day of his life.

EIGHT

The Wild West Coast

The bus took four-and-a-half hours from Nelson to Punakaiki on the West Coast. The mountains were shrouded in mist and the lush rainforest dripped with another downpour of rain. I had planned to WWOOF at the Te Nikau Backpackers, but when they told me that I'd have to sleep in a freezing cold garage I decided to be a guest instead. There were already four WWOOFers and they seemed to be working all the time. It was supposed to be a retreat but I did not find the atmosphere relaxing as they liked to work to the accompaniment of loud pop music and were unfriendly and cliquey, except for Hamish, an amiable Scottish lad.

I walked along the Truman Track through the rainforest to the sea which was spectacularly rough, with huge waves crashing on the sandy shore. I got a lift to the Pancake Rocks and Blowholes to the south. The limestone rocks resemble stacks of pancakes as a result of weathering and at high tide the sea surges into the caverns below them, squirting out geyser-like through the blowholes.

One night was sufficient at the Te Nikau and I took a bus south to Greymouth where I was met by Jane from the Formerly the Blackball Hilton. This old hotel, now a backpackers, was such a threat to the Hilton hotel chain that they took legal action against them, hence the inclusion of 'Formerly'. We travelled 25 kilometres north of Greymouth to the town of Blackball which began as a service centre for gold diggers followed by coal miners. New Zealand's trade union movement was born here after a mining strike in the nineteen-thirties. The 'Hilton' was an incredible place, overflowing with historical information, faded black and white photographs and news clippings covering the walls. The only downside for me as a vegetarian was the stink of meat fat which permeated the air from the constant frying. The backpackers were allowed to use the hotel's kitchen and I prepared my meatless meal quickly in order to escape the smell of sizzling sausages. I ate in the bar by a cosy open fire, drinking my first pint of Kiwi dark beer – delicious.

The following day I went for a wander around the tiny town and peered inside the other hotel bar's door. One of the male customers spotted me. 'Come in, come in,' he cried, beckoning to me. There were three other men and a woman sitting round the bar and I was immediately offered a drink. They were a friendly, jocular bunch and the woman, Glenda, invited me to play pool with her against two of the guys. She was extremely good and we won, much to the consternation of the men.

Glenda looked in her late forties and was striking, with long, red curly hair tied back with a turquoise chiffon scarf which matched her eyes, a jade necklace hanging round her long neck. After the game she told me a little about herself. 'I live in a house bus near here,' she said, her laughter lines creasing up with the thought. 'It's a great life, Margaret. I can just up and go wherever I want, whenever I want.'

My gypsy blood quickened with excitement. 'I'd love to live like that and it's so easy and safe here in New Zealand,' I said wistfully.

Glenda took a gulp of her beer and regarded me earnestly. 'Just do it Margaret! Follow your dream and go with the feelings in your heart.'

I might do just that. 'You're right, Glenda – maybe on my next visit.' I'd already decided that I'd return. New Zealand had captured my soul.

'Well, make sure that you do and then you can come and join our bus people's New Year gathering at Collingwood.' This gave me something to aim for, although I'd have to brush up my driving skills.

Back at the 'Hilton' bar an inebriated local, who said he'd played for the All Blacks, sat next to me and insisted on talking, so I retired to my dorm room. Two Kiwi women were busy settling in there. 'We're having a weekend away from our families,' one told me, 'and boy, do we need it!'

*

Hokitika, further down the coast, was my next stop. After checking in to the Beach House Backpackers by the sea I explored the beach. It was long and wild and full of driftwood; massive trees, huge branches twisted into strange shapes, their bleached stems pointing majestically towards the sky – it was an artist's paradise. I sat on a log watching the sun set into the Tasman Sea, a fiery orange ball, the sky glowing for many minutes in its aftermath. The beach was 'busy' (for that deserted place); it was Saturday night and the main entertainment was to congregate in the shelter of some large driftwood, light a fire, down some beers and have a smoke. I began chatting to a young lass feeding the seagulls. 'I'm in a band,' she told me, throwing crusts of bread to the hovering, shrieking birds. 'There's four of us and we make good money. We've got two CDs out and they were produced for free cos one of us is Maori.'

'Sounds great,' I responded and told her about my son's band in Canada.

The next day I was off south again to the Franz Joseph glacier. By the time the bus got there it was too late to see it. The female on reception at my hostel told me, 'You can only really appreciate this glacier by walking on it and it's a two-hour return hike from here.' This sounded too much for me and disappointed I decided to move on in the morning.

My small dorm was mixed sex and smelt of smelly trainers. When I entered the kitchen I stopped still in amazement when I spotted a young man busily preparing his dinner. He turned and saw me. 'My God! I know you – you were on my Delhi flight last September, remember?'

'Yes, I do, and you came with me to the Hare Krishna Guest House.'

'It's all flooding back,' he grinned, putting some pasta into a pan of boiling water. 'We were lucky to meet you, a seasoned traveller of India – that was a good, cheap guest house and the American girls liked it too.'

'Hmm. They went on to Agra after a couple of days, I think.'

We sat at the table reminiscing while waiting for our food to cook. When I told him my room number he said, 'That's funny – I'm in the same dorm as you – what a coincidence!' It was indeed. I usually think that there is something significant in coincidences, but for this one I drew a blank; maybe it is yet to be revealed.

After dinner I walked up the track behind the hostel for a few minutes. It was very dark and I saw hundreds of glow-worms under the fern leaves, shining light blue, like little stars. I breathed in the fresh, piny smell of the bush after the recent rain. What a heavenly country!

The Southern Alps' craggy snow-capped peaks were clearly visible against a blue sky in the morning, a perfect rainbow arcing across it and the rain-forested mountain slopes below. It took less than an hour by bus to reach the Fox Glacier and after checking in to a backpackers I started to walk there, taking a short detour through the rain forest, where a rich variety of ferns thrived in the warm humidity. Fantails followed me, attracted by the insects which were dislodged by my tramping. The glacier was too far away for me to walk – I saw it in the distance, jaggy cliffs rising at either side with huge boulders strewn across its path.

Back at the hostel I relaxed in their hot outside spa pool which soothed the pain in my knees and feet. Later I was joined by an American girl and two Englishmen, one of whom took off his artificial leg before expertly manoeuvring himself into the water. We began chatting about our travels. 'I walked on the glacier today and I've bungy jumped near Queenstown,' the one-legged one cheerfully told us, which made me feel like a wimp. At another hostel I'd met a man with a false arm who was motor biking and trekking around the country.

*

The next day I travelled on down the coast to Haast, where the bus turned inland, across the steep Haast Pass, south-east to Wanaka. Immediately over the eastern side of the mountains the landscape changed from lush green rainforest to brown, barren mountain slopes – the result of a dramatic reduction in rainfall. Wanaka is a pleasant town situated on Lake Wanaka. I walked round the lake to a waterfall, suddenly aware of autumn, the tall poplars glowing brilliant yellow in the afternoon sunlight, the earthy smell of leaves permeating the air, reminding me of home.

From Wanaka it was a short distance south to Queenstown, a busy, touristy little place in a stunning situation on Lake Wakatipu, The Remarkables Mountains, aptly named, creating an impressive backdrop. I stayed at the Resort Lodge Hostel near the centre which had been described as 'a quiet place' in my guidebook. It wasn't, at least not on my first night. A bus load of noisy youngsters had arrived, intent on all night partying and adrenaline-pumping activities, such as white-water rafting, jet-boating, river surfing, paragliding, parachuting and the inevitable bungy jumping.

For me it was a total nightmare, with TVs blaring in every room – even the dorms, while the two tiny kitchens overflowed with folk eating carry-outs, drinking cans of beer and leaving unwashed dishes on every available surface. Around ten they all headed out, some to a medical fancy dress party, four of the girls made up convincingly as pregnant mums. Complete with earplugs I snatched some sleep, then somehow made breakfast in the cluttered kitchen, creeping out early before bedlam began. I took a day trip to peaceful Arrowtown to see the beautiful autumn colours, walking in a loop around the Arrow River to where the old huts of a Chinese gold miners' settlement stood forlornly under the trees. Back at the hostel it was much quieter, the bus load having moved on, and I managed to get a good night's sleep.

Te Anau, two hours south of Queenstown, is the gateway to probably the most photographed location in New Zealand – Milford Sound. I went with Trips 'n Tramps to experience the area's superb scenery, the minibus equipped with roof high windows to view the dramatically steep mountain slopes on either side. A few kilometres before the Sound we passed through the Homer Tunnel and joined the numerous tour buses at the cruise wharf. Despite the massive tourist activity the scene was breathtaking; Mitre Peak towered 1695 metres into the cloud-studded sky, its reflection perfectly mirrored in the calm waters of the 22 kilometres-long fiord. Our small group of six Australians, one Japanese girl and one Englishman clicked their cameras, then gazed spellbound at the view.

We went on a two-and-a-half-hour boat trip on the fiord. It hadn't rained for a week, an unusual occurrence, with waterfalls cascading less powerfully down the vertical rocky mountainsides as a result. The rain, a steady drizzle, began while we were on the water, which at least kept the monster sand flies away. Back on land we went on the Chasm Walk, to peer through a rocky window at the Cleddau River plunging through a narrow chasm, massive boulders all around. Large greenish-brown kea parrots hung out there, waiting for tourist tit-bits. They are inquisitive, cheeky and fearless; one flew onto the top of my stick, attacking the wood viciously with its strong, curved beak, squawking furiously, much to the amusement of the group.

Further down the convoluted south-west coast lies Doubtful Sound. I had been advised to take the overnight cruise, which is regarded as even more spectacular than the one on Milford Sound. It was quite a journey. First I took a bus to Manapouri, followed by a two-hour boat trip across the lake. I sat outside, well wrapped up against the cold, gazing at magnificent mountains and breathing in the fresh air. Finally a coach transported us over a high pass to a deep cove in Doubtful Sound. The impressive Fiordland Navigator boat was waiting for us. I was shown to a bunk in one of the quad cabins, then sat on deck admiring the scenery. The weather was dry but chilly with high cloud, the mountain peaks clear against the sky. Little blue penguins' heads bobbed in the fiord, while dolphins swam under the hull and leapt high out of the water. Further out in the Sound we were given kayaks and after a brief lesson were allowed out onto the water, where for over an hour we paddled, unfortunately without stopping, as whenever we paused sand flies bit us mercilessly. To be alone on that still water, mountains with cascading waterfalls towering up on all sides, was an incredible experience. Once or twice I stopped, despite the flies, simply to absorb the total stillness and silence. I ruminated on why, in that wondrous wilderness, there should be sand flies to spoil the experience. The answer came: *this manifestation is held together by opposites.* There can be no 'good' without 'bad'; no 'beauty' without 'ugliness'. It depends on your viewpoint: from the sand flies point of view it was heaven – plenty of skin to bite and blood to suck.

On our return to the boat we were given bowls of warming tomato soup with hot rolls, after which we went on deck to watch colonies of fur seals lying on rocks at the fiord's mouth as the sun set. Dinner was splendid with lots of vegetarian options – salads, roast pumpkin, potatoes and sweet potatoes as well as vegetable pasta, while the carnivores had plenty of meat to choose from. For afters there were four different desserts, fruit salad and biscuits and cheese. We were stuffed! After our meal we were shown an excellent slide show of the Sounds' scenery and wildlife. The vessel dropped anchor in an arm of the fiord with towering mountains rising up on all sides – a splendid sight as the morning light hit them.

NINE

Rainy Riverton

My next WWOOF was in Riverton, a tiny town way down in Southland. Overnight rain had left low cloud covering the autumnal landscape of the Southern Scenic Route from Te Anau. Two hours later the bus stopped for me right outside Riverton Highland Flowers, which was on the road out of Riverton to Invercargill.

I walked up the muddy driveway disconsolately observing the general air of neglect. Wet washing hung from a line, the sheets dragging on the ground, while chickens scratched for food in the undergrowth. Gulls constantly circled in the heavy sky, flying low and cawing. A strong smell of rotten vegetation and animal excrement hung in the air. I was startled by the loud barking of a huge black Rottweiller, who was ferociously trying to break free from its chain. A large woman, followed by two yapping terriers, came out of the bungalow to greet me. 'Don't mind Lolly. She's a sweetie really,' she said, observing my fearful face, then added ominously, 'I need a guard dog round here.' She continued: 'You must be Margaret. I'm Gillian, pleased to meet you.' She held out her hand which was grimy with dirt. I shook it uncertainly. My new host was a daunting-looking lady – six-foot tall and solidly built, with longish, untidy red hair, a ruddy complexion and a manic grin. She was clad in the usual WWOOFing host garb of muddy wellies, dirty trousers and a filthy waterproof jacket.

She led the way into the porch, the floor of which was covered with footwear – shoes, trainers, slippers and wellies, as well as overflowing poly bags, cardboard boxes and other items, all of which made progress somewhat difficult. 'Excuse the mess. I never have time to clear up and my sons don't know the meaning of 'tidy',' she chuckled in a sad kind of way. The terriers ran around, wagging their stumpy tails in welcome, while two Manx cats eyed me suspiciously from their cosy chairs. 'Look over here,' Gillian instructed. In a corner, huddled together in a cardboard box, was a furry group of kittens, along with their mum – another Manx.

'Oh, they're gorgeous,' I enthused, watching as they blindly groped for their mother's teats, their little paws rhythmically clutching her belly.

'Yes, aren't they,' she agreed, bending down to stroke them. 'I breed Manx cats – they're quite popular and I've already got homes for these little ones once they're weaned.'

The porch led into the kitchen. I stood surveying the scene – it was a mess! Every surface was covered with mounds of stuff, not all kitchen-related, such as odd socks, toys, a hairbrush and a hammer. On top of the cupboards dozens of packets of instant noodles were stacked precariously. 'Make yourself a sandwich,' my genial host suggested, vaguely pointing to a grimy bread bin, which contained out of date white sliced bread. I was hungry and managed to clear a small space on one of the worktops, carefully cleaning it with a soapy cloth when Gillian wasn't looking. She brewed up some tea and we went through to the lounge where her two sons sprawled together on a threadbare sofa, noisily using a play station game. They looked up briefly when we entered. 'This is Kevin – he's seven and this one's Sam, the baby at four,' she said, almost tenderly, ruffling his curly, carrot-coloured hair.

They regarded me with little interest until Kevin pronounced, 'I guess you're another WWOOFER.'

'Yes. My name's Margaret,' I told him helpfully.

'Right, no worries,' he replied without enthusiasm, returning to their game, which made my head pound, it was so loud.

Gillian showed me my room, which was relatively tidy, the bed made up with clean bedding and even an electric blanket – quite a luxury! 'You'll be glad of this,' she informed me, 'as the nights can get right cold down here, especially when the south wind blows up from Antarctica.' She looked at her watch, then out of the window. 'Great, the rain's holding off. Why don't you get changed and I'll give you some work for the afternoon?'

I quickly put on my old clothes and went to find her. She was in a large shed near the house, next to a pile of potatoes. 'Oh good, there you are. First you can bag up these tatties.' She showed me a pile of cloth sacks. 'Then you can start digging up clumps of garlic and planting them out,' she said showing me where they were and the cleared ground in which to plant them, then disappeared. I worked steadily, glad to be busy, and quickly finished the potatoes. The clumps of garlic were plentiful, the cloves fat and healthy. As I pressed them into the dark, fertile soil I wondered what she was going to do with so much garlic. Later I found another large shed which had many dusty bunches of desiccated flowers hanging by strings from the roof, along with bundles of dried garlic. *So this is where it ends up. Maybe she's hoping to sell them?* There was a weather beaten sign at the gate announcing, 'Produce for sale', which I presumed included the garlic and flowers.

At the end of the afternoon I found my host tinkering in the bonnet of her truck. When she heard me she lifted her head, pulling a strand of hair away from her face and leaving a smudge of oil on her forehead. 'This damn thing's always breaking down – guess the spark plugs need a clean,' she said.

'Is it OK if I stop now?' I asked hesitantly.

'Sure. You can have a bath if you want. There's plenty of hot water.' This was a welcome offer which I accepted immediately and, after a thorough scrub of the tub, lowered myself into the hot, soapy suds, relaxing and thinking, *this isn't such a bad place after all.*

Afterwards in the kitchen Gillian said, 'I don't know if you're a veggie; I know a lot of WWOOFers are, but we eat meat.' She stood staring at me.

'Well, yes I am vegetarian, although I do eat fish,' I responded, aware that this was not what she wanted to hear.

'OK, you can have some leftover veg and heat it up in the microwave,' she suggested.

I peered in the fridge and found a dish of greasy-looking vegetables, which smelt disgusting. 'I think I'll make a tomato sauce for some pasta,' I told her, having found the ingredients, including fresh tomatoes, and, naturally, garlic.

She nodded absent-mindedly. 'Me and the boys are having sausages 'n mash, but you go ahead and make your stuff.'

I managed to surreptitiously clear a wider area on the counter before preparing my dinner. Soon the distasteful smell of frying sausages filled the room, overwhelming my garlicky sauce. We ate together in front of the TV, which was on at full volume, annoying me considerably and causing indigestion. New Zealand TV consists of adverts, interspersed with poor quality programmes which have a soporific effect when the volume is down. After our meal I did the dishes and tidied up the kitchen as best I could, trying not to focus on the mounds of mess and filthy floor. Gillian told me that she was a single mum. 'The boys' dad liked the drink too much, know what I mean?' she confided later after they were in bed.

*

In the morning, after a bowl of cornflakes and some toast, I was shown the field at the back of the house where the pigs, geese and chickens lived. It was a smelly, muddy mess. 'Give this bread to the chooks and the seed to the pigs,' Gillian ordered. 'You can also scatter this grass seed over the muddy patches.' The 'muddy patches' were numerous and after I'd thrown mountains of mouldy bread to the chooks, and buckets of seed to the pigs, I squelched around scattering grass seed as directed; the chooks scrabbled to eat it while the gulls hovered above, waiting to swoop on the bread once I'd gone. It was cloudy, but warm and dry so after a short tea break I planted out more garlic. Later on I refused Gillian's offer of a trip to Invercargill to buy more bread with the boys. I was suffering from a headache, possibly as a result of dehydration from the warm humidity.

The next day was Saturday and my host had a lie in, while the boys were busy with their play station. Heavy rain, accompanied by icy blasts of southerly wind, battered against the windows. The previous evening I'd been told to empty the bread out of its wrappings and place it into sacks. There was a whole trailer load of it, and after I'd fed the animals I stood at the back of the trailer, sheltered somewhat in the entrance of the shed, and began ripping open the poly bags. It was a tedious job, my hands icy cold, my fingers clumsily tearing at the bags. Four hours later I decided to take a lunch break, planning to finish the trailer load afterwards.

Gillian was just returning from a shopping trip to Riverton as I made my way towards the bungalow. She saw the trailer. 'Have you not finished yet?' she asked grumpily.

'No. I'll do more after lunch. I'm so cold – need a warm up,' I replied.

She stomped off and I went inside, grateful for the warmth of the kitchen range, and made myself some tea and toast. I was about to go outside again to finish the job when in stormed Gillian, her cheeks glowing red with cold. She began unpacking one of her shopping bags. It contained still more packets of instant noodles. 'Come here and help,' she shouted to Kevin, who appeared reluctantly from the lounge.

'Stand up on this chair and put these up on top of the other ones,' she ordered, handing packets quickly to the boy, who wasn't quite tall enough to reach the growing mountain. 'Hurry up, hurry up! Don't drop them,' she admonished as a couple of packets fell to the floor, the stack wobbling precariously.

I had been watching helplessly, feeling pity for the lad, but I could stand it no longer. 'He's doing his best, poor thing. He's not tall enough to reach up there,' I said, looking at the boy with sympathy and at his mother with anger.

Gillian's face went even redder. 'You stupid boy! Why can't you do anything right?' Kevin stood on the chair stiffly, starting to sob. Then her rage turned to me. 'And as for you – what's it got to do with you? Consoling that useless idiot! I'm knackered from putting away all that bread, which you were supposed to have done.'

I was shaking with emotion at the unfairness of it all. 'I was going to finish the bread after lunch. I told you.'

She suddenly seemed to deflate. 'I'm off to have a bath,' she said, scuttling exhaustedly from the room.

Once she'd gone I offered Kevin a drink of juice and a biscuit, feeling unable to give him a hug, there was such an impenetrable wall around him. 'No thanks,' he muttered and disappeared off to his bedroom, where Sam must also have gone. I lit the fire in the lounge and waited nervously for my host to reappear.

The bath seemed to have calmed her. She emerged smelling sweet in what looked like freshly laundered clothes. 'Thanks for lighting the fire, Margaret,' she said. Then as a peace offering, 'Would you like my bath water?' It took two hours for the water to heat up again. I looked at the bath. It was full of filthy water, covered with a brownish scum.

'No thanks. I'll wait 'til later,' I politely answered.

'My new bloke, Martin, is coming round tonight,' she said nervously. *Maybe that's why she got into such a state?* I watched her attempts to 'tidy up'. She moved a pile of dirty clothes from the settee to an armchair, then vacuumed round the mess on the floor, narrowly missing stray socks and other items. When she had finished she asked, 'Would you like to come with us to the Rugby Club? We're picking up *hangi* that they've cooked for our tea.'

'OK, that'd be nice,' I replied, glad of a chance to escape the house. We all rushed through the rain, which had turned into a steady drizzle, to the truck, Lolly barking plaintively in the background, the terriers getting under our feet.

'Stay!' Gillian ordered. 'You guys have to stay here. Good dogs!' The terriers sat on the driveway, mournfully watching our departure. The club was full of folk drinking beer and eating *hangi*, stuffing the steaming meat and vegetables hungrily into their mouths from tin foil cartons. I bought us a couple of beers, then she bought another. We both mellowed out considerably with the beer, laughing and chatting like old pals, as the boys ran around excitedly, snatching crisps and other titbits from the tables. My host was enjoying herself. 'Guess what the competition of the night is, Margaret?' I couldn't even begin to surmise what it could be. 'They have to guess where a cow shit first on the rugby field!'

'No way!' I spluttered.

'It's true and the first prize is five hundred dollars!' This was an impressive sum of money, about £250, so I had a go, after much deliberation placing a coloured pin on a map of the field, with no luck. Gillian looked at her watch. 'We'd better be getting back. Martin'll be there soon. We'll go the back road cos the cops are crawling around.' The narrow back road wound its way up into the hills; we had a rough ride as she tried unsuccessfully to navigate the truck round numerous potholes. On our return we discovered Martin sitting on the settee in the lounge. He had very blonde hair and white skin, almost like an albino. My host suddenly became coquettish, sitting down next to him, really close, flashing her eyes and laughing a lot. We consumed our *hangi* together and I found the vegetables tasty from the meat juice. *Oh well,* I reflected, *this WWOOF is teaching me tolerance I guess.*

Another dank day dawned, the rain pouring down and a freezing wind howling through the branches of the trees. There was no sign of Martin, and Gillian revealed that he was younger than her and shy, so they were just good friends. 'There's no way you can work outside in this weather,' she said, and gave me a huge pile of odd socks to match as best I could. There were no actual pairs and many were full of holes. I placed these in a separate pile and showed them to her later, assuming she'd tell me to throw them in the bin. She stared aghast at the vast pile. 'Just put them back in the draw and I'll darn them later,' she said, adding, 'you've no idea how many socks we get through. You need two pairs in your wellies for a start.' I did my best to cram them in the draw, but gave up as it was already too full with the other socks.

Next she led me into her bedroom. There was another pile of old clothes, nearly as high as me, in the middle of the floor. She asked me to clean round her bed and to dust a rail which had clothes hanging from it. On closer inspection I discovered that the clothes and their hangers were covered in a thick layer of dust and cobwebs, which I half-heartedly dusted while trying not to breathe in the clouds of dust which were released into the air. It was a pointless task; they needed to be washed, or better, thrown in the rubbish, along with the rest of the stuff. Gillian appeared, however, and remarked enthusiastically, 'Oh, Margaret! How you've transformed this place!'

Carried away with the excitement of having her abode cleaned she directed me towards the hallway, which was lined with bookshelves, filled with books, papers, magazines and what I can only describe as rubbish. I found this task most therapeutic as she gave me a free rein. I worked my way along the shelves, throwing rubbish in a bin bag and carefully wiping everything with a wet cloth. After a couple of hours the job was done and I stood admiring the only really clean and tidy place in the house. My host came and stood for several minutes in stunned silence. I began to worry that she'd miss the rubbish I'd removed, but instead she cried out in wonder, 'Oh, what a lovely job you've done, Margaret!'

Later that day she went to the next village to see her mum with the boys, telling me that her father farmed there. The place was blissfully peaceful without them and my headache went after soaking in a hot bath and reading an interesting book by the fire, which I'd found while dusting. On their return the boys went straight to bed and Gillian announced, 'The boys' dad's coming later but I won't be letting him in.' When he arrived, however, she did let him in. His presence filled the lounge with an animal scent; he was a big, strong sexy man, and he knew it. It wasn't long before they retired to bed and I smelt dope wafting from their room.

It was time for me to leave. I'd been there four nights – it was enough. The morning dawned bright and sunny at last. I awoke to sounds of frantic calling, followed by loud phone conversations. Lolly had broken her chain and run off and Gillian and her man were looking everywhere and phoning everyone. I fed the animals and planted yet more garlic, the supply of which was never ending. A neighbour turned up saying that he'd seen a dog matching their description up the hill in the bush. They went off in the truck and returned later, complete with a very happy, but muddy, Lolly. 'She'd been hunting possum up in the bush,' Gillian guffawed. 'Looks like she got some too, the blood that's on her.'

At 2pm I left for Invercargill on the shuttle bus, waving goodbye to her, happy to be moving on to hopefully quieter and cleaner places.

TEN

Biodynamics: Kunekune Pigs and more

After a brief stay in Invercargill, where I was caught in a hailstorm, I headed north-west towards Dunedin for my next WWOOF. My new host, Alice, met me off the bus at lunchtime. She was immediately likeable, my age, short and sturdy with long, fair hair, streaked with grey. The usual mud-spattered truck stood waiting as she chatted away, telling me that she worked part-time as a career advisor in the local school and had trained as a yoga teacher in India. Immediately we launched into a conversation about our Indian travels and in no time reached her place, a large lifestyle off the road near a river with gorse-covered hills glowing yellow rising up behind the property.

There was a small cottage in front of the large house. 'This is where our WWOOFers stay,' she said, leading the way through a heavy wooden door, which was in need of a coat of paint. 'There are two bedrooms. You can have the smaller one at the back because we have a couple in the larger one. The cottage is one hundred years old and is a bit cold and damp, but I've put an electric blanket on your bed and there's a fan heater. You're welcome to be with us in the house anyway.' She showed me the bathroom and then said, 'It's time for lunch – let's go up to the house.'

The lifestyle property was wooden and looked as if it had been made by hand. When I commented on it Alice told me, 'Well, actually you could say that. This was our place the other side of Dunedin, and when we moved here we took it to bits and re-erected it – there's still stuff to do. My husband Peter's a builder and he's too busy with other folks' building to spend time on ours.' We walked up some wooden steps into the house, along a hallway into a large, cosy kitchen, full of the smell of freshly baked bread. *This is more like it!* I thought as I met the WWOOFing couple, Mark from Wales and his girlfriend, Sophie, who was a mixture of American and Sri Lankan. We sat down round a large, rectangular table, on which was olive bread, home-made by Alice, butter, cheese and pickles, with plenty of fresh salad from the garden. I felt myself relax. This was how a WWOOF place ought to be and the memory of Riverton receded in my mind.

After we'd cleared up, Sophie showed me how to feed the animals. The Kunekune pigs were adorable, their hairy, rotund little bodies mottled colours of sandy-brown, white, black and grey. These pigs were originally kept by the Maori but have spread to other countries due to their popularity. They are the smallest breed of domesticated pig and enjoy human company. We were greeted by excited grunts as they poked their snouts eagerly through the fence, slobbering and sniffing at the food. We also fed chickens and geese and later, at dinnertime, we fed the three cats: Grey Guy, Ginger Bitch and Rosie and two cute Jack Russell terriers – a mum, Sally, and her young puppy, Betsy.

Over dinner I learned that my host was a Greek Orthodox convert, although she also believed in reincarnation. She was an accomplished cook of Greek food, and we tucked into vegetarian moussaka. My body began to glow with healthy food once more. After our meal Mark and Sophie retired to the cottage while I stayed with Alice, enjoying the warmth of the stove, Grey Guy on my knee, watching the antics of Sally with her pup. Alice was good company and there was even an interesting programme on the television: a hilarious Kiwi soap involving a man who shared his home with a Kunekune pig!

At breakfast I met Peter, an imposing-looking individual, tall and slim with a long, reddish-brown beard and a strong Scottish accent; many Scots have settled in the Dunedin area. It rained hard all morning. The farm was biodynamic as well as organic, applying a holistic approach to agriculture, the livestock, plants and soil nutrition being viewed as one interrelated entity. Rudolf Steiner was the first proponent of this method, which uses a special calendar for seed sowing, planting, harvesting and soil enrichment. It was the day for putting a special liquid manure, composed of animal compost, minerals and medicinal herbs, on the land. Before this was done we had to stir the preparation. It was in a large container in the kitchen. A long, thick wooden pole was tied to the ceiling and for an hour we took it in turns to stir it, first one way and then another, to get a vortex going. The pole was heavy and it was hard work, made easier by our constant banter at the strangeness of the situation. When it was ready we all went outside with large paintbrushes, dipping them into smaller pots of the mixture and throwing it all over the land in tiny amounts. Apparently it was very strong, and judging by the quality of the produce, effective. We were all ravenous by dinnertime. It was Mark and Sophie's last night and Alice had made a scrumptious fish and scallop curry to celebrate.

The next day I was by myself, with the departure of Mark and Sophie, and my hosts at work. I was busy all day, weeding, cooking the dinner and feeding the animals. When I fed the Kunekunes, the large orangey-brown coloured one almost knocked me over in her attempt to eat the chicken food, until Sally dashed in and sent her off, barking furiously.

It was Good Friday and after dinner Alice took me to Dunedin for a Greek Orthodox service. Although I'd been to Greece, I'd never experienced an Orthodox service before. It was long, very long. The audience was composed of us plus an Israeli man, his Kazak wife and three-year-old son, who caused a pleasant diversion during the two-and-a-half-hour service by sitting on my knee and playing. The three priests busied themselves swinging incense, chanting and carrying an icon underneath the Bible round the small church three times, kissing it reverently. Afterwards we went for a well-earned coffee and cake in a café which offered free email access.

Another WWOOFer, Chris, from Australia, arrived the next day. He'd also been to India and had studied yoga in Rishikesh, like myself. We had a session with Alice before dinner – it felt good practising it once more. It had been extremely windy in the night, blowing off the pigs' roof, which Chris helped Alice to fix. I made hot cross buns, content to be warm inside, smelling the cinnamon aroma of the buns baking in the oven, then covering them with butter before the warm dough melted in our mouths.

Easter Sunday morning dawned dry and sunny and I continued weeding and bulb planting. In the afternoon we went with Alice to Dunedin again for a Greek Orthodox Easter party in someone's house. We picked up a ninety-year-old Greek Cypriot lady on the way. There was a lot of Greek food, washed down with champagne and I chatted with a few folk, in particular an acolyte (a priest's assistant) from Christchurch. We arrived home at sunset and all settled down to watch TV, a cat on each knee with the terriers playing their comical games around us.

The following evening, after another hard day's work, we discovered that Peter was an accomplished accordionist. He sat on the stairs, producing fine Scottish tunes, which made me a little homesick. Chris joined in on an improvised drum – a saucepan lid, while Alice tried to watch *Coronation Street*, as the animals careered around, getting in the way and causing much merriment. They were simple, but fulfilling pleasures, and once more I felt sad at my imminent departure.

All too soon the day arrived. Peter dropped me at a backpackers in Dunedin, where I'd arranged to meet an old friend and colleague, Dermot, who was also travelling around the country in his holidays.

ELEVEN

Karekare – 'The Piano' Beach

I spent a pleasant couple of days in Dunedin which reminded me of home. Dunedin is Celtic for Edinburgh, named by its Scottish settlers who also called the main thoroughfare Princes Street, with George, Hanover and Frederick Streets close by. Its streets were also steep like those in Edinburgh, if not steeper: Baldwin Street is listed as the steepest street in the world.

In Oamaru, north of Dunedin, I saw both the blue and yellow eyed penguins and then travelled on to Christchurch, the South Island's capital. Unlike Dunedin, Christchurch has a distinctly English feel, with its huge Anglican cathedral and punts gliding down the picturesque River Avon.

I was due to fly to Auckland from Christchurch but first I spent time exploring the scenic Banks Peninsula and Akaroa with its splendid harbour. I stayed at Le Bons Bay Backpackers, on another, smaller harbour, and was picked up along with two German girls from the Akaroa bus stop. They also took WWOOFers but were full, but as I 'd heard about their gourmet dinners I was keen to stay there. The meal exceeded my expectations: Groper fish in crab sauce, tamarind sauce with raw Groper, mussels in garlic sauce, cheese sauce mixed with mushrooms and broccoli, honeyed pumpkin and kumara and roast vegetables; then, if you had space, plum crumble and cream. All for only ten dollars! Garry, the owner, loved cooking and produced these meals every evening in the season. His fame had spread and the hostel was always fully booked. It was all served on a long table in their gorgeous garden, with splendid views of the valley below.

Garry's culinary skills were also evident at breakfast, with delicious home-made bread and muesli on offer. He also ran boat trips in his small boat, which held about eight people. We saw the rare, smallest Hector's dolphins (only four-thousand left in the South Island's waters), blue penguins and fur seals who peered at us inquisitively from their rocky swimming pool. Red and grey-coloured volcanic cliffs, cut by jagged caves, rose steeply above the sea, on which floated large fronds of kelp.

*

On 20 May I was back in Auckland, but only for one night. I had arranged to WWOOF at a place called Satyavan, deep in the stunning Waitakere Ranges bordering the Tasman Sea west of Auckland. Satyavan stood high on bush-covered hills above wave-pounded Karekare Beach, where Jane Campion's *The Piano* was filmed.

I took a bus to the outskirts of Auckland where I was met by my new host, Jenny and a young woman, Pamela, who'd recently moved to Satyavan. Jenny was in her mid-forties and not very chatty. She stopped to pick up her ten and twelve-year-old daughters, Prashanti and Prima, from school. It took around forty-five minutes along a windy road, thickly bordered by bush towards the end. Jenny told me that it was a Sai Baba ashram, a fact which had not been mentioned in the *WWOOF* book. Sai Baba was a controversial Indian guru and I began to wonder what this would mean. As we drew up outside I noticed that the lovely house had large windows with stained glass religious symbols engraved on them. My small room was down some steps on a lower, separate level, with a platform bed and a large poster of smiley Sai Baba, resplendent in his orange robe and brown beads, his hair like a thick, frizzy halo. I felt unnerved by the poster, the bed and the absence of an easily accessible loo. It had also begun to rain heavily. At dinner I met three other female residents and Philip, Jenny's husband, who lectured at Wellpark Natural Therapies College. The meal was vegetarian and tasty – corn fritters with potatoes and broccoli. Afterwards I did the dishes with the help of the girls, who kept me amused with tales of their school. Everyone went to bed early, as did I, and despite the eerie presence of Sai Baba, I managed to sleep reasonably well.

Jenny also worked part-time at the college and showed me what to do before leaving. I began planting beetroot, lettuce, broccoli and calendula seedlings until a storm came and soaked through my 'waterproofs', forcing me to stop and change. After an early lunch the sun came out and I finished the planting. The land was steep, with terraces for the vegetables and herbs and I found the slopes difficult to negotiate with arthritic knees and back. By 4pm I was on the verge of collapse but revived after a snack and shower. Jenny brought another WWOOFer, Mona from East Germany, back with her from college.

The next day I was given all the large windows to clean both inside and out. It was a morning of blustery showers and Mona was given a heavy job lifting stones from the pond. In mid-afternoon Jenny gave us a lift downhill to the beach, where she left us to go and see a horse. Once she'd gone Mona said, 'My back's killing me after lifting all those stones. They were too heavy and I got soaked. Jenny didn't even thank me or show any interest in how I'd got on at lunchtime.'

I commiserated with her. 'I know what you mean. She's the same with me and I've never seen her smile. They seem to be lost in their own world, her and Philip.' We soon forgot our grievances as we strolled along a grassy path through the bush to the beach in brilliant sunshine. Karekare Beach was dramatic, with gigantic waves crashing onto the black volcanic sand, a tiny craggy-looking island offshore and steep cliffs. Luckily we got a lift back up the long, steep road by the owner of a black Labrador dog who had decided to follow us. At dinner nobody asked us about our afternoon and afterwards we were treated to a short film about Sai Baba. He mingled with his devotees, giving each nectar and holy ash, which, we were told, materialised in his hands. They had all been to his ashram and experienced it, so we were in no position to argue. It all seemed very strange. I'd heard about him on my Indian travels but had never been tempted to visit.

There were more squally showers in the morning, but I managed to plant out some herbs and bulbs. I was also given their big jeep to wash. Jenny was at home and remarked over lunch, 'Maybe you, Margaret, should find another WWOOF because of this weather.' I wondered if she were displeased with me, or that I hadn't done enough work, but it was impossible to ask.

Later Mona said, 'I'm going to leave as well tomorrow. I'm too cold here and I'm fed up with their unfriendly behaviour. We can go together.' We tried to find another place but most hosts were no longer taking WWOOFers with winter coming.

I had an idea. 'Do you fancy going to Waiheke Island?' I asked Mona.

'What a good idea!' she enthused so we booked the Hekerua Lodge Backpackers.

*

60

Before our lift with Jenny at nine the next morning we had to strip and make up our beds and clean our rooms, as well as wash everyone's breakfast dishes. The atmosphere was tense and Jenny drove in silence to Henderson, from where we could take a local train to Auckland. We waited for a farewell smile and a 'thank you', but neither manifested. As she drove off we both heaved a huge sigh of relief. 'Well, I hope she's not a typical WWOOF host,' Mona said. It was her first WWOOFing experience and I felt sorry for her.

'Don't worry. This is the first unfriendly, ungrateful host I've had. All the rest were lovely people,' I assured her.

We boarded the train and then took a bus to the ferry terminal for Waiheke Island. We had an hour to wait and went to Starbucks for a coffee and a muffin. 'This is more like it,' laughed Mona. We both felt light and free and ready to party: it helped that the sun was shining, the air warm and balmy. The boat took fifty minutes to reach the island, stopping at Devonport on the way. Flotillas of racing yachts, their large, multi-coloured sails ballooning out in front, sped past us, the tangy sea air making us feel even higher.

A bus was waiting at the ferry terminal and it took us to the backpackers where we got a three-night deal. It was a lovely place with a spa pool, plus a cold one for when the heat got too much. We walked back to Oneroa, the main tiny town, admiring the clean, sandy beaches. We dined on fresh fish and chips and stocked up with food supplies and a bottle of cheap champagne, to celebrate our freedom. The spa pool was just what we needed to soothe our aching muscles, and after hot showers we drank the bubbly, sitting either side of the pot belly stove, feeling warm and pleasantly tipsy. 'This is the life,' Mona sighed, 'but I will need to start WWOOFing again as I can't afford to travel like this.' I was planning to return to my favourite WWOOF in the Hokianga while she was heading southwards.

The three days sped by, exploring the island, swimming and hanging out in the aptly named *Lazy Lounge* in Oneroa, which made the most delicious carrot cake I'd ever tasted, served with cream or yoghurt. All too soon it was time to return to Auckland and Mona and I went our separate ways. The Dalai Lama was in town and I had arranged to see him, having been unable to do so in India. I saw him twice – once in the theatre in the morning and then at Eden Park Stadium in the evening, where ten thousand people assembled to hear him. I gazed at his jolly face through my binoculars, joining in the crowd's laughter. His merriment was contagious – what a wonderful human being.

While in Auckland I walked barefoot through lush green grass to the summit of Mt Eden, with its deep volcanic crater. It was a clear day and there were superb views all round of the entire Auckland area, with its many bays and harbours. Another day, in Devonport, I walked to the top of Victoria Hill and was treated to more fine views of Waiheke Island, the Coromandel Peninsula, Auckland's Skytower and harbour. There was also a free performing arts festival on in the centre of Auckland and I met Angela and Brian from Kohu Kohu there. Folk were dancing to the beat of samba from a large group of Maori, and there were Flamenco and Pacific Island dance performances. It was all very lively, colourful and exotic, but I was looking forward to be being back in Hokianga Heaven.

TWELVE

Hokianga Reunion

Angela and Brian gave me a lift back to the Hokianga. This time I was to WWOOF partly at Angela's place and partly at Brian's, which was called 'Bag End' and was a small backpackers near Kohu Kohu. There were two reasons for this arrangement: Angela already had WWOOFers and Brian needed some help, although the hostel had no visitors at that moment. Most of them headed for the Tree House and Brian took their overspill. Angela spent half her time at Bag End and half at her own place.

We went to a supermarket on the way where I also bought provisions. I was to do two hours a day at Bag End with free accommodation but no food. We just missed the ferry at Rawene, so sat sipping lattes in the Boatshed Café, glad to be sitting in the unseasonably warm June air, gazing at the calm waters of the Hokianga again. Angela's two WWOOFers, Ziggy and Geraldine from Germany, were also on the ferry. Ziggy was returning from doing a Vipassana meditation retreat near Auckland and could not stop talking after ten days of silence. 'It was great!' he kept enthusing, brimming with vitality after his experience.

'You should be still and calm after that,' Brian said, 'not chattering away non-stop! What are you on?'

'Life! I'm high on life and love,' Ziggy beamed, doing a little jig on the ferry's deck.

Wally was waiting for them in his truck and I continued to Bag End with Brian and Angela. It was another adobe built house in a lovely spot surrounded by thick bush, and I had my own comfortable room with a double bed. We were welcomed home by Brian's two big, sloppy, ginger and tabby cats, Frodo and Bella, who wound round our legs, purring loudly and meowing for their supper. Angela made a tasty tuna pasta while I got settled in and afterwards I did the dishes. Then we all retired, tired out by travelling.

The next day Brian was working in his building business and Angela was off to her cleaning-cum-counselling and massage job in the village. I'd just finished my yoga exercises when Mick appeared.

He told me about his latest venture. 'I've bought this old yacht, Margaret. She's a beauty, at least she will be once I've done her up. Then I'll take tourists for trips around the harbour.' The last time I'd seen him he'd been talking about setting up an EFL college in the old school in Kohu Kohu, with me as the English teacher. I knew he was an Aquarian, an airy type, as Angela had warned.

'Don't believe a word he says,' she had told me, 'he's always hatching some hair-brained scheme, none of which ever get off the ground.' In fact, Brian was now considering turning Bag End into an EFL school. There were plenty of Asians, particularly Japanese, who would be interested in learning English in such an environment, he believed, and again I could be their teacher. It sounded like a great plan to me. After Mick had gone I did the housework then went to visit Leah, the singer from Bruce's party. She lent me a singing book with voice training exercises on a tape, assuring me that with practice my voice could sound as good as hers. I returned to Bag End and began the training in a large, airy room upstairs with Velux windows overlooking the bush. The acoustics were incredible and I could make as much noise as I liked, with no-one nearby to complain. This room was to be the classroom and I fantasised about teaching small groups of enthusiastic students in such a wonderful space. *If I visualised it hard enough, it would happen.*

After three days Angela, Brian and I went to her place. It felt good to be back in the high hills above the Hokianga, although winter was coming and I needed a hottie at night. This time I was in the bunk room, but I had it to myself. We made a large circle around the meal: myself, Angela, Brian, Wally, Geraldine, Ziggy, Claire (a kiwi WWOOFer) and Tiana, Lillavarti's older daughter. When I asked Tiana where her mum was she said, 'She's away on some crusade with a monk after going to see the Dalai Lama.' The food was as delicious as I remembered, the conversation as stimulating.

I walked across the large expanse of lawn towards the Whale Lodge in the cool early morning air, glad to be back in heaven. A great feeling of oneness enveloped me as I stood on a yoga mat gazing at the rolling bush-covered hills, listening to the Tui birds' melodic calls as I raised my arms to greet the sun. After breakfast I cleaned the WWOOFers' accommodation, then, just before lunch, Emery (the American pianist from Bruce's party) and his wife, Dawn, turned up in their battered bus. Hearing the commotion, I emerged into the sunshine and was greeted enthusiastically by Emery, followed by Dawn.

'It's great to see you again, Margaret,' they chorused, each giving me a large hug. Another man appeared at the door of the bus and looked around hesitantly. 'Come on down, Patrick,' Emery commanded and he hopped agilely from the bus, grinning widely. 'Meet Patrick, Margaret, my old friend from Nelson on the South Island.'

This wiry little man, with sparkling brown eyes, a greyish-white beard and thinning, longish hair, immediately caught my attention as I felt a warm, calm connection with him. He held out a bony hand, 'To be sure it's great to meet you, so it is,' he said with a charmingly mixed Irish-Kiwi accent.

'Pleased to meet you too,' I replied, feeling foolishly felicitous, adding, 'so what brings you to the Hokianga?'

'My pal Emery,' he chuckled, looking at his friend.

'Sure thing,' responded Emery. 'We met at Nelson's Saturday craft market. Patrick made beautiful carved wooden signs and now he plans to settle here and maybe carve some more.'

'Maybe,' Patrick said, 'but my hands are so arthritic I'm not sure that'll be possible.' He held up his hands, the fingers horribly bent, twisted and swollen. I felt a rush of sympathy, my own hands being unaffected by arthritis but my knees were periodically prone to painful swelling. Then he asked, 'Do you know how to play Hacky Sack?'

'Never heard of it,' I said, wondering what on earth it was.

He began to jig around doing strange contortions with his legs. 'Come on, Margaret! Join in, I'll catch you if you fall,' he assured me, but I was not convinced. Certainly his knee and ankle joints appeared to be unaffected by arthritis. 'You can do this with a wee soft ball, called a foot bag. You have to keep it off the ground without using your hands.'

They disappeared with Angela and later she told me that Patrick would move into the Cabin in the Sky: a tiny hut high on a hill above us which had been inhabited by one of her sons and was now sadly in need of repair. He would live in it rent free and in return would give it some tender loving care.

We were in the middle of dinner when Lillavarti, her younger daughter, Kaishalah, and a Filipino monk arrived. Lillavarti was on a high and entertained us to hilarious tales of her travels with the monk, who sat in silence, a beatific smile upon his round face. It was bedlam and I soon escaped to read in bed, unwinding from the day's excitement.

*

Surprising events happened in Kohu Kohu. On a Saturday evening I attended a recital by a famous pianist called Ramon. It was taking place in one of the villager's fine old wooden houses and we all crammed into the lounge, sitting wherever we could find a place – on the arms of chairs, curled up on floor cushions or outside on the deck where an impressive spread of nibbles was laid out, along with soft drinks. Chilled wines and beers were to be found in a large fridge in the kitchen. This was all included in the small price of our tickets.

Once we were settled, including the house's two tabby cats, who sat ears alert on the sideboard, Ramon, who had performed in seventy-five countries, began to play. We listened, entranced, as strains of Mendelssohn, Debussy, Chopin, Beethoven and Prokofiev whirled around us, a cascade of sound, transporting us to other, higher realms.

On our return to Angela's in Wally's car, Tiana's birthday party was in full swing. We consumed more food – pizza, salad and birthday cakes: a carrot cake which I'd made and a carob one from Ziggy. Tiana's teenage friends were there, including a Nepalese lad. Later, after the food had settled, we dressed up in colourful old clothes, which were kept in a large wooden chest, and danced around to pop music. One of the girls did a sensuous belly dance to some Arabic melodies and we all joined in with much merriment. It was after midnight before I got to bed. What an evening!

Dawn and Emery dropped by for a chat on Sunday afternoon, our free day. 'Patrick's poorly, Margaret. You should go and see him – he's resting in our bus.' I didn't need much encouragement and walked up the hill to a small camp site where the bus was parked. I tapped tentatively on the door which was partly open.

'Come away in,' Patrick's voice called. 'Good to see you, Margaret,' he said, sitting up from where he'd been lying on the bed at the back of the bus.

He looked bleary-eyed, his clothes and hair ruffled, but still managed a sunny smile. 'How are you feeling?' I asked, sitting down on a bench by the door.

'Oh, not so bad. At least I can make it to the loo in time now!' The loo was a long drop one, a short walk away through the bush.

'That's good. It must've been awful for you. Do you know what caused it?'

He gave a rueful grin. 'There's no fridge in here and I reckon that they sometimes keep food hanging around for too long. I can't wait until I can move into my own place. Would you like a cuppa?'

'Yes, thanks. Shall I put the kettle on?'

'Go on then. There's matches over there on the shelf.' I turned on their two ringed cooker's calor gas while Patrick hunted for clean mugs. As we sat, cradling the steaming mugs in our hands for warmth, he told me about how he'd travelled overland from Ireland to India at the age of twenty-five.

'So you're an old hippie then,' I laughed and then told him about my Indian journeys, when I was twice his age.

'You're an even older hippie then,' he retorted. We both chuckled, remembering our respective trips with pleasure.

'You should visit my future home on your way back,' he suggested.

'Yes, I will. I've never seen it close up,' I said. 'When do you think you'll move in?'

'The sooner the better. I just need to get some stuff, like a kettle, some pots and pans and bedding. There's a second-hand shop in Rawene where hopefully I'll find what I want.'

We had a goodbye hug and I strolled along the track feeling light and happy. The Cabin in the Sky was situated above the road on the right and I scrambled up a narrow path towards it. It was tiny with three small windows, faded sky-blue paint and a sunny yellow chimney sticking out of the roof. I opened the door easily and peeped inside. It was all kitted out with a double platform bed at the back, a stove and a sink, with a rainwater butt attached to the outside wall. It was a fine evening and I walked to the hilltop above the hut. There were rolling green hills all around, dotted with fields in which sheep and cows grazed, and a scattering of trees, the harbour a smudgy grey in the distance, with higher hills, wreathed in puffy white clouds, behind the water. I sat on a boulder and watched as the sun set, turning the hills and distant water pink, imagining myself living there with Patrick, a romantic but not a practicable prospect.

Two of Angela's WWOOFers had moved on which meant that I

could stay at her place. One afternoon I went in Wally's van with Angela and Ziggy to a place for sale not far from them called The Herb Garden. It had once been a herb garden but the fifty acre piece of land had become overgrown, although there were some beautiful mature trees as well as a two-bedroomed wooden house and a small studio. I was tempted to buy it, but it would have been too much work for me. We had gone to get Girlie the Goat, who was easily enticed into the back of the van with a persimmon. She was docile for the short ride back to Angela's, no doubt busily munching on the sweet fruit. She was tethered up on a steep bank which was covered in brambles and long, thick grass. She would make a fine job of clearing the area, while simultaneously fertilising it. Before bedtime Angela gave my feet a wonderful massage with lavender oil – the perfect end to a hard day's work.

The days passed with autumnal work clearing beans, peas and other vegetable crop remains from the beds, then shovelling compost from the heap into a wheelbarrow and depositing it on top of them. They used a 'no dig' method, similar to many of the places where I'd WWOOFed, to prevent damage to the soil structure.

Lillavarti was a keen member of the Green Party and was busy preparing for a rally in Rawene for the upcoming elections. After days of rain the Saturday morning of the rally dawned cloudy but dry. I helped her load up her car with banners and then she gave me a lift to the ferry. A friend of Angela's, Rob, was there with his lovingly maintained old yacht which had green canvas sails.

'Come aboard my gorgeous green yacht,' he said, giving me a hand as I stepped onto the deck. As we set sail a vivid rainbow curved across the sky, while a kingfisher perched on a pole, as if to bid us farewell. As we sailed over to Rawene I helped Rob hang banners from the side, emblazoned with, 'Vote Green' and 'GE free New Zealand'.

Rawene village hall was full of stalls, which included a large Green Party one, laden with leaflets, stickers and badges. Leah was there selling her home-made wines and Patrick was advertising his wooden signs. I went over to say 'hello'.

'How ya doing, Margaret?' he asked, treating me to one of his enchanting smiles. 'I've moved into the cabin. You should come up and visit. Emery's parked his bus there as Dawn's gone on a retreat and he wants some company. I'd rather be by meself, but it won't be for long.'

'That's great, Patrick. I'll come up tomorrow as it's my day off.' I looked at his signs. 'These are really good. Are your hands feeling better?'

'Sure, they are Margaret. I reckon it's something in the Hokianga air,' he said, examining his knuckles which looked less swollen.

Lillavarti arrived and organised us all to march down the road to the ferry landing, banners held high, chanting 'Vote Green' and 'Keep New Zealand GE free'. We were less than twenty in number but we made up for it with plenty of noise and the onlookers, which included many Maori families, cheered us on. Back at the hall there was live folk and jazz music and I met Heide, a new German/Irish WWOOFer, who'd just arrived on the Auckland bus. She informed me that she was a sixty-two-year-old shaman, and she looked the part, her ebony hair, tied back with a bright red scarf, a long, black skirt and a ruffled red and white patterned blouse. From her ears hung large hooped silver earrings, while her fingers were adorned with silver snake rings and round her neck was a wooden tree-shaped pendant.

We went to the Boatshed Café, where other friends of Angela's were congregating, for more live music, coffee and cakes. In the late afternoon we all took the ferry across to Kohu Kohu and headed for Angela's. It was the winter solstice and a big party was planned. Angela had been busy cooking roast stuffed pumpkin and kumara and we were greeted by a mouth-watering aroma as we entered the communal area.

The rain had held off, the night black, but we lit it up with home-made lanterns – candles in coke bottles, as we began to walk up the hill to the sanctuary, an area of flat land just below the Cabin in the Sky. Angela and Brian led the way, followed by Wally, Claire, Geraldine, Emery, Lillavarti and her daughters and other friends. There was no sign of Patrick. As we walked we sang, 'Ah poor bird, take thy flight, far above the troubles of this dark night'. Our chants became more powerful, more melodious and more magical as we approached the sanctuary and formed a circle round a huge bonfire, which by a miracle lit, despite the recent rain. A three-quarter moon shone in and out of scudding clouds as we slowly danced round the flames, holding hands and singing other songs. It was all extremely pagan, primeval even, as we threw handfuls of dry grass into the fire, saying our own prayers. Mine was: 'Goodbye inner and outer war.

69

Hello peace'. We then drank glasses of hot mulled blackcurrant wine, rejoicing in our togetherness on this, the shortest day of the year. On our return we had fresh fruit salad and ice-cream, followed by more live music and singing. I went to bed and was woken up at 3am by the sound of loud thunder and flashes of lightning, followed by rain pelting down on the roof.

I went to visit Patrick the next day, as promised. When I asked him why he hadn't been there the previous night he replied, 'I was tucked up all cosy in me bed listening to your lovely music. Then I heard the possum trap outside go "snap!" You know I'm catching two of those devils every night. That was enough.' Then he showed me some yellow cloth. 'I'm going to line me ceiling with this, Margaret. What do you think?'

'Hmm. It's a cheerful, sunny colour – just what you need to brighten up the place in the long, dark days of winter.'

'Yes. It's not my favourite time of year, but it's a lot warmer here than down in Nelson.' He bent down to put another log into the pot-bellied stove, prodding it with the poker making sparks fly up.

'So you don't miss it?'

'Not at all. I'm content to be here, for a time at least,' he said.

There was nothing more I could say. It was only another two days before I had to leave on the bus to Auckland, from where I would fly to Vancouver, the second to last stage of my round the world trip, on 2 July, 2002. The last stage would be a flight to Toronto, followed by an internal one to Sault Ste Marie to visit my son. It was already in my mind, however, to return the following year for another six months in glorious New Zealand.

PART TWO

NEW ZEALAND WITH VANNIE

THIRTEEN

The Return

New Zealand was calling to me so strongly that I returned to Auckland on 3 December, 2002, only five months after I'd left. I stayed in a hostel near Mount Eden and sat in the evening sunshine, breathing in the heady scent of spring flowers, listening to the birds singing in the trees. It was perfect. I was back where I wanted to be and had already contacted immigration about getting a business visa to set up a language school in Kohu Kohu. They had told me on the phone that they looked carefully at the merits of each case. Several of the hostel's guests were in the process of applying to immigrate, including a Dutch chef and we sat chatting in the garden, sipping cool beers while attempting to unravel the intricacies of the process.

I was also planning to buy a second-hand van and had taken refresher driving lessons back in Scotland as it had been several years since I had driven. My confidence was still low and I decided to wait until I was on the South Island to buy. It would be much quieter there, with less traffic, although not so easy to find anything suitable. Most travellers bought from the large Auckland car sales and then sold the vehicle in Christchurch before flying home. The tourist buses that I had used covered the main parts of both islands but I craved to see the wild wilderness, only accessible along rough and unsurfaced minor roads, or unmetalled, as the Kiwis call them.

Before I left Auckland for Kohu Kohu I went to see an immigration consultant. He quickly dashed my hopes of obtaining a business visa. 'You need to have proper business experience which you don't have,' he told me bluntly, 'but you could come in with a relevant job offer in teaching. You'll need to get evidence of all your previous jobs though. Then you'd have enough points.' I thanked him but went away feeling bereft. I had pictured myself so strongly running the small school at Bag End, Brian's place in Kohu Kohu, and the thought of having to teach in a busy city like Auckland or Christchurch in order to obtain residency was not nearly so appealing.

Four days after I'd arrived in Auckland I was once again heading to Northland by bus, which stopped as usual to allow the passengers

71

to view the big kauri tree in the Waipoua Kauri Forest. I never tired of seeing this huge 'Lord of the Forest' and craned my neck to look closely at its towering height, festooned with lichens, ferns and other creepers. The splendour of it somehow put my paltry plans into perspective and I felt lighter, stronger and more able to simply be in the present moment, accepting that whatever happens is how it should be.

Rawene looked the same and I boarded the ferry to Kohu Kohu with mounting excitement. A group of Harley-Davidson bikers stood leaning against their powerful machines, helmets clasped to their muscular chests, allowing the sea breeze to cool their long, straggly-haired heads. They smoked and chatted as the ferry headed out into the harbour, while I sat on the outside bench, backpack at my feet, enjoying the rhythm of the boat's engine, the salty tang of the sea and the rolling green Hokianga hills all around. Angela was waiting for me at the small jetty and as we hugged I could smell her earthy fragrance. She looked as beautiful as ever and seemed delighted to see me.

'Welcome again to the Hokianga, Margaret,' she said on releasing me.

'It's great to be back, Angela. I feel like I'm coming home,' I replied, loading my pack into the back of her car. I was staying at her place full time as there was a lot of work to do. I shared the bunk room with a friendly twenty-two-year-old German girl called Kaitaia, while Katy, a pleasant young Kiwi, was in the other room. Claire, Wally and Gwendoline were all still there as part of the core community. Brian was at Bag End. Angela had made a delicious meal with a huge garden salad and we stood in a circle around the table, holding hands, and with our eyes shut experienced a few moments of silence as we unwound after the day's events, allowing an atmosphere of peaceful calm to envelope us. Angela said a few words of welcome and thanks to Mother Earth for providing the food and then we loaded our plates and went to sit at the long table by the window, chatting amicably like old friends.

The following day was Sunday, their rest day, and it dawned windy and showery, with short spells of bright sunshine in between. Margo, a friend of Angela's, had an exhibition of her photographs down in Kohu Kohu and Angela drove us there after lunch. The photos, which were of cubic shapes, were excellent, and there was quite a crowd in her tiny garden studio. Afterwards we went to the village café for ice cream and then visited Brian at Bag End. I felt sad remembering my fantasies about teaching there, but realised that I was probably too old to start up a new business; I'd just relax and enjoy myself. On our return Katy began to show Kaitaia how to weave flax, which she had cut from the numerous plants scattered around the place, into baskets.

I managed to get up early and do some yoga in the Whale Lodge before breakfast, a fine way to start the day. A crop I'd had no experience of was being grown on a piece of land which had recently been cleared by the goat's grazing, followed by smothering with black polythene for several months, which effectively killed off the weeds. Kaitaia helped me to remove clear polythene from the ginger, which was keeping it warm as the bright green shoots burst through the soil. I then watered it with a hose and went on to water the mandala garden nearby. I tidied up this garden and sprinkled fresh coffee grinds around to deter the slugs from nibbling the young tomato, basil, lettuce and brassicas.

In the afternoon I eventually managed to book a flight from Auckland to Nelson, in the north of the South Island. It was much cheaper than the combined bus and ferry fares would have been and I would leave on 27 December. I was busily weeding another part of the garden near the kitchen the next day when Patrick appeared to collect his post and fill two large containers with water. He was still living up the hill in the Cabin in the Sky and seemed pleased to see me. 'Come up for a visit after lunch,' he suggested, making my heart race with anticipation. As I drew near to his place I stopped in amazement. He had transformed the small area of land in front of the cabin, making raised beds in which flourished potatoes, tomatoes, herbs, celery, marigolds and nasturtiums. A banana tree was already more than two metres high while flax bushes and other shrubs were growing around the edges of the land. A charming seating area with beautifully carved wooden benches was positioned just outside the cabin and he had even built a timber extension which was his workshop. As I stood gazing, Patrick came out of the cabin.

'So what do you think of my abode?' he enquired, grinning widely.

'Oh, Patrick! It's incredible.'

'And you'll never guess,' he didn't wait for a reply. 'I'm carving loads of signs again. Look at my hands.' He held them out for me to inspect: the swollen, twisted finger joints and knuckles were almost normal-looking.

'What happened to your arthritis? Your hands look so much better,' I said in awe.

'To be honest, Margaret, I don't really know. I reckon it's got something to do with my lifestyle here. It's so peaceful and I'm really content, possibly for the first time in my life.'

'That's wonderful! I'm so glad you're happy.'

'Well, I don't know about happy, but I'm certainly content. Would you care for a cuppa?' Naturally I accepted and waited on one of the wooden benches admiring the garden while he brewed away. Once we'd finished our tea he said, 'I'll need to crack on with a sign I'm making for someone. I've got quite a few orders coming in and I must keep on top of it.' I reluctantly left and spent the remainder of the time before dinner relaxing in the sauna and swimming in the pond to cool down. It was a fine evening and as I lay on my back feeling the silky caress of the water on my bare skin, gazing up at the myriad of stars and listening to the croaking of the frogs and eerie cries of the possums, I realised that my disappointment with Patrick's lack of a romantic response had evaporated, leaving me feeling simply at peace.

*

The days glided by with plenty of garden work, cooking and cleaning as well as morning yoga, afternoon swims in the pond and sauna. Social gatherings happened regularly – people's birthday parties and village events, like the community association's wine and cheese party held, surprisingly, in the fire station. One afternoon I went with Brian and Angela to Kaiokohe, more than an hour's drive away, where we did some shopping. Afterwards we went to see the three-hour long *Twin Towers*, part two of *The Lord of the Rings* trilogy, set in New Zealand and all the rage. The small but cute cinema was packed and stuffy but I was soon so engrossed in the film that I didn't notice. We had to drive the long way back as there was no ferry, along narrow, winding roads where wild roses, hydrangeas and the crimson-flowered pohutukawa, or 'Christmas Tree', grew in abundance. A full moon blazed in a clear, light sky, but over the Hokianga Harbour hung menacing-looking black clouds, while the moon shone on its calm waters. It looked surreal and we felt the same, still affected by the film.

An English family with a five-year-old daughter were staying temporarily in their converted van, helping out with the work in return for an electricity supply. The father wrote EFL materials for a living and could work anywhere in the world as long as he could use his computer. I felt rather envious of his job and was surprised to discover that my brain still worked when I helped him with an EFL game. One morning at breakfast their daughter calmly announced that there were rats in the compost toilet. My rat phobia immediately manifested. 'Rats! Are you sure?' I asked her, terrified.

'Yes, rats,' she said serenely. 'It's OK. They're quite a long way down.' This did nothing to placate me. Rats could climb, couldn't they?

Angela arrived, wondering what all the commotion was about. 'Oh, yes. They've been in there for some time. We've been wondering how to get rid of them humanely,' she said.

With regard to rats, my eco-principles became non-existent. 'What do you mean, humanely? Just poison them. How can I sit there now?' My breakfast remained untouched, my tea getting cold.

Angela sighed. 'Well, I suppose we'll need to do something now,' she conceded.

I felt relaxed enough to resume eating and tried not to dwell on my usual post-breakfast visit to the compost loo.

Christmas Eve dawned mild, with cloudy skies and the promise of showers. I went with Angela and Brian over the ferry to Rawene, with Aniko, a new Japanese WWOOFer. While our hosts were busy we went to explore the mangrove walkway – a short excursion through the muddy mangroves just outside the village. These plants fascinated me with their strangely twisted roots rising out of the water, their ability to live between the salty sea tides an incredible feat of nature. We all had lunch in the Boatshed Café, watching as the clouds lifted from the harbour and the sun came out. That evening we decorated a large branch of a pine tree which Brian had cut and tied to a pillar in the communal area. Aniko showed us how to make origami paper shapes to which we glued on glitter and then arranged them on the branch – a marvellously simple Christmas Eve. On our way to bed we stood for a while gazing up at the stars, the Milky Way palely shining, while shooting stars or satellites shot across the sky. There was nowhere else I'd rather be.

I learned to cope with the loo rats by not looking down, shutting my eyes as I threw in handfuls of dry grass and twigs. Wally had put poison down but they seemed to be immune to it. It was a good test for my phobia, and Christmas Day began with such a test. The second test was Patrick's appearance. He looked dapper in a collarless checked shirt and waistcoat with clean and pressed blue jeans. Angela had invited him to lunch but he had accepted another invitation from two lone women who lived near him, a female farmer and a Maori lady from the Bay of Plenty. He would be the only man and was obviously looking forward to it.

A male friend of Angela's, who ran another small organic community which took WWOOFers, arrived with a huge Pavlova that he'd made with fresh strawberries and passion fruit syrup from his land. It was the tastiest Pavlova that I'd ever eaten. I attempted to make sushi with Aniko's expert guidance and Angela concocted vegetarian kebabs and baked bananas – all from the gardens. I picked and made a large salad, decorated with marigold petals and nasturtium flowers. Gwendoline had made special German biscuits and there were nuts and dried fruit. What a splendid, unusual feast.

Boxing Day was quieter and I spent time packing and preparing for my trip the following day. It felt like the right time to be leaving and as I planned to return after my travels I wasn't too sad. On 27 December Angela drove me to the ferry, wished me *'Bon Voyage'* and 'come back soon' and stood waving as the boat chugged out into the harbour. I waited in the Boatshed Café for the 10.30am Auckland bus, writing postcards and drinking coffee. I was becoming used to this Auckland-Rawene bus journey and the driver welcomed me like an old friend. Once more I saw the magnificent 'Big Tree' and we arrived at Auckland's Sky Tower at 5.30pm. I had a meal of Turkish *meze* then got the airport bus. The tiny 33-seater Air New Zealand flight to Nelson was punctual and comfortable and took just seventy-five minutes. We flew over the majestic snow-capped peak of Mount Egmont, bathed in the rays of the setting sun and soon after the expanse of the Cook Strait which separates the North from the South Island.

FOURTEEN

Golden Wheels

I took a taxi from tiny Nelson airport to the Trampers Rest Backpackers. This quaint little house had an avocado tree in the garden surrounded by a profusion of colourful flowers and herbs, including peppermint and lemon verbena, and was run by Alan, a helpful, friendly man in his mid-fifties.

After a breakfast of porridge, fruit loaf baked by Alan and mint tea from the garden, I ventured out in search of a vehicle. I bought a car sales magazine and found the address of a cheap dealer. Sitting in his front yard was a silvery-gold Toyota Liteace, 1986, but 'very tidy', according to the salesman, in good condition with a turbo-diesel auto engine, a skylight roof, eight padded seats and curtains. I could put down the seats and sleep in the back. I took it for a test run and found it easy to drive, having automatic gears. I was smitten and signed the forms, although I was fairly sure that it was overpriced at around £1800. I paid half the price and left it there until I had the rest of the money and all the paperwork.

The next day I withdrew the rest of the money from the bank, got change of ownership forms from the Post Office, took out six months third party insurance and joined the AA. With their membership I was given a set of detailed maps – one for each district in the country. Then I collected my beautiful Vannie; it was so exciting as I nervously managed to navigate into a petrol station to fill up with diesel. Then I collected my backpack from the hostel, went to the Warehouse for a bed roll, a sleeping bag, a one-ring gas cooker and cooking utensils, and finally the supermarket for food. It was by that time 5.30pm and I was very hot and tired, too tired to drive far.

I headed west out of Nelson to the McKee Reserve campsite, on the shores of the Tasman Sea, at Ruby Bay, with splendid views over to Nelson and the mountains beyond. It was packed, being the Christmas holidays, but I found a quiet spot sandwiched between two big converted house buses, which both had childless couples dwelling in them. There were many wacky bus and truck conversions, with extended roofs, balconies and terraces, some looking more like caravans, cabins or houses than trucks, with incredible artwork on their brightly painted bodies. I spent ages unpacking everything, dining on bread and spreads as I couldn't locate the cooker. It grew cold after the sun went down and I wriggled into my new sleeping bag fully dressed and lay looking at the stars twinkling in a clear sky through the skylight roof. I didn't sleep well on the bedroll, which was too lumpy.

The van soon heated up with the morning sun and I was up early to escape the heat. After a trip to the bathroom I went for a swim in the warm sea, relaxing briefly in the sunshine afterwards before returning to sort out the van, which took ages. My kind neighbours gave me hot water for my tea, congratulating me on my purchase. 'You're one of us travellers now,' they said, with wide, welcoming grins. It felt good to be part of this fraternity, although I thought that my tiny van didn't quite qualify. The inhabitants of the conversions were as colourful and fascinating as their vehicles and seemed a hospitable bunch.

It was too hot by eleven o'clock (strange weather for New Year's Eve I realised, thinking of the cold back home) when I finally left, then stopped at the small town of Motueka to buy a single mattress, quilt and duvet cover. I was returning to Golden Bay, near the north-western tip of the South Island, but first I had to ascend the 791 metres high Takaka Hill, which separates Tasman Bay from Golden Bay. It was a scary drive, and after receiving some incomprehensible shouts of abuse as people passed me, I began stopping in the passing places, allowing the fast, impatient Kiwi drivers to overtake. At the summit I stopped for a rest and walked to the lookout point where the expanse of Golden Bay could be seen through the hazy heat.

The road down was either not so steep and twisty, or my driving had improved, and I stopped for lunch in Takaka. I had been emailing a friend of Angela's, called River, who lived near Takaka and had invited me to join him and his girlfriend at the Mussel Inn in Onekaka for New Year's Eve. I had fond memories of the Inn from my previous visit and hoped that it would be as good as I remembered. Near the Inn, down a stony track, was the Shambhala Beach Farm Hostel, where I was allowed to park on a grassy spot with a view of the sea and Farewell Spit in the distance. Later a group of five Kiwis came to camp and I discovered that they were also going to the Mussel Inn. I showered and changed into a dress, feeling in a party mood. The Kiwis, a South African man, an Australian girl and an English nurse who worked there, were sitting in the garden so I joined them. They were drinking gin and lime and offered me one, after which the nurse ran me to the Inn. It was already busy at eight, but there was no sign of River, so I sat outside at one of the wooden tables and ordered their special New Year's Eve dinner: Dory fish, salad and a baked potato. It was a large, delicious portion and I washed it down with more gin and tonics.

About half past nine I noticed River, who I recognised by the picture he'd sent me. He was an ageing hippy – tall and lean, with long, straggly grey hair tied back with an embroidered band. With him were two women, his English girlfriend, Sarah, and a younger lady called Joe. We all sat down and Sarah, who had just immigrated, explained how it had worked for her. It was obvious that I'd have to be offered a teaching position to get the points, but I still was uncertain that I wanted to do this. They left before midnight, to my disappointment, so I went inside to dance. The large wooden dance floor was heaving and when January 1, 2003, was heralded, I received a few hugs and wishes of 'Happy New Year,' but inside I was feeling homesick, missing my children and worried about the impending black cloud of war with Iraq, despite the gins. An elderly German man, who was staying at the Shambhala, hugged me too tightly, and when I announced that I was leaving he decided to come too. He took me for a short cut through the bush, where there were hundreds of glow worms glinting through the foliage. We stood transfixed by the tiny, starry specks all around us, while through the branches above glimmered a myriad of stars. It was a clear, calm night and my sadness melted away, surrounded by the pungent aroma of earthy vegetation. I snuggled down on the comfy mattress, cosily warm in my sleeping bag underneath the quilt and was soon asleep.

I went to the toilet in the peaceful dawn light, then returned to sleep. It was a gorgeous, sunny day and later I went for a swim, stepping with difficulty over the beds of mussels to get to the sea. There was no-one there, but later I spotted a family fishing far out from a small boat and some backpackers came to forage for mussels. The Kiwi campers had left so I had the spot to myself that night. I could see the lighthouse at the tip of Farewell Spit blinking in the still night air.

FIFTEEN

The Nook

River lived in a house bus in the grounds of The Nook Backpackers in Pohara, where I'd WWOOFed before at the Sans Souci Inn. The Nook was a rendered hay-bale house and a popular place to stay, run by a German lady called Astrid. River had found me a part-time job there for a week, in return for the use of a caravan in a field and the hostel's amenities. The work involved cleaning and bed-making once the backpackers had left in the morning, and I had the afternoons free to explore and swim in the sea, which was only a five-minute walk away. I prepared my own food in the caravan and often socialised with the backpackers in the evenings.

One evening I started chatting with a Rhodesian man called Steve. 'I've been a guide in Antarctica for the last nine seasons,' he told me.

'That's incredible! How long is a season?' I wanted to know.

'Four to five months,' he replied, taking a swig of beer from his bottle. 'I've also been a guide in South America, Borneo, Siberia and even your beautiful Scotland,' he said.

'What an interesting life you lead,' I breathed, becoming increasingly attracted to this tanned, handsome man. 'What are you doing in New Zealand?' I asked, wondering if he were single.

'I'm on holiday, trying to get over the loss of my wife eighteen months ago.'

Shocked, I didn't know what to say, but he continued. 'She was only thirty-six and went suddenly with a brain haemorrhage,' he sighed sadly, and my heart hurt for his loss.

At breakfast the next morning he was sitting by the window drinking tea, looking radiant. I joined him and said, 'You look very wide awake, Steve.'

'Sure am! I was up at 5.30am for a run and then a swim. It sets me up for the day.'

'I'd be ready to go back to bed after that,' I said, thinking that he was too fit for me, or rather, I was too unfit for him.

He laughed. 'You should give it a try, it would rejuvenate you,' he said, adding, 'I'm away back to Nelson this morning; heading up to the North Island to see some more sights before I fly out in a couple of weeks.'

That afternoon I drove along a stony road to the Waikoropupu Springs, which are the largest freshwater springs in New Zealand. There was a well-maintained walkway through the reserve, which took me three hours to complete as I stopped many times to admire the views and the crystal clear waters running alongside the path. At the top there was a rail, to prevent people from plunging down the sheer drop through the bush to the valley below. The track ended at a deep pool into which cascaded a waterfall and I sat on a boulder and bathed my hot feet in the cool water. The descent was very steep and I hung onto trees at the edge of the path to prevent myself from falling.

I went to the excellent Wholemeal Café in Takaka for dinner and was beginning to enjoy a tasty fish curry and salad when a lanky-looking older hippie approached my table and asked, 'May I have your permission to sit here?' I was too polite to refuse and he sat down, smiling broadly, his bluish-grey eyes inquisitively perusing my person. He then commenced to subject me to the 'third degree' kind of chat up, firing questions at me, seemingly unaware of my monosyllabic replies. I wanted to give my sole attention to the yummy food and told him so. He seemed to accept this but yacked on at length nonetheless, oblivious to the fact that I was not responding, only eating. 'I work in a bakery here and I'm just unwinding after a nine-hour shift,' he said, by way of explanation. I was wearing a Green Party of New Zealand badge which he'd spotted. 'I see you're into the Greens,' he smirked, 'does that mean you smoke dope?' On receiving a negative response, he finally took his leave, no doubt to find someone else to unwind to, who was more responsive and maybe had some dope to share?

After work the next day River invited me to his house bus. It was well kitted out and homely, with all mod-cons, including a computer and a TV. He was easy to talk to and I found myself divulging things about myself which I usually kept hidden deep inside. It was good therapy and I left feeling considerably more positive about my life.

One day around lunchtime a Kiwi in his mid-thirties arrived and erected his small, home-made tent in the field by my caravan. I had just finished work and stopped to welcome him. He immediately launched into an intense conversation. 'Why are you travelling?' was his first question, which always potentially led on to a deeper discussion, although I resisted this, having only just met him. He, however, was not so constrained. 'I've been chasing a German woman, but she's gone to Christchurch with a guy from Belgium,' he disclosed chattily, adding, 'I thought I was gay but I felt sexually attracted to her and she had her first orgasm with me – wasn't that amazing!'

'Whoa! Too much information. We've only been chatting for five minutes and you're telling me such intimate details,' I said.

'You're right. Sorry. I know I have communication problems but I can't seem to have the usual inane conversations about the weather and what I'm having for dinner tonight. You know what I mean?'

I did know what he meant but nevertheless I was aware that one needed to participate in this kind of chat, as that's what folk generally did, initially, at least. I told him about River, recommending a therapeutic session with him.

My week's work was nearly over and I began to prepare to leave. I took Vannie to a garage, filled up with fuel and got the tyre air pressures checked. I then asked the garage attendant to show me how to check the oil and brake fluid, annoyed with myself for behaving like a daft female. I was planning to drive out into the wild Western wilderness and needed the van to be reliable.

SIXTEEN

The Western Wilderness

In the morning I stocked up with food from the supermarket knowing that there would be no shops where I was going. Black clouds hung ominously over the mountains so I decided to keep to the coast. First I drove up to Farewell Spit, remembering the wonderful café there from my last visit. I tucked into smoked salmon and brie toasties, salad, a big blueberry muffin and a large moccachino, as if it were to be my last meal on earth. The sky was a clear blue over the Spit so I took the Westhaven Inlet road. I had been hoping to WWOOF in that area, but the few places were all full. I turned off onto the Kaihoke Lakes road but it became very steep and windy, as well as being unsurfaced and in bad condition. It was tiring driving on this type of surface, requiring total concentration as you needed to keep the speed up, but not too much, as you were in danger of skidding and going off the road. The other road was also unsurfaced, but not quite as bumpy. I pressed on through an amazing landscape of bush-covered mountains, ponds and lakes, with no signs of habitation and no other traffic. It felt like I'd been transported to another dimension in time, long before the start of civilisation. Suddenly, in the middle of this wilderness, there was a tiny hamlet – Mangarakau, which to my surprise and delight had a café! I went in for a cup of tea and the friendly owners told me, 'You can camp for free on the beach fifteen minutes on from here. There's no facilities, so make sure you have plenty of food and water.'

The landscape after Mangarakau became even wilder and more watery, until suddenly, at Paturau, I was on the West Coast, the farthest north it is possible to get by road. The Paturau River enters the Tasman Sea here and I drove along a sandy track beside it towards a long, wild sandy beach, backed with stones and covered with driftwood. There was a sign instructing campers to bury their waste, with a useful shovel next to it. I stopped beside the river mouth, the rolling waves not far away. I was not alone – there was a family camping further along the beach while nearer to me a motorhome was parked. It was a relief to have company in such a wild spot. It was six o'clock by this time and I got out of the van to explore before dinner, feeling too tired to cook. A man came out of the motorhome and walked towards me. 'Hi,' he said with a strong Kiwi accent. 'I'm Keith and my wife's about to serve up dinner. You're welcome to join us.'

I was overwhelmed by his hospitality. 'Are you sure?' I asked.

'Sure! I caught a massive fish at the mouth of the river. There's far too much for us – you'd be doing us a favour,' he said, smiling broadly.

I followed him into his motorhome, where I was welcomed by his wife, Lynn. Delicious smells of her fish, potato and onion stew filled the van, and I was soon tucking in, surprised to find that I was hungry. As we ate I learned that they were from Hamilton, on the North Island. Lynn said, 'I retired three years ago. I was a Physiologist. Keith's a teacher in a technical school and he plans to retire soon.'

'That's right,' Keith added, 'we're not sixty yet but we'll sell our house and live permanently in a slightly bigger house bus. We love wild camping like this, so we'll wander around the country living off the sea and land.'

'What a great life,' I said enviously, wishing I could do that too, but with a partner.

'We've got two sons with grand kids in Nelson,' Lynn went on, 'so we'll spend time with them before exploring more of the South Island.'

We chatted until it began to get dark, so I hurried back to Vannie to close the curtains and get ready for bed before darkness descended, as I was careful not to use the light too much, fearful that it would run down the battery. It was dark by half-past-nine, so it was early nights followed by early mornings.

*

It had rained in the night, intermittently waking me up with its pitter patter on the roof, but by morning it had stopped. It was cloudy but warm so I donned my bikini and went for a swim, clutching my soap. I found a calm swim hole in the river behind some rocks where I had a refreshing wash – it was certainly an efficient way to wake up. A rain shower blew in on my return to Vannie but I had to make my tea outside, in the shelter of the van, as it was too dangerous to do it inside.

Keith and Lynn had told me that the track actually continued for

84

a while, so I drove along it to the end, where another river – the Anatori, entered the sea. There was a pleasant camping spot, but it was sheltered, so there were sand flies, the pest of the West Coast. I was better off by the sea where a strong breeze kept them away. I also discovered a recently opened farm backpackers near the Paturau River, complete with a wild-looking farmer with a thick, grey, curly-haired beard; my rough camping spot was more appealing.

I returned to 'my spot', which already felt like home and snacked outside the van in the hot sunshine, the rain having moved away. I watched Keith and Lynn fishing at the sea's edge as the tide came in and went to look. Two large fish, similar in appearance to salmon, lay on the sand. 'Those are what we call kar-why,' Keith told me. Later Lynn caught a third and I was again invited to share their catch. Keith also showed me an interesting artesian well between the rocks in the sand along the beach. He placed a bucket with its bottom cut off into it and fresh water rose up on top of the sand. 'Taste it,' he said, after collecting some in a bottle. It was cold and sweet and he filled up one of my water containers with it. I had another swim in the river, then joined them on their 'patio' – an awning at the side of their motorhome for a glass of wine before dining on the delicious fried kar-why.

Later three men appeared and came over to chat. One was the landowner. 'I've lived here all my life – seventy-six years,' he informed us. He looked at least twenty years younger which no doubt was due to living in such a remote, stress-free place.

'You guys are brilliant fishers,' one of the others raved. 'We were over the other side of the river and caught nothing.'

My morning swim at the river mouth was rather different to the previous day. My calm washing hole was no more and I got carried past it by the current, a result of heavy rain in the night, which had increased the amount of water flowing down the river. I managed to scramble out by clinging to a rock, then slithered on my backside over stones until I reached the sand. Breakfast tasted especially good after all that exertion. I packed up and said 'goodbye' to Lynn and Keith who invited me to stay with them in Hamilton, should I be passing through there on my way back north.

SEVENTEEN

Return to Civilisation

It was hot and sunny after the rain and the return drive seemed a lot easier, probably because I was more confident and driving faster on the unsurfaced road. I was planning to stay at the Inn-let Backpackers in Collingwood again and they allowed me to park in their apple orchard. I needed the comforts of a toilet, shower and fridge and made dinner in their cosy kitchen, surrounded by a babble of German, the guests all being from that country. Nobody seemed inclined to speak English, so after clearing up I retired to Vannie for an early night, tired after all the driving.

The Inn-let's resident cockerel woke me up at 6am, enabling me to have an apple-scented yoga session in the orchard before loading up Vannie and filling up with diesel in Collingwood. I drove down the Aorere River valley, hoping to find a spot to swim as it was hot and muggy, but the ground bordering the river was too rough and stony. I drove across three fords to the start of the Heaphy Track, one of the most popular tracks in the country in the Kahurangi National Park, and walked to the first hut through the bush for half-an-hour. Six middle-aged Kiwis were about to begin the 77 kilometre hike and I took photos of them posing with their packs. The thirty-minute walk had been enough for me.

I went back to Takaka and dined on salmon quiche and salad at the Wholemeal Café. Who should come in right after me – Lynn and Keith, who were heading for Pohara as they needed to do some laundry. Then Astrid from The Nook appeared – New Zealand was a small place! I stocked up with more supermarket supplies and went back to a DOC (Department of Conservation) car park with toilets near the Tui Community, which I had discovered while staying at The Nook. There was a 'No Camping' sign but Keith had assured me that I would be able to park there overnight. It was a short stroll from the car park to a beautiful, white sandy beach where I swam in the warm rain, which had just begun. It rained hard for the rest of the day so I was stuck in the van, reading and planning my trip, glad that this weather didn't happen too often. It was a popular place. I peered through the rainy windows at the arrival of two more motorhomes and a van similar to mine, who all stayed the night.

I managed to boil up some water for tea during a brief dry spell in the morning and by the time I left at nine the rain had almost stopped. I drove out of Golden Bay and up the Takaka Hill, which seemed a lot less scary than my first encounter. I was driving faster too and no-one shouted abuse at me. By lunchtime I was in Motueka and treated myself to a delicious meal in Hot Mama's Café – fish chowder with garlic bread, pumpkin fruit cake and creamy cappucino. Afterwards I drove down the Motueka River valley, the mountainous scenery and coniferous forests reminding me of Scotland, except for the hop fields, orchards and vineyards which grew abundantly in the treeless spaces.

That night I stopped at the West Bay DOC site at St Arnaud, in Nelson Lakes National Park. It was well equipped with toilets, hot showers and a kitchen. Many manuka and kanuka trees grew on the site, providing much needed shade but also attracting numerous sand flies which invaded the van. I squashed many against the skylight windows, with most unBuddhist-like behaviour, and was relieved that the hundreds remaining fell asleep as darkness descended. The site was at 640 metres altitude and it felt pleasantly fresh after the mugginess of Golden Bay.

The next day I felt tired as I drove through the heat towards Murchison. I was going to stop at a private site by a river near a hotel, where several Kiwis were parked. One of the women came over and said, 'You can stay here for the night but I should warn you that we're expecting a lot of folk. It's a fiftieth birthday party celebration and we're setting up a music system.' She nodded her head towards where a couple of guys were busily wiring up speakers in the branches of the trees. 'It'll go on all night and you're welcome to join us,' she kindly offered.

'Oh, thanks,' I said, 'but I'm not really in a party mood.' I was hot and tired and wanted a quiet night, asleep in Vannie.

'No worries,' she said, with the usual Kiwi relaxed response.

It wasn't much further to the Riverview Camp Site, by the Buller River, where I parked in a quiet spot between some bushes. I took a relaxing hot shower, prepared a light meal in their kitchen and went to bed.

EIGHTEEN

The Two Passes

It had been a frosty night and I shivered as I prepared to depart in the morning. Just a half hour's drive south I discovered a great parking spot by the lovely Maruia Falls but it was too early in the day to stop. I contented myself by taking a photo of the cascading water, a rainbow hovering in the spray. The sky was cloudless, the sun busily heating up the air.

Turning eastwards I found a large DOC site 11 kilometres before Maruia Springs at Marble Hill. It was situated in the Maruia River valley, with beech forested mountains all around. I had lunch there, sheltering in the shade of an enormous beech tree and then continued to the hot springs. The Japanese bathhouse was segregated into male and female sections. I had the place to myself, wallowing in natural hot water in the massive bath tub. There were views of the river and mountains through large windows at one end, with suitably subdued lighting embedded in the stone walls. The sublime atmosphere was perfect for yoga, the positions easily held with warm, relaxed muscles. Small stools with round buckets made from bamboo were provided to wash oneself, as well as traditional showers. A naked Japanese girl, slim and white-skinned came in, and I went outside to the smooth rock pools, which were luckily in the shade as the water was roasting. I entered the icy-cold plunge pool, followed by a hot water stream, where you were supposed to massage yourself against the smooth rocks and stones.

There was a small camp site there but I decided to return to Marble Hill (my lunch spot) as it was getting busy and I craved peace and quiet after the relaxing springs. I parked underneath the spreading branches of an ancient beech tree at the forest's edge and watched, spellbound, as a grey-breasted robin came and perched on a rock next to the van. He was my companion for the evening, entertaining me with his shrill songs and charming behaviour, cocking his head to one side, looking expectantly at me, waiting for any tit-bits to come his way. I prepared dinner on a picnic table, closely watched by my friend, and dined on a tin of Thai tuna curry with rice. It somehow tasted better in that peaceful setting as I sat watching a hawk circling in the fields nearby, the sun shining on the mountain peaks as shadows crept up them. There was only one other occupant of the site who I could not see, but I heard the faint sounds of a guitar being played from deep in the forest.

I had enjoyed an exceptionally good night's sleep after the hot springs relaxation and peacefulness of the beech forest, and bid a sad farewell to Mr Robin, who had joined me for breakfast. The road twisted upwards to the Lewis Pass, at 907 metres the northernmost pass through the Southern Alps, where I stopped to do a short nature walk and admire the snow-capped mountain peaks all around. On the other side of the pass the scenery changed dramatically. There were few trees and a wide valley through which ran a blue-green river, split into many ribbons separated by greyish-white expanses of shingle and stubbly grass.

There was little traffic with lots of good, straight road; Vannie emitted a loud 'ping, ping', for the first time. I looked at my speed – I was doing 105 kilometres-per-hour, exceeding his speed limit. Most daring! I stopped to look at a deep river gorge where jet boats zoomed through the fast flowing water, their inhabitants' screams drowned by the noise. I reached Hanmer Springs in the early afternoon and found the AA Tourist Camp, which had good facilities but I missed my lovely spot of the previous night. It was too hot and too busy and I felt stressed. A visit to Hanmer Springs later did nothing to relieve my stress. The shady parts of the pools were crammed with people and the cool swimming pool was crowded with children. After a short time I returned to the site to cook and do my laundry. I phoned a few WWOOF places in the area. They were all full but I managed to get one in Fairlie for two weeks later.

The next day I drove south to Mt Thomas forest, where Vannie navigated a tricky creek to a DOC site with toilets and water. I had done 166 kilometres that day, the longest daily distance so far. I awoke to a gloomy, cloudy sky, quickly packed up and continued southwards to Oxford, a tiny, quiet place. The post office was located in the library where I caught up with news in the papers as well as posting some cards.

Not long after leaving Oxford I turned north-westwards in the direction of Arthur's Pass (924 metres). I passed many free camp sites with toilets and finally stopped eight kilometres before the pass at

Klondyke Corner DOC site, situated in a wide expanse of flat river valley with mountains all around and the snow-capped peaks of the pass in the distance. The name 'Klondyke' presumably originates from the West Coast gold rush in the nineteenth century. The *TranzAlpine* train line crosses this river valley on its way from Christchurch to Greymouth on the West Coast. I was forced to retire to the van to eat supper due to the sand flies. One of the most spectacular views from the road at Arthur's Pass is of Mt Rolleston, which I was fortunate to see, unshrouded by cloud. The viaducts after the pass are an incredible feat of engineering, along with many bridges, rock shelters and waterfalls, which have been redirected into chutes. As I plunged down the other side of the pass the weather changed into the typical West Coast rain, so I pressed on to Hokitika.

NINETEEN

All the Way to Jackson Bay

I stayed in the Just Jade Backpackers in Hokitika for one night, sheltering from the torrential rain. It was a pleasant, homely place, run by a Kiwi and his Japanese wife and I settled in front of a blazing fire in the lounge, listening to the sea roaring outside, happy to be away from Vannie.

It didn't look like the same place in the morning, a hot sun shining in a cloudless sky and the sea much calmer. I drove inland to pretty Lake Kaniere, glad to be back in lush bush country. There were many paths there and I did the ten-minute kahikatea (white pine) walk, stopping to gaze up at these incredibly tall trees balancing on their narrow trunks, swaying gracefully in the breeze. They take hundreds of years to reach maturity and these were magnificently mature. A group of Kiwis were playing cricket in a large glade nearby, until they lost the ball.

I picnicked by Hans Bay, soaking up the sun, but it was too cold to swim. An unsealed road continued through wild bush and I stopped to photograph Dorothy Falls, which tumbled down a steep bush-covered cliff next to the road into a pool which glowed greenly with the surrounding bush's reflection. Near the end of this unsealed road I stopped to watch a kiwi amble slowly across it, my heart pounding in excitement with my first sighting of this rarely seen bird in the wild.

By 5pm I was tired from driving and stopped at Lake Mahinapua DOC site. It was quite crowded, but I still managed to find a spacious spot. After dinner I wandered up the track, where living and dead trees dripped with many types of lichens, mosses and ferns, to the main road and saw the Mahinapua Hotel. I was vaguely wondering about getting a drink when a Kiwi Experience bus drove up and disgorged its contents of young, rowdy travellers. *Guess that's my quiet drink away,* I thought regretfully and headed instead into an empty room next to the bar. The wall was covered in amusingly strange newspaper cuttings. One that caught my eye was about the existence of a man-ape animal which had been spotted several times in the dense West Coast bush. I found this quite plausible as the bush is so dense and inaccessible on the steep terrain that all sorts of beasts could be sheltering in it, undiscovered.

No-one stirred, not even the sand flies, as I sat drinking in the magical view of lake and mountains, festooned by wisps of cloud, sipping my breakfast tea. By nine, when I left, there were signs of life, but I was soon on the road south again. I reached Ross mid-morning. This place was established in 1860, during the West Coast Gold Rush, and I walked uphill through an old cemetery, where miners from all over the UK were buried. Further on, at Wanganui River, I stopped at a small place where they were still working the gold. There was a bush walk and a barbecue, where I sampled whitebait, cooked in batter and sandwiched into a burger – very tasty. The friendly female owner said, 'You're lucky to have just missed two Kiwi Experience buses.'

'Lucky indeed! They're so noisy,' I replied with relief.

Afterwards, Kevin, one of the gold workers, showed me how it's done. 'The gold comes down the river when it floods. It gets deposited in lines and, because it's heavy, it sinks to the bottom of my sieve in this trough of water.' I bent down and saw tiny specks of glinting gold.

'You'd have to be extremely patient to find enough to get rich,' I observed.

'Yes, right. Well, you can see in the cemetery that plenty men came, tried and failed,' he chuckled.

That evening I stopped at Okarito, a wonderful little hamlet with glorious views of the Southern Alps poking through cloud in the distance and a calm lagoon. The population was just twenty-four, with no shop or bar. Keri Hulme, author of *The Bone People,* her powerful novel which won the Booker Prize in 1985, built her own house in Okarito and the isolated environment inspired and influenced her work.

There was quite a choice of accommodation for such a small place: a busy camp site, with no kitchen, a cute YHA with beds in the kitchen and the Strand Hostel, recently opened and run by an American and her German husband. They had met there on holiday and had managed to immigrate, presumably on a business application. They allowed me to park on grass at the back, where huge blue, pink and white hydrangeas grew in abundance, while the sea crashed on the shore beyond the lagoon. I spent a lovely evening chatting with them and two other couples staying there, toasting my toes by a massive wood stove.

Heavy rain was falling as I drove slowly along the steep and twisty roads which led to the glaciers. The Franz Josef visitor centre was a welcome respite from the weather and then I went on to Lake Matheson where the sun came out and I thought I saw the tip of Mount Cook above the clouds. Several large, plump Kereru pigeons were busily foraging, or flying heavily around, their bright green heads, white breasts and pinkish-red beaks making them far more attractive than the common grey ones. Later I stopped at Bruce Bay to photograph the wild-looking beach, covered by huge pieces of driftwood and battered continuously by the Tasman Sea. When I stopped for the night at Lake Paringa DOC site, the rain had begun again. I hoped that it would stop long enough for me to heat up a tin of soup, which it obligingly did for about half-an-hour.

I awoke late having been disturbed by mosquitoes in the night, then continued on to Haast, where I filled up with diesel and oil and put air in the tyres, knowing that it was the last garage before driving the 46 kilometres to Jackson Bay. The road was surprisingly good – mostly straight and quiet, with bridges over huge rivers entering the sea. Jackson Bay itself is a tiny, sleepy fishing village, with a real end-of-the-road feel and a population of ten people, vastly outnumbered by seals and penguins. The road has to terminate here because after the bay the coastline becomes steep mountain ranges which plunge directly into the ocean.

There was a cute little wooden hut, called the Cray Pot, which sold wonderful fish 'n chips, tasty and fresh from the sea. After sampling some I walked through bush round the coast to Ocean Beach, where it was extremely windy and the sea spectacularly rough. Back in the calmness of the bay I found a tiny café and ordered a cappuccino. I got chatting to a Canadian and asked him about camping spots. 'You should head back a bit to Neil's Beach. It's a magical spot, loads better than the car park here,' he advised. He was right – it was indeed magical and I voted it my best scenic remote stopping place. I explored, wondering at the vast Arawata River Estuary, with Mount Aspiring's 3027 metres snowy peak rising majestically above other glistening mountain tops inland. I also found a long drop loo, set in a small garden, which was clean and supplied with toilet paper! I guessed that it was for the whitebait fishermen who arrived in significant numbers in the fishing season. Further on, half hidden in the scrub, was an old car and a blue tarpaulin. I didn't venture near it, as there was maybe someone living there. Later a young couple came to camp some distance away from me and I told them about the loo.

TWENTY

The Sunflower Café

The magic of Neil's Beach evaporated somewhat in the morning with the appearance of sand flies. They invaded the van and I was forced to walk around eating my breakfast. As I drove off thousands died having exhausted themselves trying to get out of the skylight roof's windows. Later I stopped and shook out my quilt which was covered in a thick layer of them. I did the Hapuka Estuary walkway which was sand fly-free and quiet with the vegetation dripping from the night rain in hot sunshine. Soon I was back in Haast, where I once more turned inland, following the same road up to the pass as I had by bus on my previous trip. It was so much better with my own transport. I stopped at each of the three short walks to waterfalls from the road and at the Gates of Haast watched the Haast River as it sped spectacularly to the sea, the huge volume of water an incredible sight. That night I parked at DOC's Boundary Creek site, which had a superb view up Lake Wanaka to the Minaret Peaks, Mt Albert and Mt Awful, all over 2000 metres, with snowy summits. It was clear and sunny when I arrived, but as I finished dinner I saw black storm clouds being blown up the lake and soon I was sheltering in Vannie, being battered by hurricane-strength winds and rain. New Zealand's weather was certainly dramatically changeable, especially in the mountainous regions.

Wanaka looked very different from my last autumnal visit. Now the mountain tops were covered in snow and the poplar trees lining the lake were green, not yellow. For some reason I was feeling homesick and decided that I'd been too long on the road with only my own company. I was looking forward to WWOOFing again and continued on to Queenstown, after stopping at Wanaka for provisions and email. I had not been impressed with Queenstown itself on my first visit – it was still horribly busy, so I drove about 15 kilometres along the road to Glenorchy and stopped at a lakeside DOC site. By morning my mood had improved, the weather was good and the dead end road to Glenorchy enjoyed wonderful views of the mountains at the head of Lake Wakatipu. Driving back through Queenstown I didn't even stop it was so crowded, with parking meters everywhere. At Kawarau Bridge I stopped to photograph a bungy jump: something exciting to watch, but definitely not to do! I stopped at Cromwell Holiday Park, which was quiet as the Kiwi school holidays had just finished, and had a much needed shower, after which I watched a film on TV. It was spoiled when a rather manic young man came in and asked, 'Where are you from?' On hearing that I was from Scotland he began raving on at length about Billy Connolly.

Mount Cook, the highest mountain of New Zealand at 3755 metres, was beckoning to me and I sped along the fast road next to turquoise Lake Pukaki, where sheep grazed on its steep banks, until I reached the luxurious Hermitage Hotel, where I sipped a hot chocolate, admiring the majesty of Mount Cook through its large windows which gave an uninterrupted view of the peak. Large groups of Japanese tourists milled around, taking numerous photos of their groups striking various poses, with the mountain as the backdrop. I drove 2 kilometres to the campsite for the night. It was even nearer the mountain and I walked up to the monument to fallen climbers, which had a marvellous view of the place they had perished. I was fortunate to get a photo of the summit as the sun set, glowing salmon-pink in brilliant light, the peak shining above dark scrub, with keas flying around and screeching with all their might. I stood mesmerised for ages, staring in awe at the mountain, feeling warm despite the cold.

I awoke to the sound of two big keas on Vannie's roof, pecking loudly at the metal with their sharp beaks, screeching and squawking in great delight. I was scared that they'd damage poor Vannie and rapidly pulled on some warm clothes, slid open the sliding door and peered up. Two sets of beady eyes stared back at me and then they resumed their attack, totally unperturbed by my presence. I got rid of them with difficulty, shouting many oaths and waving my stick menacingly at them. Eventually they flew to the roof of the nearby toilets and watched me balefully while they considered who to annoy next.

*

Fairlie was named after the town in Ayrshire, Scotland, the birthplace of Fairlie's first hotel owner and had pleasant tree-lined avenues, planted by the first settlers. My next WWOOF host, Val, owned the

Sunflower Café in Fairlie so I went there to eat. It was a cute wee place serving tasty vegetarian meals and was full of local information.

After lunch I went to Val's place, which was on the outskirts of Fairlie. She came out of her bungalow when she saw my van, and, wiping her hands on her blue-striped apron said, 'You must be Margaret,' looking intently at me with her bright, brown eyes, which I felt would never miss a thing. She was seventy-three, but looked younger, upright and petite with short, white hair. I learned later that she was half-Indian, but had been born in New Zealand. 'Come in and get settled while I prepare supper,' she said, so I followed her inside. Her abode was full of Eastern-looking ornaments, pictures and wall hangings and over a simple meal of fresh garden salad with vegetarian salami she told me a little about her life. 'I opened the first vegetarian café in New Zealand, in Timaru, on the east coast, between Christchurch and Dunedin. Now I just have the one here. You'll need to try it,' she advised.

'I already have and I met Suzanne who was very friendly.'

'Oh, that's good. I work there some days with her,' she said, before taking a mouthful of salad. 'This evening is our meditation night. You're welcome to join us.'

'Thanks, I'd like that. I used to meditate regularly after studying it in India, but I've got out of practice living in the van.'

'Yes well, that can't be too comfortable but you can meditate anywhere, you know.'

'Yes, I know and I do sometimes, especially when I'm sitting gazing at a beautiful view – it just seems to come naturally then.' There was a knock on the door and in came a woman who resembled Val, with the same bright eyes.

'This is my sister, Tui,' she said, as the door was knocked again. An elderly couple came in and after greeting each other Val led the way into a small room, with a wonderfully peaceful atmosphere. She lit an incense stick and we all settled ourselves on cushions, with blankets wrapped around us. They said a short prayer and then began to meditate. They were followers of Benjamin Creme of Share International, and believed in the second coming of the Maitreya, or World Teacher. I read a book about it while staying there and found it fascinating, but hard to believe. They sat in deep meditation for over two hours, but I began to fall asleep after half-an-hour and quietly left.

After the meditators had gone my host caught up with her

answering machine, showing no signs of tiredness.

I prepared my own breakfast in the morning but Val didn't eat until lunchtime. She told me, 'It's not good for your system to overload it with food. I work for twelve hours a day and I don't need much sleep because I eat little but healthily. The meditation also keeps me energised.'

While I worked in the garden weeding and cutting back shrubs, I chatted with a man called Morris, who was doing some outside painting. 'I've been coming to see Val for the last twenty years,' he told me, as he paused for a rest. 'I'd had a heart attack and she helped me and other members of my family a lot. You know, she can tell what vitamins and minerals you are deficient in by doing something with a piece of your hair.' Always sceptical I wondered what he could mean, but Val was certainly a good advert for her health treatments. After seeing clients all day she was out mowing a vast area of grass with a small tractor mower. We sat down to a dinner of salad and two pitta breads.

'We had a big lunch,' she said. *That lunch of spicy rice soup and salad, though delicious, was NOT big,* I thought, remembering the scarcity of food at Paraparaumu's Yoga Centre. Nevertheless, after dinner I had enough energy to wash Vannie and went to bed without obsessing about my empty stomach.

Val was away at the bank in Timaru the next day and I met her farmer neighbour who grazed his organic bullocks on her land. When he heard that I was from Scotland he said, 'My son married a Scottish lassie and now he lives just outside Edinburgh in Gorebridge.'

'Oh, it's a small world. I used to stay in Bonnyrigg which is just down the road from Gorebridge,' I told him.

'Well, that's funny, but I'm not happy about it as now I've got no-one to take over the farm when I get too old to work it.'

'That's too bad but maybe he'll come back here – it's so much lovelier than Gorebridge,' I enthused. It was a hot and sunny day and I couldn't imagine why anyone born in such a wonderful place should want to leave. I was in charge of dinner and made pasta with a fresh tomato and herb sauce with salad from the garden, which Val enjoyed, and filled me up, to my delight.

I didn't see much of my host: she was either working in the café or running clinics. One day ten of the bullocks escaped onto the road and her sister plus a neighbour managed to herd them back into the field with their cars. After a week I was on the road again, feeling fortified by healthy food and energising meditations.

TWENTY-ONE

Folk Festival Fun

I stopped at the pleasant town of Geraldine, north-east of Fairlie, for provisions. On the information centre's noticeboard was a poster advertising a Folk Festival at Waihi Bush Farm, which was in the *WWOOF* book. *Maybe they need WWOOFers to help with the festival?* I wondered. The book entry looked interesting and it began two days later, so I decided to go and investigate. It was easy to find and David, the handsome organiser of the festival, and his dad, were in their office. 'Sorry, Margaret, but we're full of WWOOFers. You're welcome to come to the festival though and camp in your van. It's 50 dollars for three days, including camping and use of our facilities.'

I felt a little nervous about just turning up alone and not knowing anybody so went away to think about it, staying on Peel Forest's DOC site and exploring the lovely forest walks there. The festival began on Waitangi Day and I overcame my shyness and attended. I parked Vannie at a shady spot by the river and immediately started chatting to my neighbours – Carol, Liz and Jade, who were all teachers. Everyone I met was very friendly and I was glad that I'd gone. It was hot and I swam in a water hole in the river before dinner. That evening there was a welcome concert in a big marquee. The music was excellent and included groups as well as solo singers, accompanied by guitars, drums, fiddles, banjos, wind instruments and keyboards.

Each morning there was a communal yoga session in which I joined, enjoying being in a group situation again. The contra-dance session sounded intriguing so I went along and was immediately approached by a tall man with bright red hair and bushy eyebrows. 'I'm Quentin,' he announced. 'Where are you from?' When he heard that I was from Scotland he laughed. 'Well, I don't need to explain this dancing to you. It's similar to Scottish dancing.'

'Oh right,' I said, before being immersed in a group of people and flung around the floor from partner to partner, to the rapidly increasing rhythm of the accompanying fiddlers.

When I tried to sit down and catch my breath I was pounced upon by another keen man who insisted, 'Oh, no! You're not allowed to grab a rest during this dancing.' Eventually I escaped to the swimming hole to cool off before lunch. It was too much action for a morning. The afternoon became stiflingly hot and I half dozed while listening to various musicians. One lean-looking fiddler with a neatly-trimmed black beard and a nose stud began chatting.

'My wife plays the accordion and together we tour with our three daughters. The oldest is six and we're home schooling her. Last year we toured the States and Canada doing concerts. We buy a van to live in – it's a great life.' I told him about my van and gave him Wally's phone number in case they wanted to visit Kohu Kohu and give a concert. There was a barn dance until late that evening with incredibly difficult dances so I sat watching for most of the time, chatting with my teacher neighbours.

I joined the African djembe drumming session in the morning which was superb – a great way to start the day. All afternoon I listened to live music followed by a swim and a wash in the river. The final concert that evening built up to an amazing performance by the Twa Jimmies – two Glaswegians playing small bagpipes accompanied by a Kiwi guy on guitar. It was electrifying and had us all stamping our feet and clapping our hands, while others in the audience found spaces in which to leap about to the rhythm.

*

When I pulled aside Vannie's curtains the next day I was greeted by grey skies and drizzly rain. The weather matched my mood. I didn't want to move on and say goodbye to all the folksy folk, but it had to be done. It was still drizzly when I reached Mt Somers so I decided to keep heading north-east to Akaroa on the Banks Peninsula, which I'd enjoyed on my first trip. I reached there early evening and stopped at the Top Ten Caravan Park, situated above Akaroa with fine views over the harbour, in the now clear and sunny sky. A wonderfully warm, starry night followed, complete with a half moon.

One of my memorable places from before was Le Bons Bay Backpackers, near one of the small bays of the peninsula, north-east of Akaroa. I stopped there to ask whether it would be all right to wild park in the area and they assured me it would be OK. After driving along a scary, snaky narrow road towards the sea, I found a large field through a gate next to a sports pavilion with a barbecue area. There was no-one around and ignoring the 'no camping' signs I parked under a huge old pine tree. On the gate was a notice: *This gate is locked from sunset to sunrise.* I was planning to stop there overnight and spent the hot afternoon swimming in a nearby sea lagoon, then doing yoga on the shore. It was completely deserted and I felt magical in such a wild, lonely spot. It was the first time that I had slept in Vannie entirely alone, which made me feel a little uneasy, especially because of the notice. *Would someone come to lock the gate and would they say anything to me?* After dinner I went for a walk along the beach and when I returned the gate was locked. It was 8.15pm and getting dark. I prepared for bed and slept undisturbed all night.

When I awoke at eight the gate was open, to my relief. A man came by looking for his dog and told me that an old man was in charge of the gate when I asked him if it was OK to park. 'No worries, as long as it's only for one night and you leave the place as tidy as it was,' he said, before wandering off, calling for his dog. I returned to the backpackers and parked outside their garage for the night. They were still cooking their evening banquet dinners for the same ludicrously cheap price. Twenty of us sat down at a long table in the garden again and dined on freshly grilled fish (groper), scallops, roast vegetables in lemon sauce and garden salad, all washed down with chilled dry white wine. The conversation centred a lot around the coming Iraq war and a German girl told me that there would be world demonstrations for peace on February 14, which was three days away. It was the usual story – elected governments going to war when the vast majority of the people who had elected them were opposed to their actions – and this is democracy?

My other neighbours at the table were an Englishman and his South African wife. 'We live in New York,' she told me, 'and it was incredible to see how the community changed after 9/11. Suddenly people were communicating with each other, helping and caring for each other, like they'd never done before.'

'So something good arose from the bombings,' I said.

'Yeah, you could say that. I guess we humans are a decent bunch deep down, but it takes something like that to reveal our better nature,' she replied, squeezing her husband's hand.

From Le Bons Bay I headed north-westwards round the peninsula, visiting Okains, Little Akaloa and Pigeon Bays, which were all accessed by tricky, steep and often unsurfaced roads, before returning to Akaroa.

*

Next morning I awoke early to see orange-edged clouds drifting round the hill tops surrounding the harbour; it was going to be another scorcher. I reached the outskirts of Christchurch in a couple of hours and got directions on the quickest way to Diamond Harbour, from a helpful young man at the garage. I drove along Summit Road, which had glorious views of an azure sea against golden brown rolling bare hillsides, with glimpses of Christchurch and the Southern Alps in the distance.

The scenery was superb all the way to Diamond Harbour, where I found a big park with toilets and water above the wharf. There was an absence of 'No Camping' signs so I parked underneath one of the wondrous oak trees, which were wider, stumpier and more luxuriant than our British ones. I had a refreshing swim from the wharf to a small, stony beach and back, around one kilometre, then sat and watched the sun setting behind the Port Hills, with glimpses of blue sea through the pine trees. It was a warm, calm night and after my meal I sat on a bench watching the moon shining on the sea, the lights from Lyttelton glimmering in the distance, while faint noises came from ships sailing on the harbour, their lights glinting on the water.

Late the following afternoon I had my first real taste of traffic as I hit Christchurch and somehow found the South Brighton Motor Camp. It was a huge shock to my system after the peacefulness of the previous night's camping, but I needed to be there to attend the Peace Rally in the centre of Christchurch the following day.

I got the bus to Victoria Square in the centre of Christchurch the next day where there was what the Kiwis called a 'Peace Picnic', rather than a rally. It was reasonably well attended and the sun shone obligingly from a clear blue sky, but it was all a bit tame for me, with groups of relaxed-looking people eating sandwiches, drinking juice, laughing and chatting. The Scottish CND (Campaign for Nuclear Disarmament) rallies that I had been on were much more vigorous, with marching, chanting, banner waving and fiery speeches. There were some speeches towards the end of the afternoon when the crowds had dwindled considerably but they lacked vibrancy. I signed petitions to the American Ambassador and to Helen Clark, New Zealand's

Labour Prime Minister and hoped that the combined world demonstrations would result in a positive peaceful outcome. Back at the camp site Vannie was made pretty with a 'Nuclear Free Pacific' sticker on his back window.

As the next day was Sunday there was little traffic and I easily navigated out of Christchurch northwards along the coast to the mouth of the Hurunui River. I found a small council site where the river entered the sea, with brown cliffs on the other side. The river had a deep pool but when I began to swim in it I was carried away by the current to a shallower part and had to wiggle my way over slimy stones to the shore.

It was so fine in the morning that I could see all the way south to the Banks Peninsula, the sea glistening in the sun, the air already hot. There was little shade up the coast to Kaikoura, which was, as I'd expected, an horrific wee place, swarming with tourists, all there to go on the over-priced whale and dolphin boat trips. I decided not to join them and instead headed inland to the Mt Fyffe walk's DOC car park, the last part on a rough gravel road. There was no-one there, except for another friendly robin who dragged my used tea bag away and pecked at leftover pieces of macaroni cheese from my spatula.

Next morning as I was eating breakfast I heard the sound of footsteps crunching on the gravel. I looked up to see a tall, tanned, stubbly-chinned man, clutching a trekking pole, with a small backpack. 'Good day,' he said with a strong Australian twang. 'I'm gonna trek to Mt Fyffe. Have you done that walk?'

'No I haven't. I just stopped here overnight, but it tells you about it on the board over there.'

'Thanks. So you're driving round New Zealand by yourself, staying in your van?'

'Yes. I'm taking time out from teaching,' I said.

'Oh, you need time out from that, I guess. I track colonies of albatross for a living, which brings me to cool places like New Zealand.'

'What a great job,' I breathed admiringly, wishing that I'd done something like that.

'It is, that's true. See you around,' he said as he began to head for the track. When he'd gone I realised how good it had been to chat with someone, even for such a short time. It got a bit lonesome in the van.

I went for a short circular walk in the forest before continuing northwards to Ohau Point, where I stopped to peer down a steep cliff at the bottom of which was a large fur seal colony, with many pups playing in small pools. A young woman was standing there, busily writing something. 'Are you making notes about the seals?' I asked her.

'No. I'm counting the numbers of tourists,' she laughed.

'Why on earth are you doing that?'

'It's for my doctorate studies,' she explained. 'I'm doing it in different places where there are seal colonies to see if it impacts on their numbers and behaviour.' *Another great job,* I thought.

It was very windy as I drove further up the coast, with Vannie rocking too much in the wind if I went faster than seventy kilometres per hour and I became extremely tired. I stopped at a café in Ward for a milkshake and the waitress told me about a good DOC site further on at Marfell Beach. There were four campers there and plenty of space, right beside the sea, which was wildly rough with waves crashing onto the beach. It was too windy to cook my meal outside so I was forced to make it in the toilet block where fortunately there was a bench, quickly returning to Vannie to eat it before it got cold. All night the sea pounded and crashed on the shore just a few metres from me and my dreams were full of drowsy drownings. I woke up relieved to still be safely on the land.

TWENTY-TWO

Nelson and Beyond

It was still windy as I continued northwards to Blenheim, Havelock and on to Pelorus Bridge where I stopped at their DOC site. Back in Nelson I went to the Green Grocer to buy a new *WWOOF* book, on the advice of Val in Fairlie who had told me that mine was out of date. The woman there phoned the WWOOF organisation who assured her that I did not need to buy another one. This was the only reason that I'd returned to Nelson so I was not pleased. The Brook Valley Motor Camp was five kilometres out of Nelson, surrounded by bush-covered hills. There were two parts to the site: one for permanent residents by the river and another higher up near the facilities, which was smaller and too crowded. I wasn't used to this and thought longingly of my previous night's stop at Pelorus Bridge in a spacious, grassy area edged by tall tree ferns and kahikatea (white pine) trees.

I used my time in Nelson productively by checking out the college for possible job vacancies in their ESL (English as a Second Language) department. Fortunately, the Assistant Director was available and she was positive about the possibility of employment, showing me around and inviting me to attend a student gathering. It was the end of term and they were giving farewell speeches. They were mainly Asian – Chinese, Japanese, Korean and Taiwanese, and all seemed to have enjoyed their time at the college. Nelson would be a great place to live and I planned to send my CV when back in Scotland.

In the afternoon I headed out of Nelson towards the Marlborough Sounds where I hoped to drive the incredible road to French Pass, which my sister and her husband had ecstatically described to me. The road was surfaced to Okiwi Bay and I made good progress, but then slowed down considerably on an unsurfaced road to Elaine Bay where I stopped for the night. It was bitterly cold, but the view of small boats bobbing on the bay with stunning scenery all around distracted me. I parked in front of a small jetty, the only vehicle there until a Dutch couple arrived in a small camper van. It was an isolated spot with few dwellings and no signs of any life, except for an old, grey-haired boxer dog, who nevertheless was still playful and who seemed glad of the company, accompanying me on a short stroll to the end of the road. The Dutch couple were listening to the radio, in Dutch. 'Bush says he's ready for war,' they told me angrily, and we had an animated political discussion about the stupidity of war. That night my cosy bedding was not sufficient to keep me warm.

I was up at seven, in time to see a magical sunrise, with fish leaping on the lake's surface, while a heron stood watching motionlessly and a shag swam and dived continuously, both assured of a plentiful breakfast. I sat inside Vannie, warming myself with a mug of tea while watching this marvellous scene as the sun rose, gradually heating up the air.

The road to French Pass was indeed spectacular and I stopped to take many photos at the viewpoint, where there was a memorial to the men who had made the road. On my way there to my left the mountains and sea were dark with heavy showers of rain, while to my right the sun shone brightly on the turquoise waters of the Sounds. On my return the weather had reversed, with sunshine on my right and forbidding rain clouds on my left. I had hoped to go on a boat trip at French Pass, where dangerous circular currents had claimed many ships, but it was cancelled due to the changeable weather. I kept my speed to a steady thirty-five to forty kilometres-per-hour on the way back, which lessened the amount of bumping which I'd experienced when driving more slowly. Adrenaline kept me alert for the few oncoming vehicles, with none behind me, as I drove along the narrowest parts with steep drops on either side. I stopped at the small, well-kept camp site at Okiwi Bay where the weather was warmer.

Tennyson Inlet, according to my map, was accessed by an unsealed road, so I was pleasantly surprised to discover the next day that it was sealed. This was just as well because it was steeper and bendier than the one to French Pass. The road snaked through verdant native forest, which rose up high above it. At the top there was a viewpoint down to the inlet – a long, turquoise ribbon of clear water with an erratically indented coastline, sandwiched between green, bush-covered hills. In the distance the way to French Pass could be faintly seen through the greenery.

There was a DOC camp site at the inlet, but unfortunately it was only for walkers, with no vehicle access. I walked along a short track to the beach. The water was crystal clear, the sun shining warmly and

I longed for a swim. A lone male was sitting on the beach and we began chatting. 'Hi there,' he said in a southern English accent, inviting me to sit down next to him. 'What a lovely spot. I've left my eighty-two-year-old mother in the car because she has trouble walking, although she's driven us all round the South Island easily enough.'

'It's a pity that she can't see this view,' I replied, glad that I could still walk.

'I'm going for a swim, that water looks so inviting,' he said.

I was cursing myself for not having worn my bikini, but was dying for a swim. 'I don't have my swim stuff. Would you mind if I just swim in my T-shirt and pants?'

'No, I don't mind,' he said and quickly took off his top and trousers to reveal a pair of tight swimming trunks. He ran into the inlet and was soon swimming strongly so I joined him, relishing the feel of the silky smooth water on my skin.

Afterwards we sat drying in the sun. 'I'm from Brighton, but I was born in Auckland. We left when I was three years old and this is my first time back. I'm forty-eight now and I can't really remember what it was like.'

'I love New Zealand,' I said. 'I would like to settle here but I'll need to get a job first.' I found myself telling him about my future plans, about my children and about my life. He was easy to talk to and it was good to have some company.

'Well, it's been nice meeting you but I'll have to go. We're booked on the 7pm ferry to Wellington,' he said, standing up and waving goodbye as he disappeared down the track. I followed soon after and had lunch in Vannie. That night I parked at Carluke picnic spot by the quiet main road.

*

I had arranged another WWOOF on Queen Charlotte Drive, which runs along Queen Charlotte Sound, on the way to Picton. My host, Verena, was Swiss and lived with her Kiwi husband, Ash, in a beautiful wooden house above the drive. She made jewellery and had a small shop on the premises. I stayed there for three nights, cutting grass, pruning and weeding in their lovely garden. It felt good living in a house again especially as the nights were drawing in. It was dark by 9pm so when I was in Vannie I had to go to sleep then. Verena told me that she had met Ash when she was his WWOOFer. He was gorgeous and I fantasised that something similar would happen to me.

My last four nights on the South Island were spent at Aussie Bay, where I met an American new-age woman of around my own age in her van; White's Bay, a superb beach at the bottom of a steep hill where I stayed for two nights, and lastly the DOC site at Momorangi Bay where I did my washing in preparation for leaving the South Island.

TWENTY-THREE

North Island Revisited

It dawned bright and sunny for the two-and-a-quarter-hour crossing to Wellington on the luxury Lynx boat. I drove Vannie on without difficulty, guided by the ferrymen, and sat inside on a comfy seat at the front. When the boat entered the Cook Strait I went outside to the back of the ship and watched the mountains of the South Island slipping into the distance, as the boat's engine set up two great foaming jets of spray.

I had planned to stop in Wellington and see the sights, but it was too busy and the parking charges too high so I somehow found the way out, in shock at all the traffic speeding along after the quiet roads of the South Island. It was only when I spotted an 'End of Motorway' sign that I realised I had been on a motorway – my first one. I stopped for a late picnic lunch by the Hutt River, then drove on to Featherston for food supplies, over the Rimutaha Mountain Range along steep and twisty roads, where the traffic was still fast: at least there were plenty of passing lanes. I continued past Lake Wairarapa and then on to the Putangirua Scenic Reserve's DOC site, where I stopped for the night. There was only an older Kiwi couple camping at that peaceful spot. There were fine views over the ocean to the Marlborough Sounds and the Kaikoura Mountains, blanketed with snow, and I suddenly missed the South Island. It was a calm, windless evening and as I watched the spectacular sunset a group of American quails with their chicks strutted by. At dusk a possum came and stood eerily near Vannie, fixing me with his strange round eyes. Normally I only heard their weird distant cries so I was quite freaked out by his appearance.

The site was near the Putangirua Pinnacles, which were formed by the rain washing away silt and sand to expose the hard bedrock, which stood like giant organ pipes. After breakfast I walked to the foot of them along a stream bed, a rough and difficult two-hour return trek, twice as long as my guidebook stated. I rested a while in the valley, which had a special atmosphere. I had wanted to continue on to Cape Palliser, but it was a gravel road so instead I went to Lake Ferry where I had a picnic lunch and took a last look at the South Island, vowing to return, before heading northwards along fast back roads to Martinborough, a pleasant little town with a central tree-filled square. My camping spot that night was at Mt Holdsworth's DOC site in Tararua Forest Park. It was large with no less than three toilet blocks and use of a fridge and freezer. It was surrounded by forested hills, with lush green grass all around and a rushing river. I was the sole camper until a German couple showed up later in the evening. I found a swim hole in the river near Vannie and had a refreshing dip and wash.

I made my way northwards to Tongariro National Park, a World Heritage area with a spectacular volcanic landscape. At Waiouru I stopped for diesel and saw the 1953 train disaster memorial: Crater Lake had suddenly discharged loads of water into the Rangitikhei River, causing the railway bridge to collapse just before a crowded express train arrived. One hundred and fifty-three people lost their lives in the crash.

I stayed at the Mangawhero Camping Ground, two kilometres up the road from Ohakune to Mt Ruapehu, a snow-capped active volcano of 2797 metres, whose tip could be seen from the toilet. There was one Kiwi house bus there and the inhabitants, an English couple called Pete and Ann, came over and invited me in for a cup of tea. 'Did you buy your bus here?' I wanted to know, admiring the cosy interior.

'Yes, we did and we've found somewhere to store it when we go,' Pete said.

Ann explained, 'Pete's retired and I'm a supply teacher. We love New Zealand and plan to come every year and tour in our home on wheels.'

'It's a great idea,' I said. 'I'd like to do the same but it's a bit lonesome on my own.'

'You'll need to find a Kiwi guy to marry, then you can live like this all the time,' Ann said, a gleeful glint glimmering in the depths of her eyes.

'I've been thinking the same, but I think it's an impossible task, especially at my age,' I sighed.

'Not at all! Be positive,' Ann advised, offering me a digestive biscuit.

Later, as I was brushing my teeth in the toilet block, a strange-looking woman came in and muttered, 'Just checking the facilities,' before she disappeared. I went outside but there was no sign of her or a vehicle. I saw Pete and Ann who were returning from an early evening stroll.

'Did you see that woman?' I asked them.

'What woman?' they wanted to know. I felt foolish and later began to think that I was hallucinating when I almost stumbled across a young man sleeping at a picnic spot which was a few minutes from the camp site. His backpack lay beside the open book he'd been reading. He didn't stir. It was getting dark and cold as the site was 800 metres above sea level so I went and told Pete and Ann.

'So, you're seeing more strange folk,' Pete joked and I felt embarrassed. 'I'll go and look once I've got the dinner on,' he assured me.

Twenty minutes later he turned up at Vannie's door, a mischievous grin on his face. 'Well, there was nobody there,' he said.

'Oh! You must think I'm mad,' I replied, feeling stupid.

He laughed. 'Sorry, couldn't resist that! He was there and was just leaving for the village. He told me that he'd been doing the Northern Circuit, including the Tongariro Crossing for four days and was exhausted.'

'What a relief! I was beginning to think that I was going mad, what with that weird female earlier.'

In my dreams that night the young lad with his backpack and the strange woman slipped, slithered and slid down the steep sides of Mt Ruhapehu's steaming, bubbling Crater Lake, their cries waking me up in the cold light of dawn.

I drove on to Whakapapa on the northern side of Mt Ruhapehu. It was higher up with no native forest, the landscape covered with lava flows and fantastic rock formations. My neighbours at the fully equipped holiday camp there were Pete and Ann. 'Any more strange sightings?' Pete quipped when he met me in the kitchen.

North-east of Whakapapa lies Lake Rotoaira, on the shores of which are excavations of a pre-European Maori village, so my guide book informed me. All I could see were burnt bits of wood and metal – hardly remains of Maori dwellings, but there are so few sites of historic interest in New Zealand that any tiny piece of evidence is carefully kept. The views of the lake were better, with red-beaked black swans calling and chasing each other across its calm surface, while a line of shags sat on a small dam, watching for fish or preening themselves.

Between Lakes Rotoaira and Taupo lies the beautifully secluded

Lake Rotopounamu, surrounded by podocarp forest. The two-hour walk up to it from the highway and then round it was easy, at least it would have been if I hadn't got lost in the bush. I was following a Kiwi couple, Dave and Lynn, who I'd met on Half Way Beach. We should have walked along the beach to pick up the track but instead we took a smaller path into the bush, which promptly disappeared. Dave led the way, bending branches to ease our passage, at the same time confidently proclaiming, 'This must be the right direction. We'll be back by the lake in no time!' I stumbled along behind him, cursing myself for having trusted that they knew the way. We saw open space between the trees and emerged onto a dried-up swamp: it wasn't the lake. 'We'll just have to head through the bush again,' our gallant leader announced as we reluctantly followed, unable to turn back. After what seemed ages, but was only about half-an-hour, we again saw patches of light ahead and suddenly there was the lake, glinting in the sunshine. I collapsed beside it but my companions were keen to finish the walk, so we said our goodbyes, relieved to be back on the track.

That night I stayed at the Oasis Motor Camp in Tokaanu, near the southern shore of Lake Taupo. There were thermal springs there and the camp had a hot mineral bath, spa baths and a warm swimming pool. It was my idea of heaven and I spent the early evening swimming and soaking my muscles, which were aching after my bush hike. On my return to Vannie I realised that this heaven was full of mosquitoes who had invaded my sleeping space through the open skylight roof. I hadn't seen many mosquitoes – they must have liked the thermal springs as much as me. I had to put my earplugs in to deaden their whining attacks through the night.

Before breakfast I relaxed in the spa pools then showered, soothing the mozzie bites. It was a fine day and I stopped at various picnic spots on my way north along Lake Taupo. I visited the Huka Falls again which were just as spectacular as I remembered them. A couple were standing on the bridge with outstretched arms. I did the same; I could feel the energy in them pulsating like pins and needles and told the couple about the sensation. The girl replied, 'Yes, it's a great feeling, isn't it?'

That afternoon *Whale Rider* was showing at the cinema in Taupo and I went to see it. What a wonderful, spiritual Maori film. It was set in Whangara, on the east coast, north of Gisborne and I planned to go there.

It rained continuously the following day so I drove fast all morning to Napier on the east coast. Napier was an instantly likeable town with its fine Art Deco architecture and a Marine Parade with colourful sunken gardens by the Pacific Ocean. Best of all it had a huge spa swimming complex next to the ocean with a large free car park. Vannie watched me as I swam and then soaked in the hot pools, enjoying the powerful water jets. There was no available toilet at the car park but further along the parade was a beach domain with free camping. It was a bit tacky with many motorhomes and house buses parked up for the night but I was keen to swim again before departing in the morning, so I found a spot near the facilities.

The rain unfortunately persisted for most of the day, only giving brief glimpses of the superb scenery on the way to the Mahia Peninsula. To escape the rain I stayed at Pukeko Lodge Backpackers, which was run by a half-Maori woman with her three young daughters. I had the dorm to myself and a young German couple and his brother, who arrived later, were given the other one. We sat and chatted all evening and the husband kindly checked Vannie's battery after breakfast. 'Your battery's nearly dry,' he told me and showed me how to fill it up with water. He also checked the oil which he said was half full.

The rain had cleared enough for me to see the peninsula's pristine white sandy beaches, but Vannie had begun to judder slightly so I went to a small garage in Opoutama. After examining Vannie the mechanic said, 'You may need a wheel alignment. Beau Repair in Gisborne will fix it for you. Just drive carefully until you get there.' This was worrying news: the first time Vannie had given any bother. The mechanic also filled up the oil, which was lower than the previous oil checks had revealed.

The sun was shining by the time I reached Gisborne. The chatty mechanic at Beau Repair gave his verdict, 'I'm afraid you need new front tyres and a wheel balance and alignment. I've looked for an oil leak, but I can't find one. The folk who checked the oil before were wrong. It's tricky with these vans – I'll show you how to do it.'

TWENTY-FOUR

Highway 35

Lighter in wallet, but not in spirit, I set off up Highway 35 which runs along the east coast north of Gisborne through an unspoilt, ruggedly remote landscape, home to the Maori and not frequented by many tourists. This coast is a surfer's paradise: huge waves crash onto white sandy beaches in a long, even line, but I saw few surfers as I drove along. I'd been advised not to visit Whangara, where *Whale Rider* was filmed. The Maori inhabitants were fed up with the publicity they'd received and could be hostile to visitors. I sped past the turning and stopped at Tolaga Bay to walk along the old wharf, the longest in New Zealand at 660 metres. It was opened in 1929 because the bay is shallow and had been busy with visiting vessels since the 1830s as a result of the flax and whale trades, there being no road at that time. It takes half-an-hour to walk to the end of the wharf, from which there are splendid views of the bay, islands and surrounding hills.

I had arranged a week's stay at a WWOOF place just north of Tolaga Bay, at Anaura Bay. The view from the top of the steep hill down to it was breathtaking: I had to stop and gaze and gaze at it before descending. I found the large, rambling house situated at the end of a track by the sea. As I approached a black Labrador ran towards me, wagging her tail, then lay on the path exposing her belly, gazing at me imploringly, her tongue lolling out. She wouldn't allow me to pass until I'd rubbed her tummy for several minutes. As I approached the front door a tall, wiry, grey-bearded man in his fifties appeared. His tanned, lined face split into a grin when he saw me. 'I see you've already met Lady,' he said, bending to give her a pat.

'Yes, she wouldn't let me pass until I'd rubbed her tum,' I rejoined, laughing.

'She's a real softie and she loves the WWOOFers,' he said, adding, 'I'm Scrubbs, your host by the way,' leading the way along a narrow hall into the house's kitchen, where I met the rest of the family.

A buxom Maori lady rose from her chair and held out her hand. 'I'm Louia, Scrubb's partner,' she explained, shaking my hand hard, sizing me up with bright, intelligent, long-eyelashed ebony eyes. Two pretty young girls sat at the table spooning kiwi fruit out of their skins, while regarding me with interest. 'These are our daughters, Honey Lee who's eight and Juliet's five. Don't be fooled by their angelic expressions,' their mother joked affectionately. Scrubbs had previously explained on the phone that the girls were being home schooled and was pleased that I was a teacher as part of the WWOOFers' work was to assist in their education. Also at the table were two other WWOOFers: Taka, a Japanese lad and Rebecca, a twenty-four-year-old German woman, who was travelling with her two-year-old daughter. The atmosphere was friendly and relaxed as we all tucked in to pasta with home-made pesto sauce and garden salad, washed down by an excellent Australian red wine. This was definitely my sort of WWOOF!

I was woken in the morning by the meowing of their three cats and ginger kitten, who'd lost his tail in an accident. After a hearty breakfast of cereal followed by scrambled eggs on home-made brown bread, I taught Juliet for a couple of hours and another two after lunch. The New Zealand Education Authority supplied home schooling materials and I discovered that while Juliet was good at numbers, her reading and writing skills needed attention. Nevertheless, I enjoyed teaching again, even though I'd never taught at primary level. Before lunch the girls had a quick surf, showing off their skills superbly. Although the sun was warm the sea was too cold and rough for swimming: the girls were wearing wetsuits. Before dinner I went for a walk along the beach with Lady. A group of cows followed us which completely freaked her out and I was relieved when they eventually ambled off towards some grass. Before dinner the family were all dressed-up as they were going to visit friends. We gathered to see them off, with hugs, kisses and waves, as if they were embarking on a long journey. Louia had made delicious muffins which we ate with salad and toast, spread with avocado from their tree. The avocados were so abundant that we ate them instead of butter, a healthier and tastier option.

At lunchtime the next day Louia's son, wife and adorable one-year-old daughter arrived, along with an older couple, the husband of which was an actor. Scrubbs had been a film director and knew a lot of actors. In the afternoon they all went to a birthday party in the Marae and returned in the early evening with their grand-daughter, who was staying the night. She was given a bath in a big red bucket in the sink, gurgling happily, all dimples, playing with a large blue sponge. I took a photo of her bathing in the bucket which I sent them later.

They were all off to Gisborne to watch the surfing championships the next day, leaving me and Rebecca to plant shrubs and weed the rather neglected garden. At 10pm they returned, the girls tired and grumpy after their exciting day. They had lessons in the morning but went surfing all afternoon, along with their dad and Taka, who was learning how to surf. There was a full moon that night and after dinner we took the girls to the beach to see it shining on the sea. I wondered if they realised how fortunate they were to live in such a magical place?

It was hard to leave such a perfect place and such lovely people, but leave I did after a week, with many hugs, kisses and waves as I drove off down the track.

*

I didn't go very far – only twenty-three kilometres north to Tokomaru Bay, where I stopped at a small garage to get an oil change, which Scrubbs had recommended. The burly Maori mechanic attempted to undo the top. 'I can't budge this, it's been put on with a pneumatic drill,' he grunted, sweating copiously and wiping his broad brow with an oily cloth. 'You'll need to go to a proper garage,' he advised, whatever that meant.

I went to the supermarket and bought a newspaper. The Iraq war had started, despite continuing massive peace demonstrations worldwide. I felt angry and impotent at the utter stupidity of our governments: the weapons manufacturers would be rubbing their hands with glee. A short distance from the beach was a wharf and an old brick-built freeze-works, rusting and derelict, which was established in 1911 and closed in the early 1950s. Now this area, rich in Maori culture, has attracted many artists – painters and potters, who have opened small craft shops. It was a pleasant spot so I stayed at the quiet motor camp where I met a fascinating old Maori woman who was living in a caravan. 'I've been on the road here for five years,' she told me as we prepared our dinner in the kitchen. 'I'm looking to buy some land and settle down – be self-sufficient. I'm a vegan so I can survive mainly on what I find growing wild.'

117

'But you eat shellfish,' I observed, watching her boiling up some mussels and crabs.

'Sure, I eat shellfish, but that's not strictly meat,' she said. I knew that the Maori loved shellfish and would have been surprised if she really were a vegan. She chatted away for most of the evening, regaling me with her problems of finding some land.

Tikitiki was the next place of interest on Highway 35, in particular the Anglican church with its superb Maori architectural wooden designs. East Cape, the easternmost tip of New Zealand, was reached by a mixed tar and gravel road. The car park had a toilet and water so I decided to stay the night, parking at the end where there were fine views of the ocean. I walked up steep steps to the lighthouse from which the coast stretched southwards as far as the Mahia Peninsula. Back at the car park it had filled up with three other vans and I was glad of my open view. Two Dutch girls had an older Toyota Liteace and they came over to admire mine. The other vans were inhabited by an English couple and a pair of young Swedes.

At 5am I got up for the loo and was surprised to see the others (except the Swedes) all busily preparing to climb up to the lighthouse. 'We want to be the first people in the world to see the sunrise,' they told me excitedly. I didn't fancy ascending the steep steps again and returned to bed for another hour's sleep.

It was a fine, warm day and I stopped at Waihau Bay for diesel. There were three old men there sitting smoking on a bench, obviously keen to chat. When I told them that I needed a job offer to live in New Zealand the one nearest to me nodded at the old Maori sitting next to him. 'Joe here needs a housekeeper,' he informed me, giving me a good look up and down. I'd told them that I was Scottish so he added, 'you could do the Highland Fling!'

Further on, at Raukokore, I spotted a pretty white church by the sea. It was Sunday and people were going into it. A friendly Maori lady saw me and said, 'Our service is at eleven and you're welcome to join us.' I don't normally go to church, but it felt like the right thing to do so I went. The vicar was white and female I noticed, while the congregation of twelve were half Maori, half Kiwi. Half the ninety-minute service was in Maori and I loved singing the melodic Maori hymns, discovering that it was quite easy to pronounce from the written words. I had to sit through communion and was horrified to find out afterwards that the Kiwi woman next to me approved of the

118

Iraq war. The vicar, however, did not.

When I emerged from the church it was very hot. I was dying for a swim but couldn't find a way down to the bay, so I drove back to a place selling macadamia nuts and bought some nut pesto. I parked at their gate, walked down to a beach and swam in the warm, calm water of the bay. Afterwards I had a late lunch in Vannie followed by a delicious macadamia and honey ice cream. Later I found a free camping reserve at Omaio, just past the Marae. It was a large grassy area high above the sea, with no way down. I parked near the edge where I could see through pohutukawa trees across the ocean to Te Kaha Point. It would be most colourful along that coast in December and January when they're in flower. Back at Te Araroa, near the Cape, I'd seen one of the oldest and largest pohutukawa trees in the country in the school grounds. I was completely alone at the camp site, apart from three beautiful horses grazing and the dead in a private cemetery in one corner of it.

Still on Highway 35 I paused to photograph the magnificently ornate Maori gateway of Torere Secondary School before stopping at Opape, where there was a gate to the beach. It was kept locked by the Maori between 8pm and 8am, to protect their fishing and they even had a fisher guard there.

TWENTY-FIVE

To the Northern Tip – Cape Reinga

At Whakatane I finally said goodbye to the wonderful Highway 35, changing to Highway 30 where I stayed the night at Awakeri Springs Motor Camp and once again indulged in hot spring swimming, both before dinner and before breakfast. I continued on in the direction of Rotorua and planned to stop at the DOC site by Lake Tarawera but when I got there I realised that it was only accessible on foot. I stopped near a jetty where there was a toilet and children's playground. A 'No Camping' sign was prominently displayed but I wasn't camping, was I? An aged Kiwi couple were sitting on a bench beside the lake. I asked their advice about overnight parking. The sullen-faced man said emphatically, 'No, they'll move you on.'

'Who are "they",' I wanted to know.

He obviously was unable to answer this question, so changed tack. 'Well, I wouldn't. They'll steal your van,' again giving no explanation as to the identity of the mysterious 'they'.

'I don't think they will with me inside it,' I said with spirit, trying not to laugh.

His wife quietly began voicing little reassurances. 'Oh, it'll probably be all right, dear,' and so on, to the obvious annoyance of her husband.

After they'd gone three genial old men came rowing towards the jetty in a small boat. I decided to get a second opinion. 'Do you think it's OK to park here overnight?'

'Sure lass – go for it!' they all agreed as they clambered ashore and tied up their boat. They disappeared in the direction of the road and I was left alone in the gathering darkness. The clocks had changed so it was dark by 7pm and I had discovered that I could use Vannie's light for an hour or two without running down the battery significantly. I sat inside writing my diary, listening to the sound of small waves lapping on the shore and a few cicadas chirruping in the nearby trees. About 10pm, when I was in bed but not asleep, a car's lights shone through the van's windows. The car stopped and peering through a gap in the curtains I watched a man get out. He walked to a building, which was a fire station, and went inside. That was the only disturbance and by the time I awoke in the morning, he was gone.

Rotorua was as sulphurously steamy as I remembered. I spent the day investigating language schools, and the Korean Principal of one was particularly interested in employing me. My hair badly needed cut and I found a place for trainee hairdressers where I received a wash, by a trainee girl, a cut by the teacher and a finger blow dry by a cute Maori lad with a shaved head, except for a long piece of purple-coloured hair hanging down between his eyes. Afterwards I managed to find the Cosy Cottage Motor Camp, situated by the lake, where the tent sites had underground heating from the thermal activity. *Just as long as it's only heating and not erupting jets of scalding liquid in the middle of the night,* I thought. It was a warm night and I swam in their geothermally heated pool, followed by a mineral water bath. The residents of Rotorua have free geothermal heating in their houses, even in the summer.

I drove about 150 kilometres the next day, through Cambridge and Hamilton to Raglan, a pretty little place with craft shops and cute cafés on the west coast, south of Auckland. After a latte in one of the cafés and a stroll round the beautiful, sheltered harbour, I drove on to Manu Bay, a world-famous black-sand surfing beach. A few surfers, mainly Japanese, were out on the marvellously long surfs and I spent some time watching them gracefully riding the waves. There was a 'No Camping' sign, but I met a young English couple in a smart Toyota Hiace van who assured me that it was fine to park there as they had for a couple of nights. I happily settled down and cooked my pasta dinner in the surfers' changing area, out of the wind.

A council official turned up in the morning and advised me that there was 'No Camping' but he was most relaxed about it. I was moving on anyway to Waingaro Hot Springs where I spent another idyllic time swimming and soaking in warm pools. Suitably relaxed I hit the outskirts of Auckland and the motorway where I stayed in the slow lane as cars hurtled past, many exceeding the speed limit. After stopping for directions at garages a few times, I found my way back to Karekare Beach. It was a sunny weekend and crowded with people, some surfing while others were dressed-up in their best clothes at a wedding marquee on the beach: very different to my last visit with Mona, the German WWOOFer, when we were the only folk there. I continued on to Piha Beach, another popular surfing place, and stopped to take a photo of its beautiful expanse, before descending the steep hill down. I stayed at the motor camp and got a reduction from the female owner when she saw my nuclear-free Pacific sticker.

*

Surfers were already out in force early in the morning. It was a Sunday and I'd heard vehicles arriving late into the night, no doubt Aucklanders preparing for an early start. I wandered along the iron-sand beach, breathing in the sea's salty tang and watching the huge waves pounding on the shore. I had planned to climb up the 101 metres high Lion Rock, just off the beach, but the steps were steep and rail-less – too difficult for me. Instead I drove eastwards on back roads, some of which were gravel and in need of resurfacing. It was too hot and I stopped at Kaukapakapa for a drink as I was suffering from a dehydration headache. From Warkworth I took the scenic route up the coast and reached Omaha Beach, with its white sand and surf in time for lunch at Vannie. The sea was calm at Mathesons Beach, so I went for a refreshing swim which cleared my head, just before a storm blew up. A café at Leigh, just north of the beach, had excellent fish and chips, which they served with salad. Fortified I made it to Goat Island Marine Reserve as dusk was falling and parked. A young English couple were also there in a van and I enquired about overnight parking. The girl said, 'I asked the DOC official and he told me it was OK to stop here for the night but we may be disturbed by their fishing patrols, out to catch folk fishing illegally.' I never heard a thing, sleeping soundly after my hot day's driving.

The sea was too rough to go snorkelling, unfortunately, as the reserve is abundant in fish and other marine life, so I continued northwards, following the coast. When I reached Mangawhai Heads, with its fine white sand surfing beach, I went to swim on the far side at the estuary. I immediately realised that I was making no progress – the tide was going out, sucking me with it and I had to swim extremely hard to get back onto the shore. Further on I discovered Langs Beach, a smaller, pretty beach with calm sea, where I found a shady spot to have lunch and a rest. There were great views of the Hen and Chicken Islands and Little Barrier Island from the shore. At Waipu Cove, with its long surf beach, I checked out the Cosy Caravan site and the Ebb 'n Flow Backpackers, both of which were very busy so I went on to the DOC site at Uretiti, Bream Bay. It was large and quiet, with a cold shower and, what luxury, flushing toilets! The sand was sparkling white, the surf jump-able, and I spent a fun time leaping over the waves and swimming in between them before dinner.

I was back in Whangarei next day and thought sadly about Franz and my first tragic WWOOF experience. I stocked up with supplies, got diesel and oil and went to the library to email. The Iraq war was in full swing and I appreciated reading Robert Fisk's honest accounts in the New Zealand Herald, feeling helpless at the unnecessary suffering of the Iraqi people.

By late morning I was heading northwards along the beautiful Tutukaka Coast, past Tutukaka harbour with many yachts and fishing boats bobbing about. Matapouri had a lovely, curved bay and I had a swim and then lunch, after which I walked along the beach to the other side. It was a glorious place with rock pools bursting with life – sea anemones, barnacles, chitons and many different types of shell whose inhabitants were busily moving around on the white-sand bottom of the pools. These Northland beaches are as good as any on the South Island, with sunnier, warmer weather as a plus.

I drove on to Whananaki along a surprisingly well-sealed road, then on a gravel one to Otamure Bay DOC site. It was another super place, with a long expanse of vividly green grass, clean, odour-free long drops, a shower and drinking water. There was only one other van there so I drove to the other end, out of sight. The warden came as I was having dinner to collect the money. On the South Island the DOC sites mostly had an honesty box, probably because they were more isolated. It was still warm and calm after dark and I sat awhile outside, enjoying the sea view, the boat lights, rocks and jagged headlands. I felt peaceful and content, glad to be back in Northland, which, despite also falling in love with the South Island, was my favourite part of the country.

Old Russel Road is super scenic and I drove down the narrow, steep and twisty gravel road to Mimiwhangata Bay, where I was rewarded by glorious views of green, spiky hills and brilliant blue sea in the distance. Unfortunately, I couldn't stop there overnight: it was another camping place for walkers. When I walked along the beach I saw a couple nude sunbathing; the rest of the beach was deserted so I went the other way and skinny-dipped, luxuriating in the silky feel of sea water touching my whole body. That night I stopped at

Whangaruru North Head Scenic Reserve where there was another well-equipped DOC site, this time with a resident warden. He was forty-ish and handsome and was also a talented artist. I admired his charcoal sketches of the surrounding landscape which were pinned up on the walls of his office. I told him that I would have to sell Vannie before leaving the country and he expressed an interest. I gave him Angela's phone number, but he never called. The site was crowded with no less than three other motorhomes.

The weather was so good the next day that I decided to have a rare rest day from driving. The blue bay was calm and right beside Vannie so I had a dip before breakfast. I met my friendly neighbours later, first an old Kiwi couple who told me about the Caravan Club of which they were members. They showed me the club's informative book before leaving. That left two house buses and me. In one of the buses there was another older Kiwi couple who'd been there two weeks. 'We love this place, it's always quiet and last year we stayed for three months,' they told me. When I was passing the other house bus I got chatting to its occupant, a single Kiwi male of around my age. This was the first singleton I'd met and later he held up a jug of tea, inviting me into his abode. It was spacious and tidy, with a separate bedroom, complete with a real double bed, beside which were two bedside tables, complete with lamps.

'You've got a right 'home from home' here,' I remarked, amazed at the spaciousness.

'Yes, well, I like my comforts,' he said. 'I came here to see my mate Dave, the warden. We were working together this winter.'

'What were you doing?' I asked.

'We were chefs in a hotel at Mt Ruapehu. It gets really busy there in the winter with skiers.' I declined his offer of a sandwich: I'd have to eat up my food fast as my cool box was rapidly losing its coolness. Dishy Dave came for the money as I was cooking rice outside on my burner. We had a good chat about the wildlife there and I hoped for an invitation to join him and his pal for a drink later, but none was forthcoming. Too bad! I'd had enough of my own company and the presence of two single men was so unexpected – I'd got used to meeting only couples.

*

After a reluctant fond farewell to Dave I returned to Russel, then went through Paihia again without stopping and drove on northwards to Kerikeri, a busy market town, where I stopped for provisions. To the north of Kerikeri I found Aroha Island, accessed by a causeway across the mangroves, an ecological education centre set in twelve acres of beautiful land. They had a large, grassy camping area. I was in luck – a school party had just left so I had the place to myself. I found the perfect parking place by an inlet near the mangroves under a tall pine tree. The tide was way out, making swimming an impossibility so instead I did their nature trail round the island, hoping to spot the pair of kiwis and their chicks which the warden had told me about. There was no sign of them as it was probably still too light for them to be active. The island was actually owned by the Queen Elizabeth National Trust. I ate dinner watching a heron fishing while flashes of blue-green kingfishers flew by as the tide came in and ducks swam happily around. Then I went to watch a video about the island's kiwis and on my return in the dark I discovered that a large motorhome complete with a family and two noisy children had been parked close to Vannie! *Why on earth had they parked there with a whole field available?* The mother poked her head out of the door when she saw me. 'I'm so sorry for invading your space but we wanted to be near the picnic table,' she said with a southern English accent.

There was only one table so I muttered an 'It's OK' and quickly went for a hot shower – what luxury! Afterwards I drove to the other side of the field to escape the noise and lights of the motorhome.

Angela had told me about a friend of hers, Aubrey, who had single-handedly created a wonderful water garden in the bush at the turn off to Matouri Bay. I saw the sign, *Water Gardens* and decided to pay him a visit. When he heard I was a friend of Angela's he was all smiles, extended his hand and shook mine hard. 'Come away in for a cuppa. I've always got time for a chat,' he said, leading the way into his small cottage, situated near the road at the top of a steep hill which dropped down through lush bush where he'd created the Water Gardens. He cleared away some papers and magazines from the settee. 'Make yourself at home,' he invited, bustling about putting on the jug and opening a packet of digestives. 'Take a look at this New Zealand Home and Garden magazine – it's got an eight-page spread about my Water Gardens,' he said proudly.

I flicked through the colourful pages. 'It looks amazing! What a lot of work you've done,' I said with admiration.

'Well, yes, it's been a lot of work but I get help from WWOOFers. I'm not in the book but Angela sometimes sends some of hers to me. In fact I'm desperate for someone now – you don't fancy staying for a few days, do you?'

I hadn't expected this and wondered if I'd like staying there, with only him for company. 'Hmm. Maybe later I could come after I've been back to Angela's. Before that I want to get right up to the North Cape,' I explained, feeling slightly guilty at turning down his offer.

'No worries, I'll manage. You know I'll be seventy this year, but I feel fit as a flea. Reckon there's a few good years in me yet.'

'Well, you don't look it,' I said, meaning it. The work obviously suited him.

After leaving him I drove down the steep road to Matauri Bay – a glorious, curving white-sand beach with the Cavelli Islands offshore. This is where the remains of the Greenpeace boat, *The Rainbow Warrior,* are at rest, after having been blown up by French government saboteurs. It is now a popular dive site. A haunting memorial to the once-proud ship stands on top of the headland, a Maori *pa* (fortified village) site.

I was planning to have a swim, followed by a leisurely picnic at the beach, but as I drove along I saw 'No vehicle' signs all along the dunes. The place was owned by a Maori tribe and they were much in evidence, lounging around their parked vehicles. As I passed them they glared menacingly at me, as if daring me to stop, giving the place an unfriendly, heavy atmosphere. Later I discovered that there had been an accident earlier that day. A foreign diver had developed the bends and had been air lifted from the beach by a helicopter and taken to hospital in Auckland. I hoped that this explained the Maoris' unfriendliness, but later Aubrey told me that they were always like that. A lone motorhome was parked defiantly on the dunes near the end of the beach, but I just wanted to go, so I stopped at Te Ngaire, a pretty, smaller white-sand beach nearby, which was quiet and Maori-free.

I pressed on along a gravel road which was being upgraded, making driving tricky. At the quiet town of Whangaroa I stopped for an ice cream and was told the news about the diver by the newsagent. By mid-afternoon I reached the picturesque, historic fishing village of Mangonui, where I had a delicious portion of fish and chips.

126

Mangonui is on the coast of Doubtless Bay, named because in Captain Cook's logbook he wrote that it was 'doubtless a bay'. Further round the bay I passed through Coopers Beach, a built-up holiday area, before heading north up the remote Karikari Peninsula to Matai Bay's DOC site, right at the end, which Angela had recommended. The site had a lower and an upper area, from the edge of which there were marvellous views of the gorgeous beach with its twin coves and pristine white sand. It was crowded, however, and also windy so I parked on the lower area without a view. By the time I was settled rain had swept in and I was glad I'd eaten, resigning myself to an evening in Vannie.

It was rainy in the morning and I swam in the rain, the sea lovely and warm, followed by a cold shower, then breakfast. Awanui is situated at the start of the road to the North Cape and has a wonderful shop full of furniture made from reclaimed Kauri wood. The centrepiece of the shop is a huge Kauri tree staircase. I bought Angela a brooch made from a Kauri cone for her birthday and myself a keyring, picturing some of the beautiful furniture in my future Kiwi home. I reached peaceful Houhora, nearly half way to the Cape, as the rain finally lifted and parked by the mouth of the river for lunch. That evening I went off the main road to the DOC site at Rarawa Beach. There was nobody on the large site, situated in a loop of the river, and I parked by the river where six shags perched on tree branches overhanging the water, waiting for their dinner. I walked down to the long white-sand beach where a few folk were surfing in the late sunshine and strolled to the end where the river entered the sea. Clouds were scudding across the sky to the north and I hoped for a clear day to see the Cape. On my return to the site there was a large red van parked some distance from me. I stopped for a chat with the occupants – no less than three young men and two girls, all English. 'How do you all manage to squeeze in?' I wanted to know.

'We manage fine – take a look,' one of the girls said. There were two sets of bunks and a cushioned seat. 'That folds down into a bed at night,' she explained.

'It's like the Tardis,' I exclaimed, marvelling at the cleverly designed interior.

'Yeah, we were lucky to find it at the Auckland auction; these Kiwis really know how to convert vehicles.'

At dusk the shags flew away to their beds and soon after I settled down in mine. The red van's occupants probably did likewise as there was no sound from them.

*

I awoke at sunrise to a clear sky and was at Cape Reinga by 9am, even though there was a gravel road for the last twenty kilometres. There was only one other car containing two German men there on arrival. The Cape is at the northern tip of New Zealand but is not the northernmost point; Surville Cliffs, thirty kilometres to the east, holds that title. However, as I stood at the lighthouse, looking out over the endless sea, the wind tugging at my hair, I felt as if I was at the end of the world. The rugged, desolate landscape had a special feel, and I could understand why the Maori believe that their spirits leave the island at that point. In fact, the eight-hundred-year-old pohutukawa tree still grows at the Cape's tip, its roots hiding the entrance to the mythical Maori underworld. Bus tours run along the hard sand of Ninety Mile Beach, which stretches up the eastern side of the peninsula, between Kaitaia and the Cape.

After the Cape I drove down to Tapotupotu Bay, where there was a DOC camping ground. The best sites at the far end were occupied by long-term looking outfits so I stayed in the picnic area which had a view of the picturesque white-sand bay. The sea was too rough for swimming, so I swam in the river, which strangely seemed to be flowing away from the sea. There were freshwater showers outside and I stripped off and had a refreshing wash. Shortly after I'd dressed the warden came to clean the toilets – *good timing!* By noon the first of the coach tours arrived, followed closely by four more. I spoke to a Maori woman who was busily setting up a buffet for the tourists. 'There's a lot more coaches due,' she told me so I decided to move on to Spirits Bay for some peace and quiet.

At the east end of the bay was a DOC site, with one house in the distance outside of which grazed a few cows and horses. I'd read that the place was especially sacred to the Maori; a conical hill (maybe a *pa*) rose high behind the beach, on which were notices announcing that walking on it was forbidden. When I explored the beach near the hill I discovered a strange-looking rock: it resembled a face, with a mouth, nose and a huge, swollen head, my mind imagining the swelling to be its brains spilling out. If the hill was a *pa*, the Maori would have fought against their enemies from the top, throwing them down the rock face to the beach. Maybe it was my over active imagination but I felt powerfully strong vibes there. Near the head-like rock were two enormous rocks, made up of small stones, which seemed to form a gateway; the hill appeared to have bits missing on that side, so possibly the rocks had fallen down from it.

I fancied a swim and put on my swimsuit, but the waves were too strong and bashed and buffeted me about, *as if I were a dead body*, I thought, grimly. The sea even smelt strange there – a bad smell. Afterwards I had a long, hot shower to scrub away the odour. There were five other vehicles on the site, including the red vanners from the previous night. They'd managed to cram in a couple of cyclists who'd asked for a lift.

In the morning I awoke after a vivid dream, where I owned a dog, which looked like Lady. She'd chased some cows: two farmers held her up and gave her a fatal injection into her belly. I ran up to them crying, but couldn't stop them. My face was wet with tears and I lay in bed wondering about the dream's significance – I'd never had a dog.

TWENTY-SIX

Hokianga Hullabaloo

On my way back to the Hokianga I stopped at Kaitaia post office for change of ownership vehicle forms: I was hoping to sell Vannie while I was at Angela's. Kohu Kohu looked just as lovely as before and I passed Claire cycling up the road. She flagged me down. 'I thought it was you, Margaret. Great to see you, and what a cool van – it suits you perfectly.'

'Claire! It's good to see you too. Glad you like my van but sadly I'm going to have to sell it soon. Would you like a lift?'

'No worries. I'm happy to cycle – it keeps me fit,' she said, looking tanned and well.

It felt strange to be driving my own vehicle down the stony track to Angela's, but I still felt as if I were coming home. Kyoko, a young Japanese girl, was in the bunk room and I had the double room to myself. Wally and Gwendoline were still there and Angela arrived from Bag End in time for dinner, accompanied by one of her sons, the darkly handsome Ramesh.

I soon settled back into the routine of pre-breakfast yoga sessions in the Whale Lodge, working in the gardens and cooking and cleaning once a week, with Sunday a rest day. I prepared a flyer for Vannie's sale and went round the village putting them up in the post office, the shop's window and on the Tree House Backpacker's noticeboard.

Patrick was still living in the Cabin in the Sky and one afternoon I went with Kyoko to show him Vannie. He was in his workshop, busily carving, but came out when he saw the van. 'Welcome back, Margaret! You've sure got a fine vehicle there,' he observed.

'Thanks, Patrick. I was hoping that you'd know someone who'd buy it,' I said, taking in his fit appearance.

'Well, I can't think of anyone, although I'd be interested in buying it at the right price.' When I told him the price he shook his head. 'That's way beyond my budget, I'm afraid.'

'It's less than I paid for it and it's a good runner and very tidy,' I said, trying out my sales pitch.

'I reckon you were robbed,' he muttered, adding, 'you'll be lucky to find anybody round here with that sort of money.'

'Och, well, you're probably right,' I said and changed the subject. 'You're looking very fit and tanned. What have you been up to?'

'Yeah, I feel great. I've been working as a stock man for the farmer up the road. It's hard work but I enjoy it and I'm meditating for the first time in my life – it makes me feel fantastic.'

'That's wonderful, Patrick. I do it most mornings, along with my yoga.'

Kyoko had been quiet, trying to understand our English, which she'd obviously followed. 'I'm a Buddhist and for me meditation is a natural way to connect with our Buddha nature,' she told us quietly.

'Ah, yes, I've got a lot of respect for Buddhists. You've come to WWOOF at a good place to practise it Kyoko,' said Patrick, with one of his charming smiles.

'So, are you settled here now?' I asked.

'I don't know. I've been here ten months already. I'll see how I feel after a year – I quite fancy living near the sea,' he mused.

The social life in Kohu Kohu was still vibrant; the first Saturday evening after my return I went to Leah the singer's house for an arts council dinner. Everyone brought a dish and Leah's home-made plum wine made all of us merry. After the meal there was a concert, the star, Sarah Gomez. She beautifully sang songs by Carol King and Elton John, amongst others, accompanied on the keyboards by her charismatic Brazilian husband. When the concert finished no-one was in the mood to leave and we had a sing-song and jam session.

I spent time the next day cleaning and polishing Vannie, still hopeful of a sale, simultaneously accepting that I'd have to lower the price. The 4000 dollars I'd paid had been too much so I dropped it to 3000 dollars (about £1400). Two days later several visitors turned up, including a couple from Whangerai and their two small daughters. When the father noticed the 'For Sale' sign in Vannie's back window, he was immediately interested. 'What a tidy-looking van – may I take it for a test drive?' he asked. I gave him the keys with a mix of emotions: *my* Vannie being driven by someone else who might actually buy it. On his return he announced, 'It's a good runner, but a bit expensive for a 1986 model. Would you accept 2750 dollars?' After some thought I agreed as trying to sell it in Auckland would have been problematic and would have entailed me having to stay there longer, which I wasn't keen to do. They bought the contents as well and I sadly watched them drive away with the girls excitedly sitting in the back, waving at me. I'd had such good times with Vannie, but now he'd moved on to a different, family life.

Three gorgeous Swedish lads came to dinner with Claire, who'd met them at the Tree House and invited them for a sauna. They invited me but I declined as I was too full of food. *I must be getting old to turn down the opportunity of sitting in the sauna with three naked Swedes,* I thought. Later, as I lay in bed, I heard them returning from the Whale Lodge, where they'd been dancing. It was a full moon and the possums were out in force, their eerie cries piercing the night. My sleep was disturbed by images of Vannie returning to me, upset by our separation.

It was the Easter weekend and with my breakfast muesli I dined on fresh figs, fejoas, 'custard apples' and the first persimmon of the season – delicious. The April weather was similar to Scotland's, except that the showers were warmer and I was still able to sunbathe and swim in the pond. A new, young South African WWOOFer, Marianne, and her four-year-old son, Campbell, arrived on Easter Saturday. She was a widow: her husband had been shot dead and robbed in that tragic country.

I visited Patrick in the late afternoon and he gave me coffee and brandy as we chatted about our lives. It was dark and rainy when I left, so he lent me a raincoat and a torch. I was late for dinner and just managed to find enough to eat, as Angela quizzed me about where I'd been. 'Beware of that Irish leprechaun's charms,' she advised.

On Easter Sunday morning I went to Patrick's to return his torch and raincoat. 'Happy Easter to you, Margaret,' he cried, doing a wee hop, skip and jump – *just like a leprechaun.* I couldn't help laughing at his antics, forgetting Angela's advice. 'Do you fancy a wee walk to see Amla, Gera and the twins?' he suggested. I'd met this friendly, artistic family before at Angela's.

'That'd be great, Patrick, it's such a fine day,' I said, scouring the sky for signs of rain. There was a bank of cloud in the distance, hanging over the harbour.

'OK, let's go now before it changes,' he said, picking up his walking stick. I still had my trusty two-pronged hazel stick and we set off along a high ridge, with stunning views of the distant harbour on one side, while on the other grazed his neighbour's cows. We reached our destination just as it began to rain. Amla and Gera were having lunch and invited us to join them. We played with the twins afterwards, now at the adorable age of five months, until the rain passed.

On my return to Angela's I was treated to more witticisms. 'So, what have you been doing all day? Cuddling up with a leprechaun, maybe?' I laughed them off, feeling secretly pleased about how things were going with Patrick.

Angela had washed a pair of his trousers and asked me to return them late the next afternoon. I'd been skinny dipping and sunbathing nude in the hot sun after lunch, as everyone was out. When I arrived at Patrick's he was again in a sociable mood. 'Oh, thanks for bringing me trousers. Come away in for a drink,' he said. Once again I was offered coffee with brandy and then he said, 'I was down at Angela's this afternoon to borrow the wee mower and I saw you.' He paused to allow this information to sink in, then added, 'you looked real nice.'

I was flummoxed and resisted the temptation to make a sarcastic comment, such as: *where were you hiding? In the bushes?* Instead I smiled sweetly and said, 'Thank you.' Then we sat in silence, an air of embarrassment hanging over us, until he began telling me about his carvings. While he talked I wondered about my feelings for him – did I fancy him? He was older and shorter than me and possibly wouldn't smell too clean when up close, given that he only used Angela's bathroom spasmodically. I decided to hurry down the hill for dinner and he escorted me to the top of the drive, but left without a hug. I felt a pang of disappointment and wished that I'd stayed after all.

After work the next day once again I went to visit Patrick, unable to keep away. He was all smiles and Irish charm, offering me more coffee and brandy as we sat in the cabin, warming ourselves beside the pot-bellied stove. We were politically on the same wavelength and he showed me a notebook of press cuttings and photos of his campaigns. 'This one's the most spectacular,' he said, turning to a page with a photo of himself perched high up on Nelson Cathedral's spire, holding up a banner proclaiming, 'No Springboks in the Rugby World Cup'.

'That's amazing,' I said admiringly. 'How on earth did you get up there?'

'It wasn't easy,' he grinned, 'but we succeeded. They couldn't compete in the first two World Cups, back in 1987 and 1991, because of the strength of the worldwide anti-apartheid boycotts of South Africa.'

'They were allowed to take part after South Africa became democratic, weren't they?'

'Yes, in 1995 they hosted it and defeated our All Blacks in the final,' he said.

As the brandy took effect, he began to open up more. 'You know, Margaret, I'm happy with my life, but it lacks one thing: a woman to love and cherish,' he said, as he looked directly at me, causing a stab of desire to pass through me.

'I feel the same, Patrick. My life's pretty good but I'd like to share it with someone who I care about and who cares about me.' I waited for him to say something, but he just sat, silently sipping his brandy. *Should I take the plunge and ask him?* I took a swig of brandy for some Dutch courage and hesitantly asked, 'How do you feel about me?'

He moved slightly away from me. 'I really like you, Margaret, you're an attractive woman, but only as a friend.'

Damn! He was giving out such positive signals but I guess I misread them. I immediately withdrew into myself, thinking, *I don't really fancy him anyway – he's too old, too scraggy and too short for me.*

He came with me to the top of Angela's drive again. 'Come tomorrow and help me finish the brandy,' he suggested, still behaving in a flirtatious manner.

'OK, see you then,' I replied, thinking, *no way! Find yourself somebody else to flirt with, you fanny teaser.*

*

I always find that keeping busy helps at times like these and spent the next morning harvesting Maori corn and beans. Unlike our golden yellow corn Maori corn is different colours: red, black, brown, cream or yellow, and tastes delicious. I cleared the vegetable beds of tomato plants and sunflower stalks and continued the mammoth task of wheeling wood chippings from the shredder to cover the garden paths, ready for winter, to prevent them from becoming slippery and muddy.

A ceilidh was planned in the village on Saturday evening and the musicians, dancers and other guests arrived in Kohu Kohu on the Friday. We were invited to the Marae for a welcome ceremony, greeted with a *hongi,* or nose rubbing and treated to some Maori music and

134

dance. We participated in the ceremony by singing the haunting Scottish ballad, *Wild Mountain Thyme*. Afterwards we went into the large hall, where many food dishes had been placed on the long tables, everyone having contributed. Claire had come with some friends, including Steve, who had recently immigrated to start his own chiropractic clinic and Tom, to work in computers. They were both English and gave me a lot of information about the immigration process. Of Patrick there was no sign.

Angela's place was crowded the next day, with Steve's luxurious motorhome parked by the driveway, Tom's tent tucked away near the bush and then Angela's friend Buffy and her small son arrived in their hippy house bus, which she drove onto the lawn. Later, the females got together and had a fun time dressing up in Gwendoline's clothes. I chose a long, green embroidered Indian dress which I wore with my satin blouse. We all piled into Gwen's car, already in high spirits. Kohu Kohu's village hall was packed, with many children running about excitedly while their parents chatted away, happy to let their offspring run riot. I looked around at the crowd; it felt like another era, with folk in hippy-looking outfits and a relaxed, 'no worries' atmosphere. The band were brilliant and I joined in the dancing: *Strip the Willow, the Gay Gordons,* and other favourites, despite my stiff joints. There was a food break half way through, again supplied by everybody bringing a plate. I'd baked cheese scones and we'd brought a huge dish of garden salad, decorated with nasturtiums and marigold petals. A special ferry was laid on to take the Rawene folk back, after which we left, arriving home around midnight.

There were fourteen of us for lunch the next day, plus the baby twins and Marianne's son. We all helped with the preparation and clearing up and then Steve gave me an excellent chiropractic session in the Whale Lodge. 'Your pelvic and neck joints are out,' he informed me. No wonder I was sore.

Claire got the sauna going. We swam in the pond and steamed in the sauna until dinnertime. Steve was reluctant to join us in the sauna at first, but eventually shed his clothes and sat shyly with us. It became obvious that he'd taken a shine to Buffy, especially when they both volunteered to do the dinner dishes which we teased her about afterwards. 'He's way too straight for me,' she said, which was indeed true as she was a relaxed hippy, while he was a staid businessman. Still, it might have done them both good to get together, and he would have ensured that her joints remained in position.

At breakfast Angela had shocking news. Her caravan was on the far side of the pond, from where she could see the sauna. 'I was getting ready for bed and noticed a bright glow coming through my windows. It was the sauna!'

We were horrified. 'What did you do? We never heard or smelt a thing,' we chorused.

'I just ran barefoot in my nightie and poured loads of buckets of water on it from the pond. It was blazing furiously when I got there and I was scared it'd spread to the house and bush.'

'You should've come and called us,' said Claire, adding, 'I definitely extinguished the stove.'

'There wasn't time. I was frantic to put it out. I guess the stove was so hot after being alight for so long that it just spontaneously burst into flames.'

We all trooped down to look at the damage: the roof and one side of the wooden sauna were burnt out, the charred remains a sorry sight. Steve stated the obvious, 'I guess we won't be having a sauna any time soon.'

Two days before I was due to leave, everyone seemed to be going. Marianne and Campbell were getting a lift with Steve south to the Bay of Plenty, where they had fixed up another WWOOF. Buffy and her son headed for home and Ramesh, Angela's son, moved out to work on the forestry. I felt the need to say farewell to Patrick, and trudged up the hill to his cabin with a heavy heart. He welcomed me as if nothing had happened, his mind elsewhere. 'Anthony's off to the UK soon for five weeks and I'm in charge of his stock,' he said with a worried look on his lined face.

'I hope that goes OK,' I replied, in what I hoped was a soothing voice.

'Me too. It's a big responsibility and I'm not sure that I'm up to it,' he said anxiously. Then he changed the subject.

'You're off soon, aren't you Margaret?'

'Yes, in a couple of days. I'm going to WWOOF for Aubrey at the Water Gardens for a few days and then I've got another WWOOF arranged near Auckland.'

'Oh, right. So when do you leave the country?'

'Not for another month, then it's back to Edinburgh.'

'And when do you plan to return?' He looked at me expectantly.

'As soon as possible. I want to immigrate but I'll have to get a teaching job offer.'

'Good luck with that, Margaret. Maybe I'll still be here when you return.'

'I hope so, Patrick,' I said with a lurch of my heart. We'd walked to the top of Angela's drive and he enveloped me in a wonderfully warm hug, which seemed to last forever. Reluctantly I broke away: *would we ever meet again?*

My last day was April 30 and Angela told me that it was the Kiwi Halloween, although they also celebrate it on the usual day. She made a delicious meal, all from the garden, for my leaving dinner: pumpkin soup, roast kumara, falafel and salad. We made a large pumpkin lantern to hang outside the main house which gave the veranda a cosy orange glow.

I sadly squashed my stuff into my backpack in the morning, not an easy task after my time in Vannie, when I could just leave my things lying around. Gwen gave me a lift to the ferry after a big send-off with hugs all round and cries of, 'Come back soon!'

TWENTY-SEVEN

Taraire Water Gardens

Aubrey met me in Kaiokohe car park, looking fit and tanned in a much worn red-checked shirt and faded, baggy grey trousers. 'Hi, Margaret. It's good to see you again. We'll need to head straight back to my place in case we get any visitors.'

'That's all right, Aubrey,' I said as I threw my pack onto the back seat of his muddy, old van.

When we arrived at his small bungalow he explained the sleeping arrangements. 'You can have my bedroom and I'll sleep on the settee in the lounge. I've put clean sheets on the bed.'

'That's kind of you, Aubrey, but I could've slept on the settee,' I said.

'No worries. I always give the WWOOFers my room. I'm OK in the lounge.'

With that I put my bag in his room and joined him in the tiny kitchen where he'd brewed up some tea. 'My place is very special, you know,' he said, sipping his tea. 'It's never been milled, which you can tell by the giant taraire and puriri trees and the massive volcanic boulders scattered about, which are covered in lichen and moss. There are glow worms and kiwi and lots of other native and exotic species.'

'It sounds wonderful,' I said.

'Yes, it is, but it's been a lot of work, especially to create the ponds with their bog plants and water lilies.'

Before we had lunch he got me preparing Japanese water iris, which were growing in tanks near the house and would be planted out in the ponds later. One elderly man came to see the gardens and later in the afternoon we drove to Keri Keri to stock up on food. 'I'm not one of these vegetarians,' Aubrey explained. 'I eat meat, white bread, Edam cheese and tins of fruit, beans and spaghetti, but you can choose food for yourself and I'll pay, as long as it's not caviar!'

'Don't worry, I'll be careful,' I assured him, wondering how he was so fit on such a poor diet.

Nevertheless, he ate my cauliflower cheese and potatoes with gusto that evening. 'That was delicious, Margaret. I guess I just don't know how to cook this veggie stuff.'

I laughed. 'Well, I'll do the cooking while I'm here.'

'I won't complain about that. Would you like to go out and look for kiwis?'

'Yes – I've only seen one in the wild, on the South Island. It crossed the road right in front of my van!'

'What time of day was it?' he asked.

'It must've been late afternoon and it was in a remote spot, surrounded by dense bush.'

'You were lucky, they usually only come out after dark,' he said, picking up a large torch.

We ventured out into the darkness, the torch's powerful beam lighting the way. 'You can often see them here, at the edge of the bush,' he whispered, then suddenly stopped. 'Look, over there.' He shone the torch's beam on a small, fat brown bird, which was foraging in the bush, looking for worms.

I watched, my heart racing, as the kiwi stood transfixed in the torch's beam. For such an uninspiring, ugly bird it has a remarkable reputation.

A storm came the next day, heavy rain beating non-stop on the roof, until, finally in the evening it calmed down. I gave his house a thorough clean and cooked him another tasty vegetarian meal. 'You'll be turning me into a vegetable if I'm not careful,' he joked.

He had been observing my way of walking, with which he was concerned. 'I used to be a ballroom dancer and I'm still able to move well,' he said, giving a short demonstration of his skills, then inviting me to join him, showing me how to position my feet. I felt clumsy but with his support I managed a few twirls around the cramped lounge. Then he showed me how to walk, up straight, with my feet pointing forwards. It wasn't easy but by the time I left he said that he could see an improvement.

The sun was shining in a storm-washed sky and I continued to work above the garden, preparing iris and Abyssinian banana plants and weeding and staking up red sunflowers, which made a wonderful show for the visitors before they went downhill into the gardens. A coach party of eighteen retired folk from Auckland arrived in the afternoon and after they had gone I finally went to see the gardens. It was a magical, peaceful spot and I sat on a wooden bench by the largest pond, soaking up the atmosphere, while butterflies, dragonflies and birds flew around, busily catching insects or laying eggs.

When I arrived back at the bungalow Aubrey said, 'Would you like a trip to Ngawa hot springs? They're quite near here and you've been good today, working hard.' Naturally I agreed, always keen to soak my aching limbs in thermal springs. The springs were basic, but enjoyable, with mud pools at different temperatures. We didn't stay long as there was a Maori birthday party taking place in an adjoining building. When I asked him why this was a problem he replied, 'Because later they'll be coming in the pools "ticked".' I made him macaroni cheese for dinner, his response to which was, 'It's not as good as the packet stuff.'

After work the next day he took me down to Matauri Bay. The atmosphere was far more agreeable than on my first visit. There was no-one there and we walked barefoot along the beautiful, white sandy beach, Aubrey commenting that my barefoot walking was a huge improvement. He bought us ice lollies from a small shop at the end of the beach and we sat on the dunes enjoying them with no sign of any hostile Maori.

Aubrey's place faced west and I watched a stunning sunset while he made dinner; it was my last evening before returning to Auckland and I felt sad to be leaving Northland. We sat down to mashed potato and salad with tinned herring. 'So, what do you think of my cooking?' he quipped.

'Brilliant, Aubrey!'

Early the next morning he gave me a farewell hug at the bus-stop. 'The room is there for you any time,' he said as the Auckland bus came into view.

TWENTY-EIGHT

A Taste of Rudolf Steiner

I was back in Auckland by lunchtime but it took all afternoon with two buses to get to my next WWOOF in West Auckland. The bus dropped me right outside my new host's door, which she'd left open as she was at work. My new abode was a wooden bungalow in need of some tender loving care. It felt weird to be entering a stranger's house and even weirder when the phone rang. *Should I answer it?* It was my host Christine's ex-husband who left a long and garbled message about their son. Not long afterwards the fourteen-year-old son, Tim, also phoned with a message. I felt as if I knew the family already.

A couple of hours later Christine arrived with Tim, bursting in to the kitchen where I was sitting reading near the range. 'Hi, Margaret. I see you've made yourself at home,' she said with a welcoming smile as she bustled about unpacking her bags. She was about my age and had the usual relaxed Kiwi attitude. I liked her immediately and helped her prepare dinner as we chatted about her job. She was a teacher at the Rudolf Steiner school nearby and planned for me both to tidy her garden and to work on the Steiner one. Tim had disappeared into his room but emerged when he was called to eat. He was a tall, willowy lad, handsome-looking with his mum's fair hair and blueish-grey eyes. He ate quickly, as if he were starved. 'Slow down, Tim,' she admonished. 'You'll get indigestion eating like that.'

'Sorry Mum, but I've still got loads of homework to do.'

'Tim goes to my school,' Christine informed me.

'That must be fun for you Tim,' I said. 'Has your mum ever taught you?'

'No, thank goodness!'

'Watch it, young man,' quipped his mum.

We washed up together and she told me about the following day. 'It's a school day tomorrow, Margaret, so it's best if you get up after we've left. You can come up to the school in time for their mid-morning break. You can't miss it – it's straight up the road on the right, about a twenty-minute walk.'

I had the smallest of the three bedrooms; we all retired early, tired out after our long day.

Christine was away early in the morning. She'd told me that she worked a twelve-hour day, devoted to her job. When I reached the school I went to find her classroom and she was there working, even though it was break time. 'Let me show you what to do in the garden,' she said, hurrying out of her classroom. I weeded flower beds and did some digging, then joined the staff in the staff room for lunch of soup and sandwiches. Christine grabbed a sandwich and returned to work. 'You can help in Jane's handiwork class this afternoon, Margaret,' she told me. This was a relief as I was stiff and sore from the digging.

There were sixteen nine-year-olds in the class, with me, their teacher and two other helpers – a good student: teacher ratio. Their task was to make a cloth holder for their recorders, but they struggled to thread their needles and my clumsy efforts at helping them did not really help – I was useless at sewing. Christine had told me to go home after the class and tackle her mountain of ironing, which I did, wondering if it were necessary as I rarely did any. They were both back late so I had some leftovers and watched TV.

My host had left instructions to clean the bungalow's windows the next morning, which I dutifully did. Cleaning windows was a favourite task for hosts to give WWOOFers. In the afternoon I worked at the school's garden with Christine, who had the afternoon off. I had been trying to find another WWOOF for the following week, without success. When she heard this Christine said, 'You can stay here another week as long as you go somewhere for the weekend. I need to blob out so I won't be able to entertain you.'

'OK, I guess I can find somewhere to go,' I said.

She thought for a few minutes. 'Actually, there's a wonderful place near here called Whatipu Fishing Lodge. I think you'd like it. I could drive you there Friday after work and maybe you could get a lift back from someone there on Sunday.' This sounded like a good idea so I agreed to go.

On Saturday mornings there was an organic shop at the school, so on Friday morning I helped to prepare for it, weighing out loose organic teas, lentils, spelt flour, desiccated coconut and other foodstuffs, bagging them up and labelling them. We had lunch at home and Christine gave me some food and bedding for the weekend. She also took me to the supermarket where I bought supplies and a good bottle of red wine.

142

It was a forty-five-minute drive to the lodge through thick bush, the last stretch of road being unsurfaced. It was a wild and windy place with darkness descending when we arrived. Christine helped to carry my belongings inside. It was a large, rambling old place and I had my own room with a four-poster bed. The bathroom was nearby and there was a huge lounge, complete with a piano, a full size snooker table and a wood stove, which was burning brightly. The two women who ran the place told us that six more guests were due to come for the weekend. Christine gave me a hug and left and I settled by the fire with my book and a glass of wine. The other guests appeared around eight: three women and three men, although there was only one couple. They were in their forties and all from Auckland, there to unwind after a hard week's work. An English couple also arrived unexpectedly and were pleased to find a free room. 'We're usually full weekends,' one of the women told them. 'This is a popular place for folk from Auckland to come and relax.'

The Kiwis were all very friendly and in the morning one of the women, Karen, invited me to go tramping with them. 'I'd love to,' I said, 'but my back's sore from gardening and I can only walk short distances.'

'That's too bad. You should try the Alexander Technique,' she advised.

'I've tried that and just about everything else,' I told her, not wanting to elaborate upon my health problems.

The black volcanic sandy beach was a short walk away, wild and desolate, with two islands offshore: on the smaller one there was a lighthouse. There have been many shipwrecks on the treacherous sand bars in this area. There were more high rocky Maori *pas,* which looked like the profiles of heads and were surrounded by marsh, reminding me of the strangely shaped rocks at Spirit's Bay.

It rained on and off all afternoon so I rested in the lodge. After dinner I played pool with three of the Kiwis. None of us were much good at the game but we had a great laugh nonetheless. The English couple had left to catch their flight home and the others played Scrabble while their smelly spaniel, Stanley, stretched out by the stove, snoring loudly. The Kiwi couple retired early, with some sniggering from their pals. Once they'd gone Karen remarked, 'They've gone for nooky.'

We all chuckled, while the other woman, Andrea, added, 'They're welcome to it!'

One of the men, Steve, said, 'You're just jealous,' which produced a furious denial from Andrea.

The rest of the evening passed pleasantly; Roger played the guitar and sang some of his own songs, after which we read out poems from a poetry book, which was found in the lodge's large bookcase. I learned that both the men, who were fathers, had been through traumatic separations from their wives. As we drank more wine I discovered that Andrea and Karen were sisters and that both Steve and Roger were Andrea's ex-lovers from some years previously. 'How do you manage to all be friends?' I wanted to know.

'It's easy!' said Steve. 'Andrea and I were together about twelve years ago, soon after I came out here to work and before my marriage.'

'Then I came along, it must've been six years ago, before my marriage,' piped up Roger, grinning mischievously.

Andrea glowered at them over her glass. 'I wonder what would've happened if either of you had married me?'

'What indeed?' queried Roger.

'Maybe we should find out?' said Steve, obviously enjoying the banter.

Andrea eyed them both. 'Be careful, boys, I might be tempted to put it to the test.' After this outburst the poetry became increasingly lovelorn until we all finally decided to go to bed.

Sunday morning dawned warm and sunny so I went for a swim in a calm cove and sunbathed in the shelter of some rocks, lazily listening to the surf pounding on the beach further up the coast. Steve kindly gave me a lift back right to the door of where I was staying. Christine seemed pleased to see me and drew up a list of work for the week.

TWENTY-NINE

Apples Galore

The week at Christine's sped by and she took me to the bus station Saturday morning. I was off to my last WWOOF, fifty kilometres north of Auckland, high on the hills above the eastern coastal village of Waiwera. My new host, Grace, met me at the bus stop. She was in her forties, attractive, with short, blonde hair, brilliant blue eyes and a kind face. She led the way to where her muddy van was parked, walking confidently in her green wellies. It always amazed me that anyone was able to drive wearing these cumbersome boots. As she drove up the steep, winding road to her place she told me a little about it.

'Our farm's one-hundred acres and it's run as a co-operative with five houses, each occupied by families. There's always loads of work to do and this time of year it's the apple harvest, so you'll be doing a lot of apple-related jobs – I hope you like them.'

Soon her self-built house came into view. It was made of stunningly beautiful reclaimed Kauri wood and, when she opened the door, a pungent fragrance of apples greeted us. The polished wooden floor of the open-plan lounge and kitchen-cum-dining room was covered with boxes of apples. 'Don't mind the apples,' Grace said, 'sorting these is one of your jobs for the week you're here.' My bedroom was just off the lounge, near the bathroom and also smelt faintly of apples.

After a light lunch we went down to the orchard on her large quad bike. We picked Braeburn Red and Granny Smith apples for the rest of the afternoon, along with a couple from one of the other houses. As we worked I learned that Grace had lived alone since the departure of her three grown-up children. Her marriage had broken up eighteen years before. 'I've never met anyone to settle down with again, although I've had some interesting relationships, including one or two with rather attractive WWOOFers,' she confided.

Another big task for me was weeding in between leeks, which were growing in a large plot of land and would be sold in the market. I did that for a couple of hours in the morning and then washed and graded some of the apples for four hours after lunch. Then I made pumpkin soup for dinner, after which Grace transported some crates of apples to the end of the road, where they'd be collected in the morning and taken to market.

My host also worked as a Special Needs teacher in the week and left me to continue with leek weeding and apple sorting. There were also boxes of fejoas, which I loved. 'Some people will be coming for these,' Grace told me.

'What do they do with them?'

'They turn them into delicious, white tangy wine.' The egg-shaped, green fejoas had been cropping for two months and were large and juicy. Some days the wind and rain knocked a lot from the trees and we had to go and pick them up from the ground before they rotted.

One afternoon she took me to the nearby picturesque historic village of Puhoi, believed to be the first Bohemian settlement in the country, with the founders being folk from Czechoslovakia. We visited the ancient church which was built by the settlers and then went to the old pub, where we sat by the open fire, drinking wine and looking at sepia-tinted photos of the village's past life; these included ones of the Kauri tree cutters, who devastated the landscape for their farming and sheep grazing. The only other clientèle were a group of weather-beaten elderly men, who were propping up the bar, silently sipping beer, while the equally aged barman stood, slowly polishing glasses. It seemed as if the past were still present in this pub.

Waiwera has a massive complex of thermal pools and waterslides, the most expensive in the country, but after 7.30pm it is cheap, so we went one evening and swam in the largest pool, followed by wallowing in the smaller ones.

Every Friday evening the co-operative held a communal meal in one of their widely spread houses and WWOOFers were invited. Grace drove us to her neighbour John's house and we were forced to walk through thick mud for the last part, in case we got stuck. In fact, at the end of the evening we had to push a neighbour's van out of the quagmire. We opened the door of another lovely wooden house. The room was packed: I counted twenty-four people altogether, including the children who were mostly in their teens and early twenties. John, who was a widower, was an excellent cook and we dined on roast pork, baked potatoes and other vegetables, fresh from the farm, although they hadn't raised the pork. None of them worked full-time on the farm: they couldn't afford it. One of the men trained university teachers

146

while another person taught ESL (English as a Second Language) at Massey University. She gave me details of who to contact for work as I was still planning to immigrate. We all drank fejoa home-made wine and had a great time. *I'm going to return soon to this wonderful country,* I stated to myself, something that I'd been repeating over and over again, confident that things would work out if I remained positive.

*

It was another sad farewell the next morning as Grace saw me off on the Auckland bus. I stayed for three nights at the backpackers near Mt Eden and spent a frantic three days visiting language schools and following up the Massey University contact. They all had the same story to tell: they'd love to employ me with my qualifications and experience, but a combination of the Iraq War, the Sars virus, (which was affecting the intake of potential Chinese, Japanese and Korean students), and the high New Zealand dollar, were causing student numbers to drop considerably. 'Things will get better soon', they hopefully told me and I prayed that they were right.

As I boarded my Korean Air flight I thought, *I'll be back soon, no worries!* Positive thinking and daily affirmations do indeed yield results if you totally believe in them: eight-and-a-half months later I was back having been offered a job teaching EFL in a small language school in Rotorua, but that's another story.

PART THREE

SCOTLAND

THIRTY

Eigg Eggs

My dream of living in New Zealand was in tatters: the Rotorua job was a disaster and nowhere else was recruiting teachers. I stayed for thirteen months and finally left on 23 March, 2005, bound for Edinburgh, but not to live in my house, which was still rented out. I had no wish to settle down at home; the WWOOFing lifestyle was still in my blood, so why not continue to live it in Scotland? My daughter, Sarah, agreed to me using her Edinburgh flat as a base, receiving my mail and lending me a big cupboard to store my few possessions. 'As long as you don't stay here for too long, Mum', she ordered. It was a bit of a reversal of the usual roles, where long-suffering parents have to accommodate their mature offspring.

*

It was June 20 and I was off to my first Scottish WWOOF on the Isle of Eigg, one of the Small Isles of the Inner Hebrides, which I'd never visited. I'd been cycling on the mainland and excitedly watched my bike being winched onto the small CalMac (Caledonian MacBrayne) ferry boat, while a helpful employee carried my panniers on board. I sat on the upper deck for the short trip across the ten-mile stretch of calm sea. It was cloudy but mist free and the distinctive shape of Eigg, with its pitchstone peak, An Sgurr, 393 metres, rising dramatically from the central plateau, clearly visible.

I chatted to an attractive man from the Scottish Borders who made wooden furniture, just one of the day trippers who came to climb the Sgurr. He kindly carried my bags up the slipway while I pushed my bicycle. The island's small store near the jetty was a hive of activity with tourists milling about while locals busily collected or delivered goods. One of these locals was Neil, my WWOOF host, who was bringing boxes of his Eigg eggs for transport to the mainland. He met me at the store, accompanied by his four-year-old son, Struan. After a brief introduction he put my bags in his van, leaving me to cycle to Cleadale, at the north end of the island, where his croft was situated.

The island is only nine kilometres long by five kilometres wide, but the single track road wound steeply up through woodland and I was forced to dismount. Finally, I reached the top where moorland stretched in all directions, with marvellous views of the sea and mainland mountains. The primary school was on this part of the road, where Sue, Neil's wife worked. The road twisted sharply down to Cleadale and I was treated to my first sight of the Isle of Rhum Cuillins, rising spectacularly into the sky, their summits wreathed by cloud.

After nearly half-an-hour I reached the croft. There was nobody there so I explored its front garden and the narrow strip of rear land, the flat part of which was a vegetable and flower garden, after which it rose steeply, largely covered with bracken nearer the top. It wasn't long before my hosts appeared, accompanied by two young women. They were each holding an intriguing-looking tool.

'What are those strange things for?' I asked.

'They're called "bracken bashers",' explained one, adding, 'guess what they're for?'

Her friend laughed. 'It's a great way to relieve all your stress.' I learned that they were both doing a Master's degree in Human Ecology at Edinburgh University and were staying at the hostel. While we'd been talking Neil had made a huge mushroom omelette, with salad from the garden and home-made bread.

'I hope you like eggs, Margaret,' Neil queried, 'because our hens are laying loads right now. We supply all of Eigg and have some mainland outlets, but there's still a lot left over, so any new egg recipes you may have would be much appreciated.'

'Well, this omelette's delicious, but I'll think of other recipes,' I said.

My new hosts were immediately likeable and made me feel at home straight away. It was a huge relief as I'd been wondering if Scottish WWOOFs would be as relaxed as the Kiwi ones. After we'd cleared away the lunch dishes Sue showed me my accommodation, a caravan at the edge of the property, clean and comfortable, with a portaloo. 'You're welcome to use the portaloo and also the bathroom in the house, but we have a rule: no WWOOFers in the house before 9am or after 9pm,' she explained. 'This is so we can have some space. There's a long drop loo at the top of the hill which we'd prefer you use for number twos,' she added. Luckily I only needed to use the long drop once during my stay, first thing one windy morning. I toiled up the steep slope, past the pig pen, to where they had a small camp site for tents which was deserted. The long drop was at the edge of a steep drop and the faeces literally had a long drop down through the air into a wheelie bin! I sat on the loo seat, feeling gusts of cold air breezing around my bum. *You would have to be desperate to use this loo,* I thought. The breeziness of the place did have one extremely positive effect – I hardly saw a midge (the Scottish equivalent of the sand fly) the whole time I was there.

Sue went back to work and Neil showed me how to feed the chickens, ducks and the large pig, who got moved around the croft in his pen, simultaneously making an excellent job of clearing the land and fertilising it. Then he showed me how to collect the eggs and to wash and sort them in the scullery. They expected six hours work per day – two hours more than most New Zealand WWOOFs. If that had been bracken bashing I could not have coped but because I was a mature WWOOFer and an experienced gardener, I was given the tasks of weeding the vegetable and flower garden, watering the polytunnel, picking strawberries and planting out flowers and vegetable seedlings. The weather was mostly dry but when it was wet I shredded newspapers for the hens' nests, worked in the polytunnel tying up tomatoes and weeding and cooked meals. Most of the rain seemed to fall on Rhum and in the evenings I would sit in my caravan watching its ever changing mountains, sometimes shrouded in mist, sometimes with their peaks poking out of the clouds and sometimes glowing with the rosy hues of sunset. The caravan's side window also had a glorious, but very different view, of the Sgurr and the craggy cliffs behind the croft.

When I was there the croft ran on electricity produced by a noisy diesel generator, which was used for a short time in the morning and evening, both to keep down costs and reduce noise pollution. In 1997 the island had finally been bought by the Isle of Eigg Heritage Trust, following years of problems produced by absentee landlords. The Trust is a partnership between the residents of Eigg, the Highland Council and the Scottish Wildlife Trust. One of its major projects has been the electrification of Eigg. The island now has a mains electricity grid, powered by hydro, wind and solar energy, with the polluting generators only used as a stand-by.

*

Saturday afternoons and Sundays were my time off. I explored the nearby white shale beach of Laig Bay, where the Scottish Episcopal Church stands facing the spectacular view of Rhum. Adjacent to the church is the ruin of the former manse. On another sunny day I walked north across boggy ground to the Singing Sands, so called because the beach's pure quartz sand grains emit a small chirping sound when walked on, but only in dry conditions. The sand was too wet when I was there to hear the singing. The rocks are of great geological interest with lava lines passing through them and a freshwater waterfall cascading down a narrow cleft between them. The beach was deserted and the sea inviting so I skinny dipped, gasping as the cold water touched my warm flesh. After the initial shock I swam and swam, then dried in the shelter of some rocks, the warm sun's rays soon heating up my body. In June the island is covered in wild flowers and I often sat on orchid-covered mossy knolls, meditating or resting in the clean air.

Kildonan is down a steep, winding road on the eastern side of Eigg. I cycled there and left my bike near a lovely old mill house, which was inhabited. I walked up a stony track to the old burial ground and found an ancient ruined chapel, which had never been roofed. The original wooden chapel was built around 600 AD and the monastery, which was founded by St Donan, the patron saint of Eigg, was discovered in 2012 during an archaeological dig. St Donan brought Christianity to Eigg and became a martyr when he was assassinated, along with his fifty-two monks, by the Queen of Moidart's pirate band, in 617 AD. Despite the tragic history I found the atmosphere inside the chapel incredibly peaceful. I stumbled through the overgrown interior and sat on a broad stone window ledge gazing up at the sky's scudding clouds, then closed my eyes. I seemed to fall into a deep meditation and heard the sounds of sweetest singing softly on the air: it was as if I had stepped back in time and left me with a calmness which was only dispelled when I began cycling back up the hill.

I returned to the ferry where there was a busy café and had a huge, delicious and cheap lunch. It became even more crowded when passengers from the cruise ship, the Hebridean Princess, came ashore, their custom a boon to the island's economy.

Every Saturday evening in summer there was a ceilidh in the island's hall. Sue and Neil didn't often go but they arranged for the

Helliwells, an English couple who owned the Glebe Barn Hostel and who lived near the croft, to give me a lift. Karen and Simon were a friendly couple and like many of the incomers had successfully integrated into the island's life. I met other locals at the ceilidh, including Camille Dressler, a French lady whose book, *Eigg, the Story of an Island,* I had been reading with interest. I joined in some of the dances, the live band providing excellent accompaniment, until the increasingly frenzied dancing became too fast for me and I collapsed next to a couple of English women, Ruth and Joy, who I'd met at the croft. They ran photography courses on the island each summer. They pointed out an attractive man of about my age, who was dancing frantically. 'That's the postman, one of the two eligible older males on the island,' said Ruth.

'He looks quite academic,' I observed.

'Yes, I believe he is. He lives in the wee house by Laig Bay, with the well-tended garden,' Joy added.

'Oh, yes, I saw that and wondered who lived there,' I said.

The ceilidhs don't start until late, so it was 2.30am when the Helliwells dropped me off at the croft. It was a calm night after a wet and windy day and I easily found my way to the caravan in the semi-darkness. The sun would soon rise and another long, light summer's day would begin.

THIRTY-ONE

The Last Wilderness

Knoydart, often called Britain's last wilderness because it can only be reached by boat from Mallaig or on foot across twenty-six kilometres of rough moorland, was my next WWOOF destination.

My hosts, Morag and Bob, turned up at the Eigg croft unexpectedly a few days before I was due to leave. I was busy weeding when they arrived one gloriously sunny day along with their WWOOFers, an English couple and their four-year-old daughter. 'Hi, you must be Margaret,' Morag said in greeting. 'I hope you don't mind us dropping by. Our WWOOFers were hoping to stay on Eigg, but the hostel and WWOOFing places are all full, so they're going to have to return with us.'

Morag was a small, lively lady, about the same age as me, who never seemed to stop and relax. Bob, by contrast, was much quieter and calmer. I stood in the middle of the flower bed feeling confused. 'So, how did you get here?' I asked.

'We hired a car at the ferry where we left our boat,' Morag answered airily. She looked at the flower bed. 'You seem to be a good weeder. Do you fancy coming back with us?'

'I'll have to ask Sue and Neil,' I replied, not really wanting to rush away but aware of the logic of the situation.

Sue readily agreed. 'You've finished weeding, tidying and planting up the garden so it seems the right time to go.' With that I went to my caravan and hurriedly packed my cycle bags which my new hosts took in the car. As I cycled towards the ferry I felt sad to be leaving such a beautiful place, but I'd fixed up a different WWOOF on Eigg just twelve days later, so it wasn't too bad. Morag had friends to visit before we left so I sat outside the café where a group of locals were drinking beer while one played the accordion.

We finally boarded Bob's boat at 6.30pm, complete with their WWOOFers, who would leave the next day plus a German barmaid and her two young children, who'd been on an excursion. The boat glided over a calm sea with clear views all around until about the middle of the crossing when it became rough. We sailed past Mallaig and entered the calm waters of Loch Nevis, enclosed by high mountains, where we docked at the tiny hamlet of Inverie. A new jetty was being built not far from the old one. 'They seem to have been building it for ages,' Bob complained, 'but the pub and restaurant are doing very well with the workers' business.'

Knoydart is another successful example of a community takeover. In 1999 the Knoydart Foundation bought the 17,500-acre Knoydart Estate, which comprises most of the peninsula. They run a micro hydro-electric scheme which provides power to the estate. They also own the bunkhouse, which is mainly used by walkers and climbers. Morag was the hostel warden and had the task of running and cleaning it as well as managing her and Bob's market garden. They lived in a small room and kitchen in the backpackers but Bob was busily building a luxury house for them at the edge of the market garden. When I was there he was working on the foundations but a few years later it was finished, built largely from larch trees. Judging from the excellent reviews on Tripadvisor, Knoydart Lodge was a lovely bed and breakfast, but now Morag and Bob have retired and it was up for sale in Autumn, 2014.

That first night I slept in an unoccupied ten bunk-bed room, then moved into the WWOOFers' room the next day after they'd left. It was the strawberry season and I spent a lot of time picking the juicy berries, both outside and inside one of the large polytunnels, where they were growing in containers on benches at eye level, making them easy to pick. Unfortunately, the market garden was situated in a sheltered spot and was plagued by giant, ferocious midges, which were especially bad in the polytunnels. It was necessary to cover my face and hands and any other exposed flesh with liberal splashes of midge repellent, which made the produce somewhat less organic. An easier task was processing them in the kitchen and preparing the excess for strawberry jam, which Morag was somehow finding time to make in her busy day. Raspberries were also cropping in another polytunnel while blackcurrants were ready to pick outside. Morag supplied the pub and restaurant with produce as well as random passers-by and she seemed to be constantly running from place to place all day – it made me feel exhausted just looking at her! The produce for the pub and restaurant, especially salads and fruit, she liked to pick as late as possible for maximum freshness, so we were often frantically picking late in the afternoon. As a result, I was never quite sure how my day would be.

Sometimes she gave me time off if she received a message that the restaurant or pub wouldn't be busy that evening or lunchtime.

At the weekend the Old Forge Pub, so called as it used to be a smiddy's forge, and the remotest pub on mainland Britain, was the meeting place for musicians. Late on Saturday evening Bob drove me and Alan, a Liverpudlian diver who was working on the new jetty and staying in a nearby guest house, the short distance to the pub in Inverie. Sounds of folk music and gales of laughter greeted us when we entered and somehow we managed to find empty seats, squeezed up close together near the bar and the main group of musicians. Customers of all musical abilities were encouraged to join in the crack, with various small percussion instruments available on the bar. After a few sips of Guinness I chose some wrist bells and happily jangled away in what I hoped was rhythmical accompaniment, along with players of a tambourine and a triangle. There was a woman with a guitar, another on the bharang and a man playing the accordion, all very accomplished musicians. Bob had brought his accordion, but could only begin playing after downing several pints to overcome his shyness. When he did start he proved to be an excellent player. He also taught me how to play the spoons and told me that my rhythm was very good.

Bob showed no inclination to leave and by 2am I was feeling tired and hungry and decided to go. When Alan heard this he volunteered to accompany me. It was dark outside, with no moon and a cloudy sky, and became even darker as we left the village and walked underneath trees, trying to avoid splashing through deep puddles. It was made even more difficult by Alan's staggers: he was very drunk. 'Come on, Margaret, hold on to my arm,' he insisted as we lurched along. He began telling me all about his recent break-up with his girlfriend and I made sympathetic noises at suitable moments. Then he switched to holding my hand as we came out of the trees. After a short distance he stopped and tried to kiss me – he was thirty-three years old.

I backed away, laughing. 'Do you know how old I am? I'm fifty-five,' I said.

'So what! Age doesn't matter, Margaret. It's how you are inside and I feel that you're a lovely lass.'

While I found this flattering I was aware that he was drunk, which no doubt affected his reasoning. Also, more importantly, I didn't find him attractive – it was a pity. 'It's nice of you to say that, Alan, but I'm really tired and must go to bed.'

With that I quickly walked away while he staggered towards his accommodation with a reluctant, 'Good night'.

One hot, sunny day Morag gave me the afternoon off, 'To enjoy the good weather while it lasts'. She suggested that I cycle ten kilometres to the hamlet of Airor, at the northernmost end of the road out of Inverie. It was a two hour slog up and down the narrow, hilly, pot-holed road and I stopped many times to drink water and admire the spectacular views of Eigg, Rhum and Skye. Airor Bay faces the Sound of Sleat and the Isle of Skye. I stopped at a small jetty and looked around. There was a house in the distance but no sign of any inhabitants so I quickly took off my shorts and T-shirt and went for a swim in the calm, blue sea. The water wasn't cold and I swam and floated around for ages, revelling in the coolness after my hot and exhausting ride. Afterwards I sat munching an apple and eating a sandwich, to give me energy to cycle back. There didn't seem to be so many 'ups' on the return trip and I arrived in time for dinner. Morag had made a delicious dessert with the fruit I'd picked that morning: strawberries and raspberries with blackcurrant sauce and cream.

THIRTY-TWO

Eigg Lodge

E arly the next morning Bob took me over to Mallaig, where I had time to go to the bank before boarding the Loch Nevis ferry to Eigg. This time I'd be staying at the other end of the island, near the pier, shop and café, at the Gardener's Cottage in the Lodge's grounds. The Lodge is a B-listed building and was built in the 1920s for the then owner of Eigg, Sir Walter Runciman, a shipping magnate. Runciman owned Eigg between 1922 and 1966 and since then the Lodge has only been occupied for short periods. As a result it began to deteriorate and was fast falling into a state of decay. When the island was bought by the Eigg Heritage Trust in 1997 a feasibility study was carried out in conjunction with the Highland Historic Buildings Trust. Unfortunately, the study concluded that the cost of renovating the Lodge (estimated at £2.2m) was too high for the project to be viable.

My WWOOFing hosts, Norah and Bob, had taken on the challenging task of turning the Lodge into an Eco Centre and when I was there in the summer of 2005 it was in a sad state of dilapidation. Bob, who looked the part of an eco-warrior, heftily built, with a bushy, brown beard and a tanned, weather-beaten face, was waiting for me at the ferry. 'I'll take your bike bags,' he told me. 'I've got to wait at the shop for the bread and milk to come off the ferry.' A small crowd of locals, many of whom I'd already met at the ceilidh, were similarly waiting, using it as an opportunity to socialise. I continued up the steep road towards the Lodge and got caught in a heavy shower of rain. The house was surrounded by a large area of trees, including palms and other exotic varieties, which had been brought in by the previous landlords. As I cycled up the drive the Lodge came into view: an imposing, Italianate-style, two-storey building, with single-floor extensions on either side. It was painted white and my first impression was not one of dereliction; it was only when I ventured inside that I saw the decay.

I pushed my bike round the back, as Bob had instructed, to the kitchen, where Norah was busily preparing lunch. The sun had come out and her two sons, Murray, aged three and Logan, eighteen months, were outside playing. They immediately greeted me excitedly with no signs of shyness, obviously used to getting visitors. Norah was expecting a third child the following January. I peered round the kitchen door, breathing in a delicious smell of home-made vegetable soup. 'Come away in, Margaret,' she called, drying her hands on a tea towel. She was immediately likeable, with long, curly coppery-coloured hair and kind eyes. Bob soon arrived with the provisions and we sat down to eat, along with the boys, who were ravenous.

Norah took me to the Gardener's Cottage after lunch, which was along a track at the edge of the trees. 'You'll be sharing with the Scottish Wildlife Trust volunteers and Nicky, an English WWOOFer,' she explained. 'I'll lend you a sleeping bag as the upstairs rooms are cold,' she continued. 'We provide breakfast food – porridge, bread, tea and so on. You have lunch with us and get your own dinners. Please let me know if there's anything you'd particularly like for breakfast. It's too late now to do any work so you can come tomorrow after breakfast with Nicky.'

After she'd gone I sat in the cottage's small lounge, where a fire was burning, despite the warm weather. Upstairs the rooms were indeed cold – icily damp, and I wondered what it would be like in winter. Soon the volunteers arrived and began cooking dinner. They were a lovely bunch, all very young and friendly. I was sharing a room with Nicky and Alison, from Wales. There was also a Canadian, Kateland, a Dutch couple, Bass and Stefania and Jo, Stefania's sister, who was visiting. Quite a crowd for such a small cottage but everyone got on well. The fire heated the water so I had a bath while they cooked, planning to eat afterwards. 'Don't mind the bath water: it comes out dark brown, but it's not really dirty, it's from the peaty soil,' Bass assured me. He was right – it gushed out, almost boiling, a deep rusty-brown colour. I didn't care, I was happy to soak my sore muscles and relax.

The morning dawned bright and clear after a night of heavy rain. The garden was too wet to work in so Nicky and I were given jobs in the house, hoovering up large amounts of dust and dry rot spores. I lost count of the number of rooms, the place was so enormous. After lunch Norah showed me the garden, which was a wilderness. We got stuck in the small greenhouse because of the rain, so I weeded it. The following day it was again too wet for gardening so I continued hoovering while Nicky took moisture readings. They were trying to dry out the rooms which seemed to be an almost impossible task. We got our photos taken for their future web site.

After work I cycled over to Cleadale to have dinner with the WWOOFers, a young American guy and a French girl, who'd been there with me. They'd been left in charge while Sue and Neil were away and were having problems with the pump. 'We haven't been able to shower for five days,' said Nathan, the American. While I was there they finally decided to ask a neighbour for help, who fixed it.

The weather improved and Bob showed me what needed done in the garden. There were peas, broad beans and even asparagus growing amongst the weeds and I staked and tied them up, clearing away the undergrowth. The garden was in a sunken, sheltered spot and as a result was midge hell. Bob gave me one of their midge helmets, which was effective but uncomfortably clammy in the humid heat. Later I walked to the sandy beach near the pier and camp site for a swim. There was no-one around until the ferry appeared, the occupants focussing their binoculars on me, no doubt wondering how anybody could swim in such cold water. Except that it wasn't. On my return to the cottage Jo invited me to eat with them. 'We got given loads of food by some tourists who we took for a guided walk,' she said. Her sister had gone, as had Nicky, to camp on the mainland and Alison had returned home, so four of us sat down to a feast of soup, spaghetti with tomato and mushroom sauce and yoghurt.

Sunday was my day off and as it was fine I decided to walk to Upper Grulin, a three-mile return hike along a rough, stony track. It was very clear and I had marvellous close-up views of the Sgurr ridge, the mainland mountains and the Isles of Muck, Mull, Coll and Tiree, a low, blueish-grey line in the distance. At Grulin I rested my ankle, which I'd twisted and grazed my knee, eating my sandwiches and breathing in the clean, balmy air. There was a beautifully renovated croft house there, one of the previous owner's holiday cottages. There were other ruined crofts amongst the huge pitchstone boulders, neglected when the potato famine hit the island in 1847, their occupants moving reluctantly over the ocean to Canada. It was an isolated, stunning spot and I felt a sense of sadness hanging in the air, traces of the poor lost crofters and their families still lingering. A golden eagle soared majestically high above the steep Sgurr cliffs, adding to the magic of the place. The only people I met were a couple of men with fishing rods, heading up the Sgurr to a loch, a woman with two young children and the French WWOOFer from Cleadale. Back at the cottage I ate with the wild-lifers again, after which they went to Laig Beach to count bats, full of youthful vigour.

My week at the Lodge had ended and I bid sad farewells to Bob, Norah, Murray and Logan, who waved as the ferry prepared to depart. Neil arrived in a big hurry with his Eigg eggs, saw me and waved. I felt very emotional to be leaving such a wonderful place. The shop had even phoned the doctor who had come to the ferry with a tubifex bandage for my ankle.

Bob and Norah succeeded in turning the Lodge into the Earth Connections Eco Centre, which offers environmental courses and green holidays. Since the community buy-out the island has improved dramatically and in January 2010 won joint first place (and £300,000) in a competition to beat climate change, run by NESTA (the National Endowment for Science, Technology and the Arts). The Eco Centre received some of this money and was brought into being on a low budget, with the help of volunteers and the use of sustainable materials. Eigg now has the first totally wind, water and sun-powered electricity grid in the world, quite an achievement for the tiny island community.

THIRTY-THREE

To Anam Cara

The ferry I took from Eigg went on to Rhum, where it stopped to allow people to see the castle. I had yearned to visit Rhum since my first sighting of its towering peaks and was excitedly looking forward to landing on it. It was a mile-long stony road to Kinloch Castle, difficult to cycle on, so I left my bike on the boat, which was sailing on to Canna, to return later. I got a lift in a jeep to the castle, which was built between 1897 and 1900 and is now managed by Scottish Natural Heritage. I sat outside eating a sandwich and waiting for the tour to start. A Glaswegian man was also waiting and confided, 'I'm on holiday by myself. The wife's in Lanzarote, frying by the pool. Not my thing at all.' The tour was fascinating, especially the bathroom shower which had no less than seven powerful jets, including one which came up from the floor. Also, under the stairs, was an Orchestrion, a special music player, similar to an organ. It is one of only three made in the world and is the only one which can be played.

On its return to Mallaig the ferry stopped at Eigg again and I resisted the temptation to get off. I had other plans – I was going over to Armadale on Skye and had reserved a bed in the youth hostel there, which had splendid views over to Knoydart and the mainland mountains. The Skye ferry was much bigger than the one to the small isles, crammed full of tourists going to the most popular Scottish isle. Most of them headed northwards to the capital, Portree, missing the south, 'Garden of Skye' which was in my opinion the loveliest part.

I stayed at the hostel for three nights, cycling the spectacular road through Tarkasvaig, Tokovaig and Ord one day, where I swam amidst a party of schoolchildren learning to kayak. I briefly encountered the gardener at Ord and his two dogs, while changing behind the garden wall. Later, I would meet him properly and we became friends. Afterwards, sadly, the Armadale hostel closed and the Ord garden is no longer open to the public. The second day I cycled to the Aird of Sleat, enjoying more wonderful views of Eigg and Rhum, the weather again warm and sunny. The Ord gardener owned a croft house, situated right at the Point of Sleat, which I would discover later.

My next WWOOF was near Inverness and I slowly cycled there, staying at backpackers in Kyleakin and Kyle, a B&B in Strathcarron and a hostel next to the Ledgowan Lodge Hotel, Achnasheen, a long, slow uphill ride from Strathcarron. It was cold in Achnasheen and the hostel inhabitants were allowed into the hotel's lounge, where there was a roaring fire. The poorly equipped hostel was nearly the same price as a B&B, of which there were none in Achnasheen, so the concession to use the hotel's lounge was welcome. The road to Inverness was faster, being either flat or downhill and I made good progress to Beauly, where everywhere was full as the Black Isle agricultural show was on. The Beauly Tourist Information advised me to go four miles further on to Brockie's Lodge, a modern hotel, which luckily had a free room. I was only twelve miles from my destination, Anam Cara, but could cycle no further.

*

It was an easy bike ride to the bottom of Leachkin Brae, which led up to Anam Cara, near its summit. I'd been told that the road was very steep, but just how steep I could only grasp when I began to struggle up it, pushing my bike and laden panniers. To make matters worse it began to rain. I noticed an elderly man who was in his garage at the side of the road. 'Excuse me, I'm going to Anam Cara and I wondered if you'd mind phoning them for me?'

'Certainly I will. It's a terrible climb up there, especially in this weather,' he said kindly. He tried their number twice, with no answer so left a message that I was on my way, with a heavily laden bicycle. I thanked him and began to ascend, praying that Alastair, the owner, would come and rescue me.

A few minutes later an estate car appeared; a man poked his head out of the window. 'You must be Margaret. I'm Alastair come to get you,' he said, getting out and quickly putting my bike and bags in the back of his car.

'Thanks *so* much,' I said, sliding into the front seat with relief.

'Och, that's the least I could do. How far have you come today?' I told him that I'd stayed just twelve miles away.

'You should have come straight here. One day earlier would've been OK,' he assured me. I thanked him, thinking how likeable and easy-going he seemed to be, as well as being tall and extremely

163

handsome.

We soon reached the top of the hill, where there was a fine panorama of Inverness, the Moray Firth and distant mountains. Anam Cara means 'soul friend' in Gaelic and their leaflet states: 'We have chosen this name as a symbol for the "circle of being", that inner friendship which embraces nature, divinity, spirit and human world as one'. Alastair had bought the large croft several years earlier and began to develop it into a Buddhist retreat centre with the help largely of volunteers. They had built a splendid octagonal building at the top of the croft, which was covered by a turf roof and fondly called 'The Tufty'. Alastair's passion was building and he'd also constructed a small meditation chamber, made from smooth stones with a low roof, close to the ground on the sloping land further down, which faced south with lovely views.

Six years earlier this most eligible bachelor had met Twobirds, fallen in love and married her. She was beautiful, with long, glossy light brown hair, greenish-grey eyes and a willowy figure. She was interested in Shamanism and when I was there they were running Shamanic, as well as Buddhist, retreats and courses. Now they also run courses in yoga, permaculture, bush craft and other spiritual areas, as well as offering healing sessions, which are given by Twobirds or Margaret, who also lives on the croft.

It was lunchtime when I arrived and Alastair took me to the Pavilion, another beautifully built place where the meals produced in the nearby self-built kitchen were eaten. There were a lot of people there. Alastair introduced them: 'This is Eva, from Finland and Charlie from Canada – they're both WWOOFers. Then we have two helpers – Ruth and Kevin from Glasgow, along with Ian, my old friend, who's also helping. Oh, and this is Arthur, another old friend. . .'

'Not so much of the "old",' Arthur interrupted.

'OK, OK. Let's make that "close" then,' said my host.

'Hmm – I'm not too sure about that,' Arthur replied, rolling his eyes.

'Anyway,' Alastair continued, 'Arthur works in the wee office next to our office, which is part of the Crofters' Commission.'

'Are you always this busy?' I asked.

'No. It's because of the Black Isle Show. This is the height of the raspberry season and we have a stall there selling raspberries and advertising this place. I'm afraid you'll get sick of picking raspberries, Margaret, but I'll find you some other jobs to do, especially when it's raining as the rasps can't be picked then.'

By the time we'd finished lunch the sun had come out. 'Right everybody – it's back to raspberry picking,' Alastair announced. The raspberry field was further down the hill on a large area of sloping ground. The raspberry canes were kept upright by two wires running from end to end of the rows. The plants were high, often higher than me, and I found it difficult to stand up continuously, attempting to keep my balance on the sloping ground. Nevertheless, I picked punnet after punnet of the juicy berries, occasionally slipping one into my mouth. They were organic and delicious. To relieve my sore back I sometimes collapsed on the ground, stretching out my aching limbs, gazing up at the cloud-scudded sky. When I closed my eyes I saw bright pink berries on a leafy green background; this also happened at night when I was trying to sleep. When I told the others about it they all said that they were similarly afflicted.

My room was in one of two brightly painted caravans near the Pavilion, which had bamboo hedges planted along their sides for privacy and shelter from the wind. The caravans each had two single bedrooms, one double and a lounge, also with two single beds. When full this meant that six people were using the tiny toilet-cum-shower room, although there was another larger facility with a loo and two showers, near the office. This place was called 'The Blue Lagoon', naturally because it was largely blue, beautifully built with a mosaic of tiles in all shades of blue, with shapes of fish and other sea creatures picked out with the tiles. It was yet another example of Alastair and his helpers imaginative building skills.

*

The following day was the last before the show. Luckily the weather was dry so we were all frantically raspberry picking the whole day. Fortunately, there were plenty of breaks, with mid-morning tea and biscuits, lunch and an afternoon tea break. Somehow I kept going, working my way along the seemingly endless rows of raspberries, often chatting with the other volunteers. Alastair had gone over the show plan first thing and I had chosen the early shift. The show went on until evening so there were two groups of us.

We left at 9am in Margaret's car and spent some time searching for the stall holders' entrance. Once we had located our tent and stall we busily filled small tubs with raspberries. Customers were given the option of either sugar or cream with them, for £1.50. The tent became packed and later we were told that there had been between 10-12000 visitors to our tent that day! Needless to say, we sold out of raspberries.

When the second shift arrived around lunchtime I was given time to wander round the show. It was a relief to escape the swelteringly hot and crowded tent. The sun shone all day and I bought some snacks for lunch and went to see the livestock parade. We arrived back at Anam Cara around 7.30pm, too exhausted to cook dinner. Alastair gave up doing the Black Isle Show after that year, as well as looking after the raspberries, saying that it wasn't worth the effort.

*

There was great excitement while I was at Anam Cara: the BBC were coming to film for the programme, *Heaven and Earth*. Alastair was busy cutting the grass and we were given the task of tidying up all the accommodation. I also helped Margaret prepare the Sweat Lodge. We cut branches of Leylandii, took out the old ones and laid the freshly fragrant new ones on the ground inside the lodge. Margaret hung up white sheets around the walls and then we placed carpet squares on top of the Leylandii branches. By the time we'd finished it all looked and smelt divine, the large fire pit in the centre ready to emit warmth.

The filming was to take place over a weekend and Saturday morning dawned with the sun shining from a blue, cloudless sky. It was hot and continued for the whole weekend. The show featured celebrities who wanted to have a particular spiritual experience. The celebrity was 'Madge', a previous star of the Australian soap, *Neighbours,* real name Anne, who wished to delve into Shamanism.

Sixteen of us, including WWOOFers and friends of Anam Cara, assembled at the Tufty, waiting for the arrival of Anne and the BBC. Alastair came to tell us that they were filming her entrance into Anam Cara at the top of the drive. 'They're making the most of the weather, taking shots of the views. We're so blessed to have such a gorgeous day,' he said happily. At last Anne appeared, heavily made-up and exuding a strong scent of expensive perfume. She was briefly introduced to us by Twobirds who then began a Shamanic workshop.

'Please will all of you lie straight down on the floor on your backs,' she instructed, 'and position yourselves so that you are in a circle with your feet facing inwards.' We obediently did this while the cameraman placed himself as unobtrusively as possible. There were plenty of comfy cushions on the floor and also blankets if we needed warmth. Once she was sure that we were settled, Twobirds explained, 'You are going to go on two journeys, made possible by the sound of the drum. The first one will be to the lower world, the second to the upper. On both journeys you'll meet your helper, or guide. Please just relax and let yourself go. We will have a break in between to share our experiences.'

With that she began to circle us, drumming on a large African drum, at first softly and slowly, then increasing the sound and rhythm. She was a powerful drummer and soon I felt myself slipping into a kind of trance, suspended in space. Suddenly a mighty stag materialised, beckoning me to approach him. I did, then climbed up onto his broad back and, hanging onto his antlers, he careered away along a forest track. Pine trees towered up on all sides and I felt free, revelling in the speedy movement, my physical problems forgotten.

Slowly the drumming lessened, then ceased and we all lay motionless for a while, then gradually became conscious, stretching and rubbing our eyes. Once we'd all come to we shared our journeys. Twobirds began by asking Anne, who had met her pet cat and dog, and did not divulge much more information. The rest of us had met various animals, with widely different but powerful experiences. We had a break for tea, then resumed our positions on the floor. Once again Twobirds drummed around us and I imagined myself being pulled upwards. Higher and higher I went, then I looked down into the cone of a burning, bubbling volcano, molten lava spewing out in smouldering globs. I felt myself falling down towards the inferno, when a large owl flew towards me, its wings outstretched. It clasped me in its claws and carried me away, up, up into the clear blue sky. 'You are safe now,' it said. 'You are free from your pain and mobility problems. Do not be afraid.' Again it was a wonderful feeling, flying high and free and I was reluctant to return to reality. We were all again overwhelmed by our journeys, although Anne did not seem to be as overcome as the rest of us. All this without drugs – simply the beat of a drum.

In the afternoon we made masks of our helpers and danced around wearing them to Twobirds drumming. The BBC wanted to film this but Anne and half the group refused. 'We don't want to look silly,'

Anne said, despite the fact that her face would be covered by the mask. The rest of us were not so shy, including me, so we danced around a bit more while they filmed our antics. After a 'pot luck' dinner we all went down to the Tepee, where a bonfire had been lit. The drums were there and we sat round the fire, singing and drumming, while the cameraman filmed us. Soon the TV crew departed, as did Anne to her caravan, no doubt exhausted by the day's activities. We stayed longer, chatting and drumming as a huge, full moon rose, brilliantly orange, with a grey wisp of cloud across it – a perfect end to a perfect day.

*

It soon became hot again the next day – too hot for a sweat lodge. Usually the lodge continues for about four hours, but we had to halve the time as the crew were interviewing and filming Anne about her feelings so far. She had on a swimsuit, over which she wore a sarong, which she'd borrowed from Twobirds. The lodge can hold up to thirteen people, but there were only seven of us, including Twobirds, Alastair and Margaret, so there was plenty of room to lie down and relax. Before we crawled inside the lodge, a fire had been burning outside to heat up stones which were carried carefully into the fire pit inside the lodge. It was extremely hot and we were soon naked, sweat pouring from us, except for Anne who remained clothed. It was dark inside and much more comfortable without our sarongs. A jug of iced water was passed round regularly as we sat, quietly becoming accustomed to the heat and darkness. Anne, unfortunately, only stayed for about one hour as she felt claustrophobic and she sat outside praying, her make-up running down her face. Luckily the TV crew had been told that they couldn't film the sweat lodge ceremony, due to its spiritual significance. We remained inside singing and chanting Buddhist songs, as well as sharing deep, personal feelings about our lives.

I felt wonderful after the lodge, as if cleansed of all my negative emotions, until a dehydration headache began, despite my constant consumption of litres of water. By the evening it had gone, and so had Anne. The crew were still there and we relaxed in the Pavilion, chatting with them, and bursting into the refrain from *Neighbours,* which we'd been dying to sing the whole weekend. I did a piece to camera, which wasn't used in the programme, probably because I'd babbled a load of rubbish due to nervousness. I was shown prancing around in my stag's head mask, however.

After three weeks it was finally time for me to depart and everyone gathered for morning tea and biscuits to bid me farewell. It was hard to leave such wonderful people and such a lovely place, but I planned to return in the autumn, after visiting my sister in Fortrose, on the Black Isle, and my son in Canada.

*

Every autumn Anam Cara run a working week, called 'Autumn Workings', as well as 'Time for Trees', which is for two weeks in late spring. I went to both of these sessions, which were attended by around twelve volunteers. Alastair raised trees as part of the running of his croft which were sold to various organisations, including Trees for Life, who were restoring the Caledonian Forest, the John Muir Trust and the RSPB. Locally selected seeds from native trees, such as birch, alder and hazel, were sown and by late spring were seedlings which were pricked out into root trainer modules by the volunteers. By autumn these tiny seedlings had grown tremendously, depending on the weather conditions. They could be as high as 0.3 metres, their roots such a thick tangle that they were bursting out of the containers. Our task was to unpack them and lay them in rows on benches. We all worked together in a large shed with benches situated along the windows and it became quite a competition to see how high our piles of trees could grow without toppling over. Alastair and some volunteers would come along at regular intervals, packing up the trees in plastic bundles. Other volunteers were busy loading up the quad's trailer with tree modules, bringing them to the shed and then returning to the outside storage area with the packed trees. In the 'Time for Trees' session volunteers also mixed up large piles of compost and filled the modules with it.

The shed was often filled with noise as we worked, laughing, chatting and joking with each other, as well as listening to music. There was a table tennis table and from time to time we'd have a game, happy to stretch our limbs after sitting or standing for so long at the benches. Alastair had a proposal to make. 'How do you feel about having a mindfulness session after our morning tea break until lunchtime each day?'

His suggestion was met by various responses. One particularly loud Glaswegian woman asked, 'So whit's this 'mindfulness' then, Alastair? It soonds a wee bit weird.'

'It's not weird at all, Cathy. It's a Buddhist meditation when you simply are mindful of what you are doing, in total concentration, without speaking or listening to any noise.'

'Och, I cannae dae that! I cannae keep ma mooth shut fur any length o' time 'n the silence wud drive me crazy!'

At this point other volunteers chimed in voicing their approval of Alastair's idea.

'Well, it looks as if you're in the minority, Cathy. Give it a try – you might surprise yourself.' The majority of us welcomed this session and even Cathy calmed down and seemed to be enjoying it, although she would never have admitted it.

There was also a rota for meal preparation and clearing up afterwards, which gave us the opportunity to try out our vegetarian cooking skills as well as getting to know each other.

Most evenings there was a programme of activities which we were invited to. These included a meditation session in the meditation chamber down the hill: a totally different experience of candle lit darkness, compared to the ones I'd had in the light days of summer. Twobirds gave us an incredible drumming session on their djembe African drums another evening, which was extremely energising after our long day. There was a day off mid-week when some of the group went hiking up a mountain with Alastair. My walking ability could not stretch to this so instead I had a relaxing day reading and strolling around the croft. Margaret gave us a shamanic healing in the shrine room another night; we all lay down on our backs on the floor in a circle while she went round us producing various sounds, with, for example, a rattle, a tuning fork, a big white sound ball and a branch of sage. Apparently this helps our energy to flow and certainly we all felt calm and energised afterwards. On our last evening we assembled in the Tufty, along with Alastair, Twobirds and Margaret and had a farewell party, with chanting, singing and dancing as well as refreshments. I didn't want to leave and was feeling apprehensive about going to my next WWOOF.

THIRTY-FOUR

Loch Tay Vista

It was a wet and windy afternoon in late October when I got off the bus in Aberfeldy. I'd had a long journey from Inverness to Pitlochry by coach, followed by a slow local bus. There was no sign of my host so I phoned her from a call box at the bus stop. 'Oh, hi Margaret. I thought you'd be arriving later. Just wait there and I'll come and pick you up.' I waited, shivering and cursing my new host for not coming at the arranged time. Half-an-hour had passed when her Range Rover appeared through the gathering gloom.

With relief I clambered into the cosy warmth. My host, Maryse, glanced at me from under her heavy eyelids. 'Sorry about the delay but I hadn't checked your email about the bus arrival time.'

'That's OK.' I was simply content to be warm. I peered at her through the dim light as she drove. She had a fine, angular face, framed by a mass of grey-blonde hair. She looked quite old, older than I had expected. Later she told me she was in her mid-seventies which was unusual for a WWOOFing host.

After nearly thirty minutes she turned off the road onto a bumpy track, which led to Culdees Bunkhouse, her property. Soon we were pulling in outside her house, where all I could see was a light in the porch.

Maryse led me inside; she was tall, around six foot and wore a long, fawn-coloured raincoat. We hung up our coats in the entrance, where I left my bag, then followed her through a glass door into the kitchen. There was a large Aga along one wall, giving out a welcome warmth, a smell of baked bread and fresh coffee permeating the air.

Several people were sitting around a long, wooden table. 'Hi, I'm Martin from Austria.' A tall, imposing man with long, dark brown dreadlocks held out his hand. He had a wonderful smile. I shook it, mesmerised by his glittering blue eyes. 'And this is my dog, Ben.' He poked a brown shape under the table. The animal stood up, excitedly wagging his tail, nudging my legs with his damp nose.

'What kind of dog is he? He's lovely.'

'A lab/collie cross. He's a big softy but makes a good guard dog.'

171

He pushed Ben back under the table.

Next a short, black-haired woman rose to greet me. 'I'm Gwen from Germany. I just arrived yesterday.' Then I was introduced to Ingrid, a young Swedish girl and Helen, a Canadian. *That makes five WWOOFers, including me. I guess there's plenty of work for us all.*

'Please sit.' Maryse motioned me to a chair. She was Dutch, which made a total of six nationalities for dinner. This is what I liked about WWOOFing, meeting different folk from all over the world, although mostly they were from 'developed' countries. Helen served us with delicious bowls of home-made soup, accompanied by Maryse's tasty fresh bread. Following this we had pizza, from the supermarket.

Refreshed after a mug of Culdees nettle tea, Maryse broached the subject of my accommodation. 'The young ones are all outside in caravans in the barn. Martin's is way up the hill at the back. I thought you'd prefer to be nearer the house and the toilet.' Gratefully I agreed. 'It's along here.' She led me past a loo and shower cubicle to a door.

That was when I got a shock. The door led into what I can only describe as a ruin. There was a roof, but the interior walls were either half standing or lying in heaps of rubble. A narrow pathway had been cleared through a mass of furniture, rubbish and bits of building materials. I was viewing all of this with just torchlight. She tried to calm me. 'Don't worry. We've put a bed, electric fire and a lamp upstairs in one of the bedrooms. It has electricity and I can give you an electric blanket and plenty of covers and a quilt.' She led me up a narrow staircase with a rope rail. Upstairs there were two bedrooms. The one on the left did indeed have electricity and the walls and floor were intact. A curtain-less window looked out on the night sky.

What could I do? It was late and I was tired. Martin brought up my bag. There was nowhere to put anything so I just took out my night things. I made my way back down the rickety stairs, through the rubbish to the bathroom. Already I felt dirty from all the dust and filth in my abode. Meanwhile Maryse had switched on the blanket. With a parting, 'Sleep well,' she was gone.

Surprisingly I did sleep well. At 7.30 I awoke to the sound of rain pattering against the window. Outside there was a leaden sky. *At least the roof doesn't leak,* I thought. Hastily I pulled on my clothes, the cold, damp air on my warm skin forcing me to rush. After a quick wash I went to the kitchen. Maryse was busy making vegetarian breakfasts for the guests: the B&B rooms were full as it was Saturday.

Helen got me organised with breakfast. Basking in the Aga's heat full of muesli, fresh fruit and goat's milk yoghurt, washed down with a steaming mug of tea, made me feel more at ease.

Maryse told us to relax until the B&B guests had eaten. Meanwhile, Martin and Ingrid came in, closely followed by Ben, who franticly greeted everybody, with much tail wagging. They had been milking the goats and carried a bucket full of the creamy, frothy liquid. I was surprised by how delicious it was, without a goaty smell or taste.

We all gathered round the table, Gwen quietly joining us. Maryse, having finished with the breakfasts, came and told us of her ambitious plans to establish a community. She had only been there herself about two years and was finding it hard to keep people for long periods. I thought of my palatial accommodation and was not surprised.

After breakfast Martin and Ingrid went back outside to clean out the goats. Helen and I went into the large lounge-cum-dining room to clear away the breakfast things. This room was also the music room, with a grand piano and various musical instruments hung up on the wall. The view from the large windows which ran along the outside wall was spectacular, even in the rain. Loch Tay was spread out below, a long, grey expanse of water, just visible through the mist. Beyond it rose a steep hillside, covered with dense coniferous forest. In the foreground was a green field, sloping down to the road far below.

We washed and wiped up the dishes. Then we had to make up all sixteen of the bunkhouse beds. A group of folk were arriving to celebrate two fortieth birthdays. As we worked Helen complained about all the housework. WWOOFers normally are not supposed to do this: their duties should be connected with the land. Personally, I was not too bothered about it, given the wet weather; there were no polytunnels or greenhouses to work in to escape the rain. After lunch we had to rush to finish cleaning the bunkhouse as the guests were due at three. Somehow we managed and then did more tidying up around the place. It was in quite a mess and had obviously not been regularly cleaned.

In the late afternoon the rain stopped and I ventured outside. It was good to breathe in the fresh air and smell the damp earth. Strolling round to the front of the house I saw that it had two storeys. It was very long, with whitewashed walls and a slate roof. Large windows stretched along the entire length of what looked like an added extension on the ground floor. There was a swing seat from which to enjoy the view. Overgrown flower beds bordered the house and the grass was rough and quite long. There was no sign of any garden.

The evening turned out to be quite a party. The bunkhouse crowd set up a karaoke machine and invited me to join in. Fuelled by glasses of tequila we had quite a sing song. *'You're so vain, you probably think this song is about you, don't you, don't you,'* I warbled together with a very merry forty-year-old man, with a red face and curly, ginger hair. Then some local lads arrived with guitars, drums and a didgery doo. The music room was soon reverberating, our voices blending with the instruments, singing a mix of Scottish, folk and pop songs.

It was the early hours of the morning before I stumbled into bed. The down side of all that partying was that Sunday was filled with cleaning up. The guests were very good and cleared away their dishes and rubbish – they even stripped their beds. That still left the laundry to do, along with the bathrooms, toilets, floors and so on. I only had Helen for company. Martin and Ingrid seemed to spend all their time outside in the barn or with the goats. As for Gwen, she was apparently suffering from depression, and soon left without saying goodbye. We were never told to do any work: it was just obvious that it needed done. I wondered at Maryse's trust in the universe. She told me that help always appeared when she needed it and during my stay this was certainly true.

*

Some odd things happened while I was there. First there was the polytunnel. Ignoring the fact that they could be bought locally and erected for you, Maryse decided to get one from Manchester. She allowed Martin to drive her Range Rover down overnight. The next morning there was no sign of Ingrid – we guessed she had gone with him. The following day, a Friday, they arrived back at 3.30am. That weekend Maryse had organised the 'Dirty Weekenders' to come, from Friday evening to Sunday. This is not what you're thinking! They were a group of university students who went away at weekends to help people on their farms.

We had been busy getting the bunkhouse ready for them. Maryse had made a huge pot of soup and had bought in a large supply of bread, cakes, milk, oats and other high energy food. They all arrived as planned and happily settled in, dining on Maryse's food in the large bunkhouse kitchen.

On Saturday morning Martin was told to organise them to erect the polytunnel. It was pouring with rain and when it became apparent that there were no instructions with it, he disappeared in a huff. Maryse assigned one of the female students to take control. She emailed the company who, after some delay, mailed back some directions. The poor students did their best at digging holes for the poles to go in. The rain filled them up as fast as they dug them. The polytunnel remained untouched, abandoned in one of the sheds. No-one actually saw it. We had our doubts that it had even been bought!

Still, a fun time was had by all that evening. After the 'Dirty Weekenders' had washed their dirt away and eaten a hearty meal, we all gathered in the music room for a big sing song. It was a wonderful end to a wet and miserable day.

The next week Maryse went to a conference for three days. Everybody visibly relaxed. It was Halloween and Helen made pumpkin soup and pie as well as lanterns with Ingrid and hung them up outside the door. The local farmer turned up with a bottle of whisky; Maryse rented out her fields to him to graze his cows. We had a jovial time seated round the kitchen table for the feast.

The weather improved so I tidied up the flower beds in front of the house. It felt good to clear away all the weeds, revealing the damp earth and plants. Now and then I stopped to gaze down at the loch. Some people were out kayaking, enjoying the autumnal sunshine. Close by the horses were galloping round the field, glad to be dry and warm.

I went to visit a friend the next weekend, before Maryse had returned. When I arrived back I found her alone – she was very upset. Seemingly Martin, Ingrid and Helen had gone in Martin's Volkswagen van and were not coming back. I knew they had not liked her but was shocked at them just leaving. That left just me to WWOOF – an unpleasant prospect. However, with them away I was able to move into one of the B&B rooms, at least in the week. This was a huge relief as I had been suffering aches and pains as a result of being in the ruined, damp and freezing cottage. Maryse started to cook and clean, proving to be very fit for her age. There had been a group of Jews with their Rabbi there that weekend. They had had barbecues, a comedian, a singer, karaoke and large amounts of alcohol, judging by the number of bottles in the bins. Maryse was obsessed with keeping all the rubbish, convinced that it would be of use. There was a huge barn full of it. Horrible. In another barn plastic bottles were being used to build a wall, an innovative idea.

What really horrified me was the raised beds. I decided to weed them. Underneath the weeds was a thin layer of soil. Under this was carpet. And under this was rubbish: broken bottles, milk cartons, tins and cans. They were at least a metre thick, resembling mini-landfill sites, completely unsuitable for growing vegetables.

Over lunch I voiced my concern to Maryse. 'But it's a wonderful way of recycling rubbish. I thought you'd be all in favour of it,' she exclaimed. Speechless I concentrated on my food – it was pointless arguing with her.

Another strange thing was the twenty or so wheelie bins, covered with netting, by the side of the driveway. Hector, the farmer, told me they were full of human excrement. Maryse had been at the G8 summit demonstration. The camp site had compost toilets, the contents of which needed to be disposed of, so she came to the rescue. At great expense she had it transported in the wheelie bins to her place.

'What's she going to do with it?' I asked.

Hector laughed. 'She's going to leave it to break down. Then she'll grow stuff in it, I guess.'

I was stunned. 'She's got Environmental Health on her back. The neighbours complained, you see.' Hector was enjoying this. It was obvious there was no love lost between him and Maryse. In fact, I later learned that there was a legal dispute between them over his cattle grazing on her land.

I soon became embroiled in her affairs. She had a fear of opening her post and asked if I would do it. I felt more like her personal assistant than a WWOOFer. Unpaid bills, final demand notices and threats from the council planning department greeted me. It was all too much. My dreams of settling down as part of the community rapidly evaporated.

My final weekend was again filled with music. An African drum group from Fife and a samba group from Glasgow had separately booked the bunkhouse and outside caravans. They began drumming slowly early Saturday evening then more and more of them joined in, urging me to take part, and the music room once again throbbed with rhythms. Later the gas lamps were lit in the big barn and we went outside, well wrapped up against the chill night air. We drummed and drummed through the night. It was a marvellous end to my stay.

*Maryse Anand died suddenly in 2013 and Culdees Bunkhouse plus the land were sold.

THIRTY-FIVE

A Camphill Community Experience

There was a Camphill Community (Corbenic Camphill at Trochry, Perthshire) about an hour's drive from Culdees Bunkhouse which took WWOOFers and Maryse kindly gave me a lift. The ethos behind these communities is that adults with special needs are integrated into a supportive environment, living and working with each other, the employees and volunteers. At Trochry there were around eighty-five people, of which just under half had learning difficulties.

My accommodation was in a six-bunk bed dorm, my room-mates two Danish girls. Rachel, one of the house parents, met me and explained how the place worked. 'There are five separate households here and you've been allocated to Lochran, where you'll have your meals. It's lunchtime now, so I'll take you there.'

We walked along a road through green fields bordered by large trees. The community was on a fifty-acre estate, complete with their own farm. Lochran was a modern, white-painted house, with solar panels on the roof. Rachel took me to the dining room, where nine people were sitting at a long table. She was one of the two house parents and I discovered that only four of the folk eating lunch had special needs. The others were young German co-workers. At dinner two more residents appeared who'd been gaining work experience at a café in Aberfeldy. After lunch I met Anneke, a Dutch woman who was in charge of the garden. She showed me round the large area, which included two polytunnels where salad crops were growing. I was put to work planting out chop suey lettuce, a hardy winter variety and feathery-leaved, Japanese mizuna. In my four days there I forked compost into beds, ready for spring planting, pruned shrubs and weeded strawberries, as well as cutting back their runners.

I worked with an assortment of folk, including the Danish girls, German and Korean co-workers, and some of the residents. These included twin lassies with Down's syndrome, who were delightfully affectionate and had a mischievous sense of humour. We had long tea breaks mid-morning and afternoon, complete with scones and cakes from the bakery, sitting in the large garden workshop telling jokes.

One of the twins loved the smell of my hair and kept coming and burying her nose in it. One day we went on a long walk around the place, high above the river, holding hands, to where there were beehives. 'Where are the bees?' the twins wanted to know.

'They're all sleeping cos it's winter,' I said.

The twins looked disappointed and then chorused, 'What a good idea! Let's all go to sleep and wake up in spring time.' They were generally jolly – nothing depressed them for long.

Every evening I joined them for dinner and helped with the washing-up, sometimes staying to listen to one of their house parents reading a story, *Sinbad the Sailor* being the current one.

The day of my departure dawned and over breakfast the residents attempted to persuade me to stay. 'I'm sorry but I've got another place to go and help in the garden,' I explained which they seemed to accept with their usual stoicism. They gathered on the driveway to wave 'goodbye' as I got into Rachel's car. She was giving me a lift to Aberfeldy where I'd get a bus to Pitlochry, then Edinburgh.

THIRTY-SIX

The Beshara School

One of the places in my UK *WWOOF* book intrigued me more than any other. The Beshara School at Chisholme House, Roberton, near Hawick in the Scottish Borders gave courses in esoteric education. What did *esoteric* mean? I wondered and reached for my dictionary: **adj.** *intended for or understood by only a small number of people with a specialised knowledge or interest.* Well, I was still unenlightened and frustrated to realise that I was not one of the elite, but I wanted to be, VERY MUCH. When I was at Anam Cara I'd quizzed Alastair about it. 'Och, that place, aye. We had a WWOOFer here, a young lass who'd been there. She said it was a bit weird: they insisted on setting the table in a special way and I think that's all she said about it.' This isolated piece of information made me feel rather anxious but also even more curious.

After a few days in Edinburgh I boarded the bus to Hawick with a mixture of excitement and trepidation. The two-hour journey passed quickly and I was soon getting off in Hawick's High Street. I'd been told by the school's secretary to cross over the river to where the school minibuses were parked. I found the one for Roberton and was given a toffee by the friendly driver who did likewise when the schoolchildren appeared, laughing and chatting together. One of the children, a beautiful girl with shoulder-length, dark wavy hair and ebony eyes, who was sitting behind me said, 'My dad's coming to pick me up. You can get a lift with him.'

The bus stopped at the crossroads to the school where the girl's father was waiting. He got out of the car and shook my hand. 'I'm Peter Young, the school's Principal,' he said, ushering me into the car. It was easy to see where his daughter got her looks: he was extremely handsome, tall, with wavy, dark-grey hair, his brown eyes smiling at me from his tanned face. Despite his handsomeness I did not find him attractive: he had an air of reserved remoteness which prevented me from chattering as I would normally do when meeting someone new. Only a few words were spoken as he drove the mile or so to the school, which gave me the opportunity to absorb the isolation of the place.

180

After passing by a farm, rolling moors, dotted by grazing sheep, stretched into the distance on one side, while on the other coniferous forest rose up darkly.

Soon we turned into the school's bumpy, stone driveway and stopped at the front of Chisholme House. 'Welcome to Chisholme,' Peter said, adding, 'we're just in time for tea.' I stood, stunned into silence, gazing up at the four-storey building (five, including the basement). It was a beautiful Georgian house, built in 1752, with an impressive, white-pillared front entrance. In front of it was an expanse of neatly-kept lawn, bordered by mature trees, a stone wall marking the boundary between pasture land for sheep. The pasture rose up steeply to a ridge where a line of magnificent trees towered into the sky, behind which open moorland climbed up to higher hills. Chisholme was set in nearly two-hundred acres of land, with some rented out to a local farmer for sheep and cattle grazing.

My new host led the way up the front steps into an entrance hall, where he effortlessly removed his shoes and hung up his coat on a wooden coat stand. I sat down on a chair and rummaged in my bag for my slippers, while he and his daughter went through a door into the dining room. I followed and stood blinking in bewilderment at the brightly lit, spacious room, in the centre of which was a long wooden table, exquisitely laid with tablecloths, table mats, willow-patterned crockery, silver cutlery, teapots, milk jugs, sugar bowls and in the centre plates on which delicious-looking home-made cakes were standing. Seated around the table were a mixture of people, ranging in age from under five to over ninety years old, their clothes an eclectic mix of old-fashioned, colourfully hippy, shabbily chic and ultra-modern.

A tall, lanky-looking man in his mid-forties rose from the table to greet me. 'Hi, you must be Margaret,' he said, giving me a charming gap-toothed smile.

'Yes, I am. This is quite a place,' I said, sitting down next to him.

'It certainly is. I'm Walt, by the way and I'm also a WWOOFer. I've been here two months already and I'm in charge of the garden along with Julia, another WWOOFer. What kind of tea would you like? There's Earl Grey, Assam or camomile.'

'What a choice – this is the most palatial WWOOF I've been to! I'll try the Earl Grey, thanks.'

'You'll get used to it,' he said with a wry look, passing a hand through his unkempt, straight black hair, then offering me some cake. 'It's lemon drizzle, my favourite,' he confided, cutting me a large slice.

'There's no chance of losing weight here,' I said, biting into the lemony sponge.

'No chance, but I could do with gaining some. The garden's such hard work you need a large calorie intake.'

Once we'd finished our tea Walt took me to the steading, a converted stable block which bordered a courtyard on three sides. My room was on the upper floor, with a view across fields where sheep grazed. It was pleasantly furnished and I noticed a picture on the wall of an Arabic design; there had been other similar pictures in the big house so I asked Walt about them.

'The school has a strong connection with Sufism and also Turkey. The kitchen has some lovely blue Turkish tiles, which you'll see if you help with the cooking and there are pictures like this in every room. Each December the students on the six-month course visit Turkey for two weeks. The high point of the visit is a performance of the Whirling Dervishes in Konya.'

'That's very interesting. I lived in Turkey for seven years and I went to Konya to see Rumi's tomb,' I said, already feeling an affinity with the place. Walt left me to get organised and unpack, after showing me a big box.

'This is our jumble box and you're welcome to help yourself to clothes,' he said. I found many garments suitable for working in the garden and had a fun time trying them on. Walt had omitted to show me the location of the bathrooms. The place was like a rabbit warren, with doors everywhere. In my room there was another door opposite the one from which I'd entered. I opened it slowly and surprised an old man with curly, white hair and a straggly beard, who was sitting up in bed reading.

'Oh! I'm so sorry,' I spluttered, quickly shutting the door. Later I learned that he was one of the chefs and came from the Hebrides. I continued my search along a corridor with many closed doors and opened one at random. Another handsome gentleman sat in bed reading.

'Hello! And what would you be wanting?' he queried with an Irish accent. I withdrew in great embarrassment, muttering apologies. This man was also a chef and I was told later that I'd met, 'the two most dangerous males at Chisholme'. Proceeding to the end of the corridor

I found a room with an open door. It was the lounge-cum-playroom and was full of people. I met Julia and her husband David, who also worked in the garden.

Julia was very chatty and friendly. 'We've just moved back to the UK from New Zealand,' she told me, which led to a long discussion about our travels there. They had also been WWOOFers, then had settled down in Westport, on the South Island, becoming WWOOFing hosts. It had been a wonderful lifestyle but they'd become too homesick and had sold up and returned. I also met a Japanese woman, Hiroko, and her primary-aged son and daughter, Haru and Miwa, who were busily drawing pictures at a table. They lived in a part of the steading which was a separate cottage, along with David, their English father and yet another chef, called Shams. There were also a couple of students on the six-month course, who were having a self-study period. It would take me some time to learn all the names of Chisholme's residents, students and volunteers, especially as many of them had adopted Arabic names as a result of studying there. There was also a constant movement, with folk temporarily arriving and leaving.

*

Breakfast was between eight and eight-thirty and the dining room table was set as meticulously as before. 'Who does all this preparation?' I asked Walt.

He rubbed his stubbly chin and said, 'The students do all the work round here. There are six of them on the course and work is an integral part.'

'That sounds hard,' I said, taking a mouthful of their delicious home-made yoghurt.

'Yep, it sure is. They don't have a minute to spare, what with study, work and meditation periods. I wouldn't fancy it. You're welcome to help them though: laying the table, doing the dishes, sweeping the floor, whatever you feel like.'

Taking his advice, I cleared away some crockery and did some drying up; it was a good way to meet people, especially the students who chatted a lot while working.

Every week day morning directly after breakfast there was an hour long meeting in the splendid room opposite the dining room, which was called the Mead Hall. Armchairs and sofas of varying designs and colours lined the walls. The students did not attend the meeting as their study period began at nine. Slowly people entered, after removing their shoes, and sat in silent contemplation. The Principal had a special wooden chair with a leather seat and he likewise sat with closed eyes. I didn't know what to expect: it wasn't like my idea of a meeting. We seemed to sit for ages and I almost fell asleep, full of breakfast. Eventually someone spoke. That first meeting it was Julia and then David who shared their feelings about leaving New Zealand and settling down at the school. 'We feel that this is the right place for us,' said Julia, squinting at the gathering through her round-lensed glasses. Nobody made a comment, silence threatening to engulf them again.

Then I spoke, surprising myself. 'I've also just left New Zealand which was hard as it's such a beautiful country, but I'm content to be back home in Scotland and I'm especially happy to be here.' Hakim (the Principal's Arabic name) came to life at this and welcomed me to Chisholme, while the others smiled at me. Not much else was said and I felt that it was rather a waste of time, not realising that it was all part of the 'order' of the place. I would gradually understand more about this.

'Come on, time to go to the garden,' Walt said when we left the room. It was a crisp, sunny morning and I followed him across the front lawn and down some steps to the two acre walled garden. He showed me round the well-tended vegetable beds, which were surrounded by net fences – 'to keep the rabbits, chickens, ducks and geese out', Walt informed me. At that time the garden's stone wall was in good condition and there were several gates into it. However, many people carelessly left one open, (Walt being one of the worst offenders), and the geese particularly loved to gain access, quickly destroying the crops with their weight and frantic urge to gobble everything up. Ooby Dooby, the garrulous gander, would sweep inside, urging his harem to follow, chasing me away. He was a terrifying force and would have attacked me, for sure. If he appeared at the polytunnel's entrance, I threatened him with a broom. He eyed it, honking loudly, before retreating, head erect, his harem dutifully following.

There was a wonderful Victorian greenhouse along the garden's back wall where Julia was busy sowing seeds. A high beech hedge separated the garden into two halves, each with four large vegetable plots, while around the edges stretched herbaceous borders and a herb bed. Directly outside the garden was a large polytunnel and two smaller ones, where salads and other tender crops were flourishing. It was impressively well run, Julia especially having a wide knowledge of horticulture, while Walt was an enthusiastic learner. He was converting the beds in the large polytunnel into raised beds, which made it easier to work.

We finished our tour in the large garden shed, where Walt announced, 'It's coffee time!'

'But we've only just had breakfast,' I said.

'Well, ten-fifteen to ten-forty-five is coffee time. It's part of the order,' he insisted. So back we trekked to the dining room where an enticing smell of fresh coffee reached our nostrils. There were also several plates of scrumptious-looking home-made biscuits on the table, which I couldn't resist, despite still being full of breakfast. 'The students need all these breaks, even if you don't,' Walt commented. I observed their tired faces and decided he was right. Back we went to the garden where I did some weeding in a sunny area, but before long it was lunchtime, which was between one and two o'clock. A huge gong was sounded at one and it was expected that everyone would then be assembled quietly round the dining table for the blessing. It happened to be November 24, Thanksgiving Day, and a massive lunch had been prepared: turkey with all the trimmings, followed by pumpkin pie and cream. *How am I supposed to work after all that?* I wondered.

It was a Thursday – a special day at the school, for in the evening they held Zikr, or remembrance, in the Mead Hall from ten to eleven. Thursday afternoons were spent abluting the whole place in readiness. I was allotted a bathroom, a small library and a sitting room to clean in the big house. It was an easy task as they were clean anyway. Then at four it was of course teatime, complete with home-made scones. It was dark after tea which meant that we were free until dinner at seven-thirty. As I showered and then rested I concluded that this was definitely my favourite WWOOFing establishment. Where else would I be treated so kindly, fed so lavishly and housed so palatially?

The next day there were flurries of snow, with a bitterly cold wind. Chisholme was around three-hundred metres above sea level and sometimes got cut off by snow. I sheltered in the large polytunnel, planting out pak choi, spring cabbage, kale and mustard seedlings in the new raised beds, which I protected from frost with fleece.

185

On Saturday there was a silent day, which was an irregular event. Walt got into the spirit of it by using intricate sign language, which had me in fits of subdued laughter. He was bringing barrow loads of leaf mould compost into the polytunnel where I dug it into the beds. He smoked roll-ups and signed for me to stop work every time he sat down to prepare one. It was certainly preferable to being worked too hard, but it was too cold to sit still for long.

Walt loved playing games and often got a group of us together in the evenings for cards, Scrabble or Risk. At first I didn't like Risk as it was about war, but then I got into it and became very aggressive, attacking the other players' countries.

On my day off I walked up the hill in front of the house to where there was a round, pillared stone monument to Bulent Rauf, the Turkish founder of the school. There was a wooden bench to rest and meditate upon the wonderful views all around, a dense, dark pine forest spreading behind it. I always found a sublimely peaceful atmosphere there and on subsequent visits made this my first stop, as did others, all somehow connecting with Bulent and the whole ambience of the place.

Bulent had been the fourth and final husband of Angela Culme-Seymour, an amazing lady, then in her early nineties, who still lived at the school. Most fine days she would walk up to the monument, on the arm of whoever was looking after her, still upright, slim and elegant. She had been in her heyday on the front cover of *Vogue* and still dressed stylishly. Her autobiography, *Bolter's Grand-daughter,* was on sale at the school and was a fascinating read. Her first husband was Johnny Churchill, nephew of the great man himself. She would often walk through the garden, always accompanied, and would stop for a chat and a joke. Her short-term memory was faulty, but it didn't seem to bother her, and I had to introduce myself nearly every time we met. If I sat next to her at meal times she would invariably make me laugh. One of her favourite pastimes was to eye up the males around the table. 'Which one takes your fancy then?' she would ask me in a hushed voice.

I'd make a show of looking carefully at the diners. 'To be honest, Angela, none of them,' I'd say, or if, as occasionally happened, an attractive-looking male was present, 'Hmm, that one over there might do. What do you think?'

Her bright-blue eyes would flash as they had done in the past, causing many men to fall for her. 'Yes, he is rather gorgeous, isn't he?' she'd say, and we'd fall about like a couple of loved-up teenagers.

It was noticed that I got on well with Angela and I was invited to a meeting where I was asked if I'd like to help care for her in the gap between afternoon tea and dinner. Walt was also involved and I happily agreed. We'd go up to her cosy room, on the walls of which hung some of her paintings, including one of brightly-painted Turkish gulets on a blue Mediterranean Sea, which I especially liked. She remembered much of her Turkish, having lived there a while with Bulent and I loved to practise mine with her. We'd also play Scrabble, which she was rather good at, sometimes cheating guilefully, which caused us much mirth. We'd often be offered a glass or two of wine, which made me somewhat light-headed, and we'd turn up for dinner flushed and giggling.

*

On the second Thursday at the school I decided to attend the evening Zikr. After dinner I prepared and abluted myself, showering and dressing in fresh clothes. Just before ten I entered the Mead Hall shoe-less, sprinkled Turkish cologne over my face and hair and sat down in one of the comfy armchairs. We waited silently, eyes closed, as the room became full. Hakim took his accustomed seat and once everyone was settled began chanting 'Allah'. We joined in the rhythm and as I pronounced His name I felt myself relaxing, a warm flow of energy passing through my body, and as my mind cleared, the name 'Allah' totally filled my being. After this we stood up and linked arms in a circle, slowly moving round while chanting an Arabic phrase, again in remembrance of God. Various other standing and chanting movements were made, broken in the middle by sharing glasses of water. Near the end we all walked round slowly, in a line, facing each person in turn, bowing and reciting, 'Salaam', to recognise our connection. Finally, we all breathed out the sacred sound, 'Hu' several times, which I found truly liberating, the sounds of all our 'Hus' seeming to intertwine and blend together in perfect harmony. At the end tea and freshly brewed coffee were wheeled in on a trolley, accompanied by plates of intricately arranged chocolates, grapes and Turkish Delight. I did not stay to socialise, not wishing to break the spell which the Zikr had induced in me, so I went back to the steading,

187

pausing to gaze up at the starlit sky, marvelling at its vast expanse.

Two days before I left Chisholme there was great excitement: the students, Hakim and some other folk were leaving early the next morning for Manchester airport, where they'd fly to Istanbul for their two-week Turkish travel. They rushed around packing frantically as they'd been given little time to get organised. They'd been incarcerated at Chisholme for over two months, concentrating solely on their studies and the prospect of two weeks of freedom was overwhelming. The morning meeting was cancelled because many of the school's inhabitants had risen at 4am to see the group off, throwing water at the receding mini-bus to ensure their safe return. The place seemed eerily quiet after their departure, with only about twelve people remaining. I too was going back to Edinburgh to spend Christmas with my daughter but I planned to return for Hogmanay.

*

On 30 December I arrived back in Hawick. It was bitterly cold with snow showers. You were never quite sure who would be sent to meet you at the bus stop and I stood in the car park wondering where my lift was. A tall, good-looking man in his early fifties, with brown hair and a bushy moustache, came towards me. 'You must be Margaret,' he said, leading the way to his car, an old, grey Mercedes. 'I'm Kadir,' he continued once we were on our way and added in a well-spoken voice, 'and I'm a builder from Oxford.' He did not fit my idea of a builder at all, but I became used to having my preconceptions and judgements constantly challenged at the school. He went on to tell me that he'd bought a barge to live on – *what a romantic thing to do!* He invited me to Julia and David's room once I'd unpacked. I was back in the steading, sharing a room with three other females. Chisholme's always full at New Year. Julia and David were pleased to see me and we sat drinking tea laced with generous glugs of whisky. Julia kept us entertained by recounting how she'd met David through a dating site called, 'Natural Friends', which caters for people connected with the organic movement. We somehow made it to dinner after which I played 3D Scrabble with Walt and three other folk in the lounge. It felt good to be back.

The kitchen was an extremely busy place New Year's Eve as they prepared food for eighty guests. I helped out a bit after lunch, wrapping up cutlery in red paper serviettes and helping Shams prepare roast pepper and feta flans. Dinner began at 8pm. The dining room table was laden with an amazing spread: whole pink salmon surrounded by lemon slices, joints of home-grown roast lamb, roast potatoes, fennel, parsnips and carrots, flans, salads and other tasty Turkish treats. The desserts: whole pears in chocolate, raspberry cheesecake and lemon mousse, were brought in once the main course was cleared. There was plenty of wine to accompany the food and the company became increasingly jovial.

At ten we all squeezed in to the Mead Hall for entertainment. There was a glut of talent: comedy sketches, poetry readings, singing and music recitals led us towards midnight, before which glasses of champagne were passed round. We sang *'Auld Lang Syne'* holding hands in a circle, drank a toast to 2006, then circulated, kissing as many people as we could. Later the students gave a fantastic display of belly-dancing, accompanied by some fine drumming. Then pop music was played and everyone began dancing. No wonder Chisholme's Hogmanay was so popular. I awoke late but it was a sunny day so I walked up the hill to the monument and sat meditating, filled with a quiet joy at being alive.

*

At the beginning of April I was back at Chisholme, keen to work in the garden. It had changed remarkably – spring flowers were blooming everywhere: daffodils, crocus, hellebores, hyacinths and polyanthus. The trees and shrubs were bursting into bud, the air was filled with sweet smells and the sounds of bleating new-born lambs as they ran and called to their mothers. The six-month course had just ended but most of the students remained, reluctant to leave and unsure of their futures. Chisholme is part of a Millennium reforesting project and every April runs a Forestry Fortnight where volunteers plant trees and tend to previously planted ones. Walt was going to be working with the trees while Julia and David were often away. This left me in charge of the garden, which began to take over my life.

There was so much to do: seeds to be sown, onion sets to be planted, early potatoes to be planted in the polytunnel, salads and other vegetables to be picked or dug out and taken to the kitchen, while the weeds were wildly growing. I began to miss the morning meeting, coffee and tea breaks, finally collapsing on my bed late in the afternoon. Some of the forestry volunteers were sent to the garden to work and I allotted them tasks, pleased to get some help.

My involvement with the garden, which bordered on obsession, was noted quietly by the residents. No-one actually rebuked me for not following the order of the place, but somehow I was aware of it. Also in May there was to be a nine-day course, an introduction to the school's teachings, which I began to feel a slight pressure to do. This pressure seemed to be coming from outside of me and I struggled against it, simply wanting to be there but working in the garden, not studying deeply demanding spiritual matters.

Walt had recommended a WWOOFing place in Dumfriess-shire, called Parkhead Farm, of which he had pleasant memories, and I arranged to go for the ten days preceding the start of the course. I left the school with mixed feelings, still undecided.

THIRTY-SEVEN

Parkhead Farm

It was a long way from Hawick to Dumfries-shire. The Irish chef gave me a lift to Langholm where I waited one hour for the bus to Carlisle. From there I got another bus to Dumfries and then a coach to Castle Douglas, arriving mid-afternoon. My new hosts ran the Sunrise Wholefoods shop near the bus stop and I wandered down the High Street, admiring the prettiness of the place, with its country town atmosphere.

I found the shop easily, its bright yellow half-sun emblazoned on one of the large glass windows beckoning me in. Pauline was busy serving customers and briefly welcomed me. 'Hi, Margaret. Sally'll make you a coffee if you go through to the back.'

The spacious shop's back room was reserved for fresh organic fruit and vegetables, a freezer full of meat and a deli counter with an impressive array of cheeses. Fresh-faced, black-haired Sally chatted as the coffee brewed. 'I'm a WWOOF host near here, a place called Crogol Mill,' she said. I also met Pauline's husband, Steve, who was busy in the store room, measuring out bags of lentils and other pulses. They were all very friendly and easy-going, despite the huge amount of hard work it took to run both a health food shop and a smallholding. The shop closed at five-thirty so I went out to explore further, enjoying the spring sunshine.

As soon as we arrived at the farm, Pauline fed the animals, while Steve cooked dinner. 'Come and help me, Margaret,' she said, quickly changing into a pair of dirty overalls. The animals were obviously more than just livestock – they were like her family and each had a name. There were several goats with six-week-old kids, two large pigs, Jacob sheep and four abandoned two-week-old adorable Jacob lambs which I bottle fed. It was a new experience for me and I marvelled at their vitality as they greedily sucked at the teat, their little tails wagging with delight. Outside the animal pens I met Holly, their faithful black and white collie, who carried a Frisbee everywhere, her soft brown eyes pleading to be played with. There were also four cats and free-range chickens and ducks roaming around in happy harmony.

Holly and one of the Muscovy ducks indulged in a strangely comic fight-cum-dance game, circling round each other accompanied by much barking and quacking.

After all this work dinner was most welcome and we sat down to eat, almost too exhausted to speak. After helping with the dishes I had a shower and retired to my bedroom. 'There's an electric blanket on the bed,' Pauline had told me and as the room was cold it was most necessary.

My hosts were not both in the shop every day: they took it in turns and the next day Pauline was at the farm. I fed the animals with her after breakfast, had a coffee break then was shown the garden, which was downhill from the house. The farm was high up with panoramic views south across the Solway Firth to the Lake District mountains beyond. The vegetable garden had unobstructed views which I gazed at from time to time while working. After lunch we gave the lambs their bottles, which Pauline showed me how to prepare. Then we went with Holly in the car to a beautiful nature reserve above the sea, where I rested in the sunshine while Pauline took Holly for a run along the beach far below. She seemed to have phenomenal supplies of energy for a woman in her forties. I never saw her relax. After dinner she would be in her office doing paperwork while Steve dozed in front of the TV. On our return she fed the animals and washed the car while I prepared vegetables to go with a roast chicken and cleaned the kitchen.

During my ten day stay I settled into a routine of feeding the animals twice a day, working in the garden and often cooking their evening meal, which they really appreciated. What I loved the most was feeding the lambs who were usually out in the fields. When they spotted me holding the bottles of milk high and calling, 'Milky, Milky,' they'd come running across the field, bleating loudly. Bandit was my favourite, a real character and often the first to arrive. I'd feed two lambs simultaneously, while the other two jostled for attention: it was quite a task. Quirky, one of the mummy goats, was ill with diarrhoea in one of the pens, so I had to give her three kids bottles too. They were much bigger and stronger than the lambs, often mobbing me as I sat on a rock with the bottles. I was unable to crouch for long with arthritic knees. I also helped Pauline with new-born lambs, holding them while she clipped their ears with identification numbers. Their mums also needed attention: feet trimming and delousing, so I held them as they sat on their bums, their feet waggling in the air.

The weather was hot and sunny and one day Pauline asked me to help her extend the pigs' electric fence so that it included a boggy piece of land for them to roll about in and cool down. 'Did you know that pigs can get sunburned?' Pauline asked me. I thought she was joking. 'It's true, honestly! The sheeps' ears can also be damaged by the sun,' she added.

I had told Pauline that we'd often camped at Brighouse Bay, near Kirkcudbright, when my children were young and one sunny afternoon she said, 'I think we deserve some time out. Would you like to go to Brighouse Bay?'

'Oh, I'd love to go,' I said, not realising how far it was. Pauline drove along twisty country roads through lush green countryside until we reached the bay. It was unrecognisable. In place of the wide expanse of green grass dotted with a few tents and camper vans which I remembered, there was a huge, deluxe site with static caravans and a large shop, filled with noisy children and their parents. Even the beach and bay did not look the same – it seemed to have become smaller and dirtier somehow. We had a picnic there while I reminisced about rosier times.

On our return the animals were waiting to be fed and the chickens' eggs to be collected. The hens were busily laying and were finding different places in an attempt to avoid being found. There were six eggs on top of the goats' bale of hay, while many of the chickens sat defiantly on their eggs, some actually crowing as they laid them! Some, naturally, were allowed to become happy mothers.

Another afternoon Steve asked me to go and let the goats out of the field so that they could go up to the barn for their dinner. 'Don't worry, Margaret. This is their routine and they know the way. All you have to do is open the gate and then shut it after they've all gone through.' I was a bit anxious as I approached the field, knowing that Faro, the big billy goat, was rather unpredictable. I opened the gate and watched as the females calmly came out and ambled slowly up the track. Faro, however, remained in the field, waiting for all his ladies to exit. *What a gentlemanly goat,* I thought, then changed my mind as Faro came towards me, taking his time. Everything went into slow motion: he paused, bowed his head with its massive curled horns and then butted me so hard that I flew several feet into the air, landing with a thud in the mud on my bum. He gave me a look of pure disdain. *That's sorted you out,* he seemed to say as he turned and regally followed the others, his head held high. I managed to haul myself up, feeling shocked and winded, but no bones broken, and limped up to the house to tell Steve my sorry tale. He found it extremely funny. 'That's Faro for you. You should've made sure that you were behind the gate.' Pauline was more sympathetic and gave me Arnica tablets for the bruising. Over dinner that night Steve began talking about the livestock. 'Sheep and goats have a hierarchy, just like other animals.'

'Yes, well I saw that today didn't I, with Faro and his nanny goats,' I said, rubbing my sore shoulder.

'You certainly did,' he laughed, adding, 'they say that a bull or a male pig can actually break their penises if a cow or sow is too much for them: it's made of cartilage, you see.' Pauline and I went into fits of laughter, imagining this scenario.

It was soon time for me to depart and I sadly said goodbye to the lambs, which included the most recent arrivals – a pair of black, woolly twins. I also bid farewell to the goats, giving Faro a knowing look as he munched his hay. Holly was the worst to leave. She'd been my constant companion while I worked and was there as Pauline drove me down the road, looking forlorn and sad. 'She's always like this when a WWOOFer goes,' Pauline said. She presented me with a bar of delicious organic chocolate when we reached the shop. I would miss her and Steve too: they'd been wonderful hosts.

THIRTY-EIGHT

Return to Beshara

Despite the distraction of Parkhead Farm I decided to return to Chisholme for the nine-day course: something which I could not ignore was propelling me there. One of the six-month course students met me from the school mini-bus and gave me tea which we drank in the sunny steading courtyard. Anthony, who'd been helping in the kitchen on my last visit, joined us and announced that he too was on the course. Then an older man, Graham, arrived and Hannah, a lovely Israeli woman, whose daughter had been on the six-month course, joined us. I met the fifth course member at dinner. Ahmet was Turkish, married and lived in London. He reminded me of my ex-Turkish boyfriend, tall, darkly handsome, with an uncanny ability to predict my every move. When I was putting on my boots in the steading, preparing to go for a walk, he'd appear; I'd be sitting at the dinner table and magically he'd materialise at my side; at Zikr he'd be beside me, holding my hand; he loved gardening and we worked there together in the afternoons. It was a supreme test, hugely distracting, and I tossed and turned at night, burning with desire.

Our routine was similar to the six-month course. We rose at six-thirty for meditation and then prepared, ate and cleared away breakfast. From nine to twelve we read and discussed course work, with a half-hour coffee break. At mid-day there was another meditation session. From twelve-thirty to two we laid the table, had lunch and did the dishes. Two-fifteen to four was our work period, which for Ahmet and I was mainly in the garden. Four was tea time, after which there was more study. At six we had our last meditation period and then it was time for dinner. Then, about eight-thirty, we were finally free, apart from the big Zikr on Thursdays. On the six-month course the students have a short Zikr from nine-thirty to ten o'clock each evening. The sun was shining on many of the course days and I loved to walk up to the monument to watch the sunset, often with Ahmet who had the same idea. It was wonderful to sit silently meditating with him on Bulent's bench as the sun's setting rays lit up the sky.

One day we were setting the table for lunch in comfortable silence.

195

As I moved round the massive table, carefully placing the willow-patterned plates with the two doves uppermost on the spotless tablecloths, I experienced a state of suspended sensation: it wasn't like a trance, it was a peaceful clarity, a perfect moment in time, without thoughts, feelings or emotions, simply a state of being. The table laying flowed easily – every movement precise, pain-free, perfect. I looked at my fellow students who also seemed to be tirelessly present. When I told them about it afterwards they surprised me – they hadn't felt the same at all and wished that they had. It was then that I understood the significance of the place's order, which included the laying of the table: it was all designed to allow for the possibility of glimpsing the usually hidden perfection of our everyday existence.

It was hard to leave after this experience but I was booked in to Anam Cara again, so headed northwards once more.

THIRTY-NINE

Rubha Phoil Forest Garden

Rubha Phoil Forest Garden, or the Rubh, as it is affectionately called by locals, is tucked away up a steep, stony track near the Armadale ferry terminal, Ardvasar, southern Skye. I had noticed a peninsula with two tiny offshore islands over which numerous sea birds flew, as the ferry headed towards the pier, but I had cycled straight past the Rubh's entrance on my way to the youth hostel after my return from Eigg the previous year. A traveller at the hostel had told me about the garden and one evening I strolled back to the pier to investigate. The track led up to a small wooden hut which appeared to be a shop. It was closed but in the window were many notices and press cuttings about permaculture, and articles about herbs, pots of which were arranged outside the shop. A large sign, with a huge mosquito emblazoned on it, proclaimed 'Herbal midge repellent for sale: 100% effective'.

I could use some of that right now, I had thought as I ascended another steep, wooded slope. At the track's edge were painted wooden signs, some almost illegible, faded by the weather, which described various herbs and their uses. Many of the herbs were hard to locate, hidden in the undergrowth. At the top of the slope the ground flattened out and I sat down on a wooden bench to rest and enjoy the rays of evening sunshine accompanied by a sudden absence of midges. There was a wooden house at the bottom of a driveway. I heard dogs barking and soon two ferocious-looking Alsatians bounded up, fortunately penned in by a gate. Then a dumpy-looking woman with long, greyish-white curly hair had come into view from the opposite direction, where another dwelling was half-hidden in the trees.

She stopped when she saw me, putting down many heavy-looking plastic bags by her car. 'Hi there! Enjoying the sunshine?' she greeted me, her greyish-blue eyes smiling inquisitively at me through her spectacles.

'Oh, yes. It's a lovely evening,' I'd said, intrigued as to whether or not she lived there.

'Have you been on our forest walk to see Seal Island?'

It was then that I had noticed a small sign pointing further along the track into the woods, 'Path to Seal Island. Take care! Boggy in wet weather'. 'No, I haven't yet. I've just got here,' I replied.

'It's a lovely walk and we have an otter and bird hide there,' she said. Her use of 'we' was a clue.

'So, do you live here?' I asked.

'Yes, well, sometimes,' she answered vaguely.

She had then proceeded to tell me that she owned the sixteen-acre peninsula and was struggling with the help of volunteers to run it on permaculture principles. She had a marvellous vision for the land, but voiced her frustration with some of the volunteers, who treated their stay there as a holiday, rather than a place of work.

I told her that I was a WWOOFer, on my way to Anam Cara, which she'd heard of. 'I'm not a WWOOF host,' she told me, 'but I do offer food and accommodation in return for work.' When I expressed an interest in volunteering she'd immediately invited me to stay, but I was booked in to Anam Cara, so I had taken her details, promising to contact her about coming the next year.

*

Here I was, back at the Rubh, on midsummer's day the following year, after doing the 'Time for Trees' at Anam Cara, followed by a short time in Edinburgh. Cycling was becoming too difficult so I took the bus to Skye. It was a day of wild weather: The Pass of Glencoe was stunningly forbidding in a gale force wind and misty rain. At Fort William the rain eased and I boarded the small bus to Mallaig, which traversed the scenic route west, with rushing waterfalls gushing down steep mountainsides, the peaks alternately buried in cloud or shining in the sun. The driver informed us that the Skye ferry was now running, after having been cancelled that morning due to the wind. I stood at the front of the ferry, watching the sun's silvery light on the sea over to the Point of Sleat, at the southernmost tip of the island, feeling excited about this new adventure. The mainland mountains were shrouded in cloud, while Skye shone in the late afternoon sun, seeming to beckon me onwards.

When I arrived at the top of the drive, there was no sign of a car so I found the wooden building, or workshop, hidden in the trees. There was nobody there, but Sandra, or Sandy as she liked to be called, had left a note on the table, 'I'm in Inverness today but my son Tim'll be there. Make yourself at home'. As there was no sign of Tim I took her advice and made myself some tea, observing that the place could do with a good clean. A friendly black and white cat jumped onto my knee as I sat drinking and began to purr loudly. It was a comforting sound as I was feeling somewhat lonesome. Afterwards I went in search of my caravan. It was hidden from view along an overgrown path which branched off of the Seal Island track. There were two caravans in a clearing, surrounded by trees. The first one had a notice on the door, 'Welcome to your abode, Margaret'. I went inside the tiny caravan and was relieved to see that a narrow bed had been made up with clean-smelling sheets and a warm quilt. Sandy had asked me to send her a list of foodstuffs I'd like, which I'd done, wondering how much to request – it seemed a lot. There was a small supply of food in a cupboard, a gas ring which worked and a sink with water – *what luxury!*

Back at the workshop there were signs of life. A tall, lean, fair-haired young man with bright blue eyes was busy cooking. 'Hi, you must be Tim,' I said when I saw him.

'No, I'm John,' he replied, with a soft Irish accent. 'Tim might appear later.'

'Oh, right. I'm Margaret by the way,' I explained. 'Do you know when Sandy'll be here?'

He laughed and said, 'Who knows?' with a shrug of his shoulders. 'Are you hungry?' he asked and when I said 'Yes', he invited me to share his meal.

'Are you sure?'

'Sure I'm sure. You can cook for me another time,' he said kindly.

While we ate his tasty vegetarian dinner, flavoured with the Rubh's herbs, I learned that he was studying for a degree in Herbal Medicine at Napier University, Edinburgh. 'I often come here to help Sandy with the herbs and garden in my holidays,' he said. He told me a little about Sandy and Tim. 'Sandy sometimes stays up the road with her boyfriend and Tim often disappears, especially when she's not here.'

It all seemed a bit disorganised but John was pleasant company. 'Don't worry, Margaret. I'm sure Sandy'll show up soon,' he said reassuringly. He also told me that my neighbour in the other caravan was a student at the Gaelic College called Brigitte. 'She's a wee bit shy, so don't be upset if she doesn't speak to you.'

After we'd eaten I returned to my caravan with some dry kindling from John to light the tiny pot-bellied stove. With a little coaxing it lit, and after belching out some smoke was soon burning fiercely, making me a bit concerned that the roof would ignite. It quickly became cosy and I unpacked my things and prepared for bed, dozing off to the fire's crackling.

I awoke at 4am with light shining through the thin curtains and the birds singing, but I soon slept again for another three hours. I made porridge and herbal tea in the caravan glad that the sun was shining through the branches of the trees. A compost toilet adjoined the workshop, with plentiful supplies of pungent sphagnum moss from the forest to absorb any unpleasant smells. There was no sign of life in the workshop, where John slept on a narrow couch in the corner, so I did the circular walk round the peninsula, which was indeed very boggy in parts. There were carved wooden seats at the various viewpoints. One looked out to Seal Island, where many grey seals could be seen basking in the sun or swimming in the sea, while next to it was Bird Island, on which numerous sea birds were nesting, their cries mingling with the seals' guttural calls, the waves pounding on the rocks and the breeze rustling through the trees. The air smelled freshly clean with the sea's salty tang as I sat contentedly gazing at the majestic mainland mountains.

Back at the workshop John was making himself porridge. 'Good morning, Margaret and how are you this fine morning?'

'Great! I've just done the Seal Island walk. What wonderful views there are all around.'

'Yes, it's a great place. How boggy was the path?'

'It was very boggy in places.'

'Right. I'll go along it and cover up the boggy bits with old carpets from here and bracken – there's loads of that. By the way, Sandy showed up at eleven last night.'

'Oh, was she looking for me?'

'Sort of. I told her you'd gone to bed and she went to stay at her boyfriend's. She said she'd be here at 10am.'

It was already way past that time so I returned to my caravan to read as the rain had begun. Sandy finally appeared at 2pm, shouting 'Hello' before poking her head round the door. When I told her I'd been waiting for her she said, 'I usually give new folk a couple of days to settle in because of the culture shock.'

'What do you mean, culture shock?'

'Well, you know – the caravan, the compost loo and all that,' she said, looking at me with surprise.

'Oh, right, I see what you mean, but I'm used to all that, being a WWOOFer.'

That having been said she sat down and told me about her life and how she'd come to buy the Rubh. She had run a successful soft toys business in Scarborough which she'd sold, purchasing the Rubh with the proceeds. 'I was drawn to this piece of land,' she said, her eyes sparkling. 'It has a certain magic which I can't escape, no matter how frustrated I become with the volunteers and their laziness.' I thought, but did not say, that if they were left to their own devices as I'd been, she only had herself to blame. We went to the workshop for some tea. 'Let's do a mind map,' she suggested, in between giving her son, Tim, instructions. He'd appeared as soon as she arrived, rubbing his eyes as if he'd just woken up. He was tall, with short, black hair and gave the impression of not being entirely present. His clothes were dirty and worn, his face unshaven and his manner nervous. There was obviously a lot of tension between him and his mother, based largely on the fact that he only worked when she was around. She told him to go and cover up the boggy bits of the path and he disappeared. John had gone to stay with friends on the mainland for a few days. The mind map was a strange exercise with Sandy giving me a confusing picture of what needed to be done around the place. Afterwards she showed me some specific jobs, such as clearing weeds and undergrowth in what she called 'The Polytunnel Area'. This was a flat piece of land in a clearing just down from the workshop where a polytunnel had once stood. Various herbs and vegetables were being grown there but the soil was poor and acidic with a profusion of slugs, snails and other beasties all intent on eating anything edible.

It was dinner time when she'd finished and we returned to the workshop. John had left some of his soup and there was bread, cake and other tit-bits which I put together for a meal. Sandy remarked, 'You eat a lot, Margaret,' eyeing the food-laden table.

'I only have three meals a day,' I responded.

'Three meals a day!' she said in a shocked voice.

'Well, yes. This is kind of normal, I think, for most people, especially if you get up early and work hard each day like I do,' I said defensively.

Despite her criticism she joined me at the table and proceeded to eat large quantities, especially of the cake. I noticed this throughout my stay: she would rarely cook anything herself but would always join in our meals as well as snacking in between, usually on sugary items. For someone who proclaimed that she lived on raw, healthy organic food, it didn't quite seem to fit.

The food supply was erratic but I made do using the local produce. It was the time to make nettle soup, when the tips were still young and tender so I made a big pot, along with an assortment of herbs, lentils and potatoes. It was delicious and nutritious, although Tim refused it: he lived on sausages and chips, when he ate at all. A couple called Sue and Steve rented the house where I'd seen the Alsatian dogs. Sue cleaned self-catering cottages in the area and often dropped off food which had been left when the cottages became vacant. This kept me from starving, along with the meagre supplies from Sandy. She seemed happy with my work, clearing and tidying various areas and potting up herbs for sale at the shop. Sandy also supplied the café at the ferry terminal with salad, which consisted of many different herbs: fennel, thyme, marjoram, oregano, rosemary, coriander, chives, sweet cicely, sage, spearmint, Moroccan mint and even chocolate and ginger mint! She also sprouted seeds: lentil, moong beans and sunflower amongst others, which were sprinkled on top of the herbs, along with nasturtium and marigold flowers. Preparing these salads took a long time: finding and picking the herbs, then deleafing them so that tough stalks were removed from the salad. It was a pleasant, sit down job which I enjoyed, as well as delivering the punnets to the café. I could imagine the customers eating this local produce, wondering what on earth their taste buds were encountering.

*

One Saturday afternoon I was walking along the Seal Island path when two large, shaggy grey and white dogs came bounding towards me. I am wary of dogs and stood still while they barked excitedly at me. A tall man came into view and called them to him, 'Here, you two!' The dogs obediently went and sat at his command, their long, pink tongues lolling out. 'I'm so sorry,' he said in an English accent. 'They're quite harmless and only being friendly.'

'Oh, that's OK. What kind of dogs are they?' I asked, keen to keep talking to this handsome man.

'They're bearded collies which were commonly used to herd sheep up here.'

'That's interesting. I've never seen them before.'

'No, they're not very common. Are you on holiday here?'

'Not really. I'm helping Sandra, who owns this land.'

His hazel eyes twinkled at me. 'I know Sandra a little. What do you find to do here?'

I explained about WWOOFing and my attempts to garden there.

'I wouldn't know where to start gardening here. It all looks pretty wild. I'm a gardener myself.'

'Do you work locally?' I was increasingly interested in this person.

'Yes, I'm in charge of a private garden at Ord which overlooks the beach. It's open to the public for a small entrance fee.'

I remembered that hot, sunny day the previous year when I'd changed behind the garden wall after swimming, with some embarrassment. 'Oh, yes, I know that place. In fact I sort of briefly met you last summer. I was cycling and went for a swim, it was so hot, then I changed behind your garden wall.'

A slow smile spread across his face as he remembered. 'Yes, I do remember that! I hope I didn't disturb you?'

Not really, but I'm feeling disturbed now. I learnt that his name was Tom and wondered how to prolong the conversation. 'There's a barbecue and ceilidh band at Tarkasvaig village hall tonight. Would you like to come, if you're free?'

Am I free! Naturally I accepted his invitation, but how to get there? He'd guessed my question. 'I'm going home now and could give you a lift,' he suggested.

'That'd be great, but I need to change my clothes.'

'That's fine. I'll be waiting down at the ferry car park.'

Excitedly I changed my clothes and quickly told Sandy about my encounter. 'Lucky you, Margaret! Tom's one of the most eligible bachelors around here, but he's very shy, I think.'

'Well, he can't be that shy to have invited me out so quickly,' I said.

Tom drove me to his home, which was a lovely cottage at the Ord Garden. He showed me around the beautifully kept lawns and flower borders – a quite different place from the wild Rubh. 'I'm planning to have a drink so my neighbours are going to drive us to Tarkasvaig,' he said. The barbecue was in full swing by the time we arrived and I tucked in to veggie burgers, washed down with cans of Guinness. There was an eclectic mix of people at the event, including some students from the Gaelic College. I practised my Spanish with a lovely lass from Venezuela, staying close to the barbecue as the smoke was keeping the midges at bay. The view from the hall was stunning, with the most stupendous sunset I've ever seen. Dark, dramatic purple-black clouds partly hid the spectacular jagged peaks of the Cuillins, the sky glowing red and orange as the light rays turned the sea silver around the distant islands of Rhum, Eigg and Muck. Most folk gathered to watch, drinks in hand, as the sun set slowly into the sea.

After it had set we went in to the packed hall, where some people were attempting to dance in the crowded space to the band's wild music. Tom was circulating for most of the evening, obviously well known in the community and I had little opportunity to chat with him. His neighbour gave me and some others a lift to the ferry terminal and as I left he promised, 'I'll see you soon.' He didn't.

I'd been at the Rubh for twelve days but had never managed to access the sea. There was a rather dirty beach near the ferry which did not appeal to me: I wanted to swim in the clear waters between the Rubh and the small islands offshore. The day before I was due to leave dawned bright and sunny so I made my way down a steep slope near the path, which came out onto a small, stony beach. The tide was high, which meant that I only had to scramble over some rocks and stones. It was still difficult as I had to squirm along on my bottom, being unable to balance in a standing position. Suddenly as I was painfully proceeding it was as if a cosmic shift occurred within me and, like the table laying experience, everything became easy: I seemed to glide gracefully across the rough terrain, seeing everything in precise detail, until I reached the sea and finally water deep enough to swim in. Oh, the joy of it! The sea was warm, the sky blue and I began swimming towards Seal Island, the gulls circling above me, shrieking in defence of their nests. A couple of seals swam a few metres away, checking me out. The current became quite strong so I swam back to the beach, managing to drag myself out, feeling refreshed and exhilarated.

*

I met many fascinating folk at the Rubh on subsequent visits, but one which sticks in my mind was a thirty-six-year-old handsome man called Peter. He was living in his camper van with Meg, his Staffordshire terrier, but used the kitchen to prepare his meals. Sandy was in a particularly manic state when he was there, ordering him to carve and paint many signs as he was artistic. Signs were one of her passions and there was a profusion of them around the place, describing herbs and their uses, or giving directions.

One hot, sunny day Peter confided, 'I'm going crazy with Sandy's instructions: she changes her mind constantly about what she wants. I'd leave right now but I'm worried about Meg – I think she might be pregnant and there's no space in the van for pups.'

'She doesn't look pregnant to me,' I said, examining Meg's belly closely.

'You don't know her like I do,' he replied, bending down to rub Meg's tum, which made her lie down on her back to be tickled. 'I've told Sandy,' he continued, 'and she says that I can do up the hut near my van, so I've begun to prepare it for Meg's family.'

Well, that's good, isn't it?' I said.

'In some ways but it also means that I'm stuck here, at least until I find homes for the pups.'

I still wasn't convinced about Meg's motherhood. 'Don't worry, maybe you're imagining it,' I said consolingly. I'd done my work for the day and the hot sunshine was beckoning me down to the sea to swim. 'I'm off now to change into my swimsuit,' I told him, disappearing into the house where I was staying that time.

Shortly after Peter knocked on the door and shouted, 'I'll go with you if you like. The tide's going out and I can help you over the rocks.'

My heart skipped a beat. 'OK,' I shouted back, 'that's very kind of you.'

We set off along the Seal Island track, Meg happily wandering, sniffing in the undergrowth, until we came to the gully. Peter went ahead of me, holding back branches and even clearing large stones off the path. Meg was behind us as we approached the narrow cleft through high rocks which came out upon the beach. 'Meg should be in front of us,' he'd just finished saying, when she suddenly rushed past me, knocking me off balance against the jagged rock with her bulk, and I fell down in a heap on the ground.

'Are you all right, Margaret?' Peter said, calling to Meg, who'd run out excitedly onto the shore.

I examined my elbow which was grazed, but apart from that I was unhurt. 'I'm OK,' I said as he hauled me up, insisting that I still wanted to swim. The tide was going out, but not too far, and he led me carefully across the rocks, holding my hand. *This is so romantic,* I thought, *if it wasn't for me being so old and disabled.* Nonetheless, it still felt good to be in the care of this charming male.

When we reached the sea I squirmed along on my backside until the water was deep enough to start swimming. Peter meanwhile was already swimming strongly towards Seal Island, while Meg stood on a high rock, barking worriedly as she watched her beloved master swimming away from her. He shouted back, 'Don't worry, Meg, I'm all right. I'll be back soon,' but she continued to bark frantically.

We swam and swam the sea was so warm, until Peter took pity on Meg and returned to where she was standing. I soon joined him, wondering how I was going to make it back to shore as the tide had gone out considerably. The high rock where Meg was waiting was at the end of a long piece of flattened rock, which ran along to the pebble beach. I had noticed it before, when I was alone, but had avoided it, it was so high.

Peter looked anxiously at me. 'Do you think you can make it up there?'

'No way!' I was filled with fear.

'It's the easiest way back. I'll be there holding you, don't worry, you'll be OK,' he assured me.

I didn't feel assured but concentrated totally as he helped me up onto the rock. I tried not to think about the height and focussed on our feet as we stepped carefully over cracks and uneven pieces. Adrenaline was pumping through me and somehow we reached the pebbles and then the grassy, flat part of the beach, where I collapsed in a relieved heap. Meg had been very well-behaved, keeping out of our way, no doubt chastened by her previous mad dash.

'I need to get back to feed Meg,' Peter told me.

'That's OK. I'll stay here and rest a while in the sun,' I replied.

I lay feeling the hot sun warm up my body, relaxing my tight muscles.

On my return Peter came to find me. 'I've decided to head out first thing tomorrow, Margaret. I can't stand being around Sandy any longer. Please don't tell her.'

I was upset at hearing this but understood why he wanted to leave. 'OK, I won't tell her and I wish you luck and hope that Meg's not about to become a mum.' With that he was off to prepare his van and pack.

Sandy was perplexed the following day when she realised that Peter's van had gone, but I didn't say anything. In the evening I went down to the pier and on my return, there was Peter's van, with Peter and Sandy standing outside it. 'Come and see,' Sandy gushed as I approached. I peered inside the van. Meg was lying contentedly in her bed, seven small heads sucking strongly on her teats.

'She had them in the van last night,' Peter said. 'Sandy's going to let me stay until I've found homes for them.' Sandy told me later that they'd had a chat and apologised to each other, which pleased me considerably.

*

The lens in my glasses had fallen out while working and the nearest place to get them fixed was Inverness, so I'd arranged a week's WWOOF near there at the Natural Vegetable Company. I was to return to the Rubh for three more weeks afterwards.

FORTY

The Natural Vegetable Company

There was what I would call 'real' work to be done at the Natural
Vegetable Company, Torbreck, near Inverness. It was a business,
growing organic produce to sell, and extremely hard work. At the
Rubh the only thing sold was the herb salad, a couple of times a week
at the most. Also the midges and showery conditions had resulted in
regular interruptions of work. There were no midges on the east coast
and the weather was more settled. If it did rain there was plenty to do
in the two large polytunnels.

My first priority in Inverness was a visit to Boots, where they
quickly fixed my glasses. My new host, Maggie, met me at the bus
station. She told me that she was thirty-nine, but looked ten years
younger, no doubt a result of her healthy diet and active life. She was
pretty and petite, with long, brown hair and a fresh complexion. She
had to leave her car at a garage where her husband, Neil, was waiting
with his vehicle. He had his own business building wooden eco-
houses and his office was at the entrance to their flat piece of land, at
the far end of which was their beautiful wooden house, which he had
designed and built. I learned that he had been involved in the building
of the Tufty at Anam Cara. As well as their two businesses they also
had three school-aged sons, a dog, chickens and three piglets to look
after. Needless to say, they were always busy and had little time to
socialise. My accommodation was a large caravan near the house and
polytunnels. It was well-equipped, with a toilet, fridge, cooker and TV
– the height of luxury! Maggie had stocked the fridge with milk,
cheese and yoghurt and there was a good supply of food in the
cupboard so that I could self-cater. That first evening I was invited to
dinner, where I got the chance to see the wonderfully airy open-plan
interior of the house. Maggie had made delicious ratatouille with
potatoes and salad, all her own produce.

I was expected to work five hours a day, although sometimes
Maggie said I could stop a bit earlier. I worked in the polytunnels,
tying up and removing side shoots from tomatoes and cucumbers,
planting out herbs, potting up celery, sowing lettuce and weeding.
Outside I raked over freshly rotivated beds, planted out lettuce, hoed

up potatoes and weeded. Twelve-year-old Ian often helped with the planting and other tasks, although he'd sometimes stop, complaining about the heat. Some days it was indeed very hot, especially in the polytunnels and I suffered from dehydration headaches, despite drinking a lot of water. I also helped Maggie bag up about six different varieties of lettuce: green, red, curly and straight-leaved, with no sign of slug damage. 'How do you manage to keep off the slugs?' I asked.

'I plough round the edge of the field,' she said. She also told me that she sold the mixed 115 gram bags (with lettuce, mizuna, rocket, dill, parsley, coriander, basil, chives, mustard and chervil) for 90p and they were sold on for £1.20. On the day these bags needed to be done she was up at 6.30am picking and then we both filled 150 bags, which took about four hours. There was no way she was going to become rich!

I had the weekend off and on Saturday managed to get a lift from Maggie's neighbours right to the swimming pool. Afterwards I explored the Ness Islands in the River Ness, which flows through Inverness. On the Sunday night, after a day of rest, I had a strange dream. I was in a castle surrounded by a deep, narrow steep-sided chasm full of icy water. A lovely lady with long, dark hair kept coming in and out of the castle gate. I had a wooden stick, but it was magic and tried to pull me into the water when I touched the water with it. Then the stick tapped both my belly and the lovely lady's and announced, 'Now you are both pregnant'. After this we went on a big protest march, somewhere in Turkey. There were many women wearing white, cotton head scarves, with horsemen astride black horses in front of them. The whole scene seemed strangely Sufi-like, and I wondered if it had any connection to the Beshara School.

My ten days at Torbreck soon passed and I went to stay with my sister in Fortrose for a few days' rest, as well as to celebrate my mum's ninety-sixth birthday.

FORTY-ONE

Skyelarks

The South Skye Feis (Festival) was happening on my return to the Rubh, with music concerts at the Gaelic College each night, a café in Ardvasar Village Hall and weekend ceilidhs at the college campus. The weather turned scorching hot, with temperatures of 28 degrees Celsius, and I swam and sunbathed in the afternoons after I'd finished work. Tom attended the Festival every night as he'd bought a block ticket and Sandy often accompanied me to events. At other times I got the last bus and Tom or his neighbours gave me a lift back. He liked to have a glass of wine while listening to the music and was always friendly, but not too friendly, much to my disappointment.

Sandy had friends who were WWOOF hosts. They had a croft, Skyelarks, at Waternish, north-west Skye and agreed to take me for a week. I fancied a change of scene and was waved off at the bus stop by Sandy, Tim, John and Brigitte, promising to return the next year. I took the bus to Skye's capital, Portree, and was met by my new host, Hilary, at the hospital where she worked part-time.

Like most WWOOFing hosts Hilary was immediately likeable and we chatted easily as she drove homewards. The weather had reverted to the usual showery conditions but it remained dry for a tour of the croft. Hilary and her husband, Ian, who worked full-time on the croft, had transformed its narrow strip of moorland into a verdant paradise by planting trees and bushes, including fast-growing willow and colourful fuchsia, which provided shelter from the wind. The land at the rear of the croft rose up to rolling hills and Ian had mown a strip of grass to make an easy path upwards through more willow and fir trees, where there was a profusion of wild flowers. We were accompanied by their old collie, Tess, who still enjoyed a good walk. I also met Wallace and Gromit, their two ginger cats, and the free-range chickens. They grew a lot of fruit and vegetables, especially in the polytunnels – even grapes! We picked raspberries for dinner and I met Ian back at the croft house where he'd been busy making vegetarian lasagne. They were a handsome couple in their late forties,

I guessed, although many WWOOF hosts looked younger as a result of their healthy lifestyle. After dinner Ian said, 'Don't disturb me until ten in the morning as I'm at my grumpiest then.'

Hilary took me to the bothy: a large hut in the garden, furnished for WWOOFers, with a futon bed, a TV, fridge, cooker and a paraffin stove, which was smelly but necessary as the bothy was damp and cold. I was expected to self-cater most days and had been provided with a plentiful food supply. 'Feel free to help yourself to vegetables,' Hilary said, adding, 'I'll supply you with fresh eggs as our hens are laying well just now.'

At ten the next morning I went to find Ian, feeling somewhat nervous, but he greeted me cheerily and showed me jobs to do in the polytunnel, as it was drizzling. I picked runner and French beans and harvested perfect carrots. 'They don't get the carrot root fly in the polytunnels,' Ian informed me. He had a wooden box where we stored the carrots, layered with dry sand, to prevent them from rotting. He called me for a tea break, which lasted forty-five minutes, we were so busy talking. The rain stopped so I picked blackcurrants and did some weeding of vegetable beds after lunch. This type of work, picking fruit and digging up vegetables, planting and weeding, continued all week. Ian commented, 'Sandy told me that you were a wizard at weeding and she was right!'

To escape the bothy's cold I sometimes sat in Ian's beautifully designed meditation room at the front of the croft. It had a large window with spectacular views across the sea and mountains to the Outer Hebridean Isles of North and South Uist, smudges of grey on the horizon.

On my final day Ian invited me to contribute a lasting piece of work to the croft. 'I always ask the WWOOFers if they'd like to do this,' he said.

'That's a lovely idea, Ian, but I'm not very artistic or crafty,' I said.

'Well, I've an idea. I'm making a path through the front garden and I'm about to make more cement slabs. There's a lot of stones from the beach in this bucket – maybe you could decorate the slabs with them?'

'Hmm – I think I might be capable of doing that,' I said. Ian got me organised with a chair so that I could comfortably place the stones in the wet cement, carefully knocking them into it with a flat piece of wood. There were some wonderful stones of all shapes and colours and I soon lost myself in the activity, finally stopping to admire my

211

designs.

Ian looked pleased. 'I think you've discovered a creative side to yourself,' he said, smiling broadly.

That last evening we dined on vegetable curry, raspberries and strawberries, washed down by glasses of red wine. It was great to socialise with this lovely, hard-working couple, but I had to retire early, to be rested for a long day of travelling by bus to Inverness and then on to Edinburgh.

FORTY-TWO

Back at Beshara

After a week in Edinburgh I returned to the Beshara School as a WWOOFer. It was August 21 and everyone was busy preparing for the Chisholme Gathering and Open Day, when members of the public were invited to see the place, free of charge. There were 140 people at the gathering and they all had to be fed. Three huge tents had been erected on the front lawn: one with long tables and chairs for dining; another for entertainment, with a stage, the groundsheet around it covered with oriental carpets and cushions, and one for an exhibition about the school's activities.

Julia's management of the garden, along with a wet and warm spring, had resulted in a bumper crop of fruit and vegetables. Much of my time was spent frantically picking beans, courgettes, herbs and salads, or digging up potatoes, carrots, beetroot and other vegetables. Luckily there were plenty of volunteers willing to work in the garden and kitchen. The meals were efficiently delivered from the kitchen and out to the tent by a small army of the more youthful members of the school, who also magicked away the mountains of dishes, all of which were washed and dried up by hand.

Many talented artists and musicians were connected to Chisholme and in the evenings I attended concerts in the entertainment tent. The Open Day dawned bright and sunny and Julia took groups of visitors on tours of the garden, while I manned a stall selling fresh produce, all of which was enthusiastically bought by the locals. They were also treated to cream teas, with delicious home-made scones and strawberry jam, as well as cakes.

Once all the excitement of the Gathering had subsided and the guests had reluctantly departed, Julia and I had time to talk. 'You know I love the garden, Margaret, but it's a lot of work and I badly need a rest.'

'Yes, it certainly is tiring,' I agreed. 'What about Walt? Couldn't he manage it?'

Julia sighed, 'He's planning to go off cycling and might be away for months.' She looked at me and said, 'Would you be interested in staying and doing it?'

I was immediately simultaneously daunted and excited by this challenge. 'I'm not sure that I could cope with it physically,' I admitted.

'But if you got plenty of help from WWOOFers and other volunteers you could do it, because you have the horticultural experience.'

'I'll think about it,' I told her and did just that for the next few days. Most of me wanted to be the Garden Manager but a small part of my subconscious was yearning to do the six-month course which began on October 1.

My friend Mary, who also loved the garden, was doing the course and I asked her advice. 'Listen to your heart, Margaret and wait for a sign. As for help, if you ask, it'll come. I'll be here and I'll come and work in the garden whenever we have work periods,' she assured me.

I asked Hakim for advice. 'If you really feel that you want to do it, we'll make sure that you get plenty of help.' With that reassurance I made my decision: *I would be the manager until the New Year.* This I did, apart from two weeks at Anam Cara's Autumn Workings with the wee trees, and occasional trips to Edinburgh to see my daughter and open my mail. The time passed quickly, the autumn work of harvesting and clearing becoming the winter's tasks of preparing the beds for the next season. Much of this work was extremely heavy, pushing barrow loads of leaf mould and dung onto the beds but there was no shortage of strong volunteers. These included Walt, who reappeared in November, announcing that he planned to stay until spring. This took a lot of pressure off of me and I was able to take some time off for much needed rest and relaxation.

It also meant that I could leave the garden in Walt's capable hands while I went on the students' two-week visit to Turkey in December. There were about thirty of us on the trip, which began and finished in Istanbul. We visited the tombs of saints and holy and historic sites of significance, such as Mary's House, near Ephesus. The highlight of the tour was a visit to Rumi's tomb in Konya, followed by attendance at the Sema, the Whirling Dervishes ceremony. This took place in the evening in a vast hall, like an amphitheatre, with tiered seats rising steeply up from a central stage.

Christmas and then New Year celebrations quickly followed our return from Turkey, after which I left for Edinburgh and then sunny Cyprus, returning in time for spring's seed sowing. I stayed for over two months, once more sucked into the garden's never ending work and the whole place's alluring ambience: it was like being welcomed back into the protective arms of a large and loving family.

However, my feet were soon itching again for the Highlands and I returned to Anam Cara and their wee trees for two weeks, after which on 14 June I was back on Skye for more work and fun at the Rubh.

FORTY-THREE

Macleod Organics

After six weeks at the Rubh I was off to a very different place, both in the type of work and location. From an unstructured, haphazard kind of existence in a stunningly beautiful mountainous setting by the warm western sea, I was thrown into the organised labour of Macleod Organics, *'Home of the Highlands original, and still the best, box delivery scheme'*, as their 2015 website proclaimed. Their situation is also by the sea, but it is instead the cold waters of the Moray Firth on the flat east coast, near Inverness airport at Ardersier.

I had been staying at my sister's in Fortrose, which is almost directly opposite Ardersier, across the Firth. Despite its closeness it took me three hours by bus, first delayed on the Kessock Bridge by an accident and then held up in the early evening rush out of Inverness on the airport bus. The farm is across the road from the bus stop, up a short drive to a large, modern house. I was met by Miho, a former Japanese WWOOFer, who told me, 'I came here to WWOOF a year ago and now I'm engaged to Donnie's son Stevie.' Donnie Macleod was the owner of the family farm.

'How romantic!' I exclaimed, thinking that she'd done well for herself.

'Yes, it is, isn't it?' she agreed, adding, 'he's my toy boy too. I'm forty-six years old and he's just thirty-five.'

I looked at her smooth, unlined face, framed by glossy, short, straight black hair. 'Well, you don't look it, Miho,' I said truthfully.

'I know. It's my Japanese youthful skin,' she agreed.

She showed me to my room which I was sharing with a young German WWOOFer called Eva. It was 5pm by that time and I was beginning to feel hungry, but there was no sign of anyone.

'I think they must be working in the fields,' Miho said, adding, 'let's go and find them.'

We walked some way across the flat land by the road until we saw two figures bent down working in the distance. As we came closer the man straightened up from the cabbages he'd been planting. 'Hi, you must be Margaret,' he said, wiping his muddy hands on his overalls and extending one, to give me a firm handshake. 'I'm Donnie,' he said, looking directly at me, obviously sizing me up. *So this is the famous Donnie,* I thought, impressed by his height and handsomeness, already aware of his charismatic charm. He'd delivered some organic lamb to my sister and had had a similar effect on her. She'd also told me that he was a Green political activist and had been involved in the demonstration against a GE crops trial on the Black Isle, near Fortrose. It had received much publicity and successfully resulted in the abandonment of the trial. He had also stood for the Green Party in the council elections.

The blonde girl next to him stopped planting and introduced herself: it was Eva, my room-mate. 'You can stop now, Eva,' said Donnie, 'you've done enough.' We walked back to the house, but Donnie remained, planting cabbages and weeding.

As we walked Eva said, 'I've been planting cabbages since 9am so I could do with a break.' I was horrified: *there's no way I could work that hard – I'd collapse!*

Miho must have read my thoughts. 'There's no rules here for WWOOFers. We have paid workers who work a full day, but you can decide how much to do.' I was relieved at this but nevertheless felt under pressure while I was there to work as hard as the others. Eva was a typical young German – strong and physically fit, she was happy to work long hours, which I was unable to do. This made me feel guilty and inadequate, which no doubt was my own problem because no-one criticised me.

Soon after our return to the house I saw Miho and Eva disappearing in a car. *Where were they going?* They'd said nothing to me and by that time I was ravenous. An inspection of the fridge was no help – it was empty except for a piece of mouldy cheese and some limp lettuce. My stomach rumbled. I found my usual standby when food is scarce – porridge oats, which took away the hunger pangs.

Donnie rented out some rooms in the spacious house and soon one of the occupants appeared. Her name was Judith and she worked at the airport. She was about my age and we immediately got on well. I asked her about the eating situation. 'They tend to eat late here, Margaret. Donnie's a workaholic and they all eat meat because it's produced on the farm and they like it.'

'I've looked in the fridge and it's empty so what can I eat?'

'It'll be empty because it's Friday. Tomorrow they go to the Farmers' Market in Inverness and they come back with loads of food they've bought, plus the leftovers of what they couldn't sell,' she told me.

'But what can I have now?'

'You can have some eggs. There's loads downstairs where they pack them. They're lovely organic ones,' she said.

Relieved that I wouldn't starve I made myself an omelette and toasted some bread which Judith had given me. Then, as I was washing up, Miho and Eva arrived. 'We've been to Nairn for a swim,' Eva said and asked if I'd eaten. She made herself a snack and then we retired to bed. Of Donnie there was no sign. *Maybe he was planting cabbages by the light of the moon?* I thought as I drifted off to sleep.

The next morning as I was preparing breakfast, he appeared, looking more attractive than ever, freshly showered, smelling divine and wearing brown corduroy trousers and a green checked shirt. 'We're off to the Farmers' Market soon, Margaret. You can come if you like but I've got enough helpers.' Feeling unwanted I said that I'd stay behind. 'OK, Stevie can show you how to pack eggs and feed the chickens,' he said. Of course somebody needed to do this, which was probably why he'd put me off going to the market.

Stevie was a younger, handsomer version of his dad and I willingly learnt how to pack the considerable backlog of eggs. It was a sit down job, easy on my back. Feeding the chickens was a more demanding task. There were hundreds of them, all squawking and desperate to get to the food which Stevie had piled high in a wheelbarrow. The chooks smelt disgusting and feathers and dust were everywhere as they fluttered around us, fighting to alight on the barrow: it was almost impossible to wade through the mass of their bodies. Stevie showed me all the places in their large enclosure where the food was deposited and as we progressed the chickens' harassment lessened as they began frantically pecking at the grain. Then we had to collect the eggs, some from inside the hen houses, but most were outside the large hen house inside closed-in boxes, which received the eggs as they were laid and rolled along a small conveyor belt. My hands were bad by this time with the stress of it all and I dropped an egg. Before it had even smashed on the ground a mob of hens were on it, gleefully scooping it up with their beaks. 'Oh, how disgusting!' I cried, horrified that they could eat their babies with such delight.

Stevie laughed, 'Yes, it is quite horrible,' he agreed. He then also departed for the market, leaving me by myself. I packed eggs and after lunch packed some more. Then it was time for the afternoon's feed. I was not looking forward to it. The full barrow was too heavy for me to push so I had to do it in two trips, which meant double the stress, the birds being as ravenously hungry as they'd been in the morning. I had to lie down briefly and rest my back in between the trips, finally collapsing on my bed, stinking of chickens, exhausted. Fortunately, this was the only day I had to suffer alone. Eva and I did it together each day after that and sometimes she volunteered to do the afternoon feed on her own. I concentrated on the egg packing and did some work in the polytunnels, removing side shoots and mouldy leaves from the tall, heavily laden tomato and cucumber plants. I also helped the paid workers assemble the veg boxes.

Donnie arrived back from the market laden with goodies, which filled the fridge and kitchen cupboards and then went to his granddaughter's third birthday party. Judith and I dined on the market treats, Eva having gone to see Loch Ness. Donnie came in later and fell asleep on the settee while watching TV.

On Sunday evening my host revealed his wondrous cooking skills. In less than one-and-a-half hours he single-handedly prepared dinner for seven people. He roasted a chicken (one less to feed); garnished a fresh salmon; prepared potatoes with redcurrants and cream cheese and cut up carrots and purple sprouting broccoli. This feast was followed by a cheeseboard of organic cheeses from the market, accompanied by cherries. He also provided red and white wine and we all sat down to dine around 9pm. There was Donnie at the head of the table, one of his girlfriends (he supposedly had three), Stevie, Miho, Judith, Eva and myself. It was a convivial gathering, our host showing no signs of fatigue after his marathon cook up, but afterwards as we watched a film in the lounge, he tried to find a space for his head in his girlfriend's lap, already occupied by her terrier, who was lying on her back with her legs in the air, snoring gently.

Once a week Donnie drove to Edinburgh to deliver organic produce, including eggs, to shops such as Real Foods, stayed the night with a girlfriend (rumour had it) and returned late the next day. Where this man who was my age got his energy from amazed me. Maybe it was the ingestion of all that healthy, nutritious food? Too bad it didn't have the same effect on me.

My ten-day stay at Macleod Organics was soon over and I headed
north by bus to Tain, near to where I'd arranged another WWOOF.

FORTY-FOUR

Lower Arboll Croft

It only took an hour to reach Tain from Inverness. My new WWOOF host, Fugo, was waiting at the bus stop. She was a fresh-faced, pleasant woman in her forties, with long, fair hair. 'We'll go straight to the croft, if that's OK with you?' I'd done all my errands, which included buying a wind up radio, in Inverness, so I agreed with her. We drove through a flat landscape with farmers' fields lining either side of the road. The croft was along a rough, narrow track, the wide expanse of the sea filling the eastern horizon, while to the north the Sutherland mountains were clearly visible.

As we drove into the croft's parking space an attractive black-haired, bearded man emerged from a wooden hut. 'This is my husband, Geoff,' said Fugo. I learned later that he ran a business, *Woodland Treasures,* and carved beautiful wooden jewellery and combs in his small workshop, which he sold online and at fairs and festivals. We went straight in to the two-storey croft house's homely kitchen, which smelled of home-made soup and freshly baked bread. *This is more like it,* I thought, remembering the initial lack of food at Macleod Organics and the Rubh. It was the school holidays and Robert, their long-haired seventeen-year-old son was already seated at the kitchen table, which was laden with tasty spreads, pickles, cheeses and a big bowl of fresh garden salad. Geoff served out steaming bowls of soup while we cut slices of the delicious seeded brown loaf. Later I discovered that Robert was a talented young man: not only was he an accomplished pianist, he had published a children's book aged eleven.

The Kings were an easy family to be around and I immediately felt at home. After I'd helped with clearing away and washing up the dishes, Fugo showed me to my caravan, which was a short distance from the house, through some trees in a small clearing. There was another caravan there. 'That's Tree Paul's van,' she told me and waited for a reaction. *The legendary Tree Paul!* I was thrilled.

'Is that *THE* Tree Paul that I heard about at Anam Cara?' I asked.

'Yes, I guess it would be. There's only one Tree Paul,' Fugo joked.

'Alastair told me about him when I was doing their *Time for Trees.*

He had supplied them with some seeds, mainly from hazelnuts, I think.'

'That sounds like him. He's off gathering cherries at the moment; he could show up here any time soon. He uses the croft as his base.' This was exciting news to me as I was already fascinated by this character, who wandered around the Highlands with the specific purpose of spreading and conserving native trees.

Fugo left me to make up the caravan's bed and to unpack my small rucksack. It was an old caravan and became cold at night, despite the August warmth, but there was a heater plus Fugo supplied me with a hot water bottle, which kept me cosy in bed, soothing my aching back.

There were no polytunnels or greenhouses on the croft but the weather stayed dry enabling me to weed, harvest vegetables, pot up house plants and clear some ground, as well as cooking dinner when Fugo was out working in other people's gardens. After dinner I often went down to the beach where there was a fast-flowing estuary. The tide went out for miles leaving a vast expanse of sand, huge vistas all around. I would sit on a grassy tussock gazing out to sea, listening to the gulls' cries, breathing in the fresh, salty sea air, content to simply be.

There was one restriction imposed by my hosts which annoyed me. I loved to have a shower at the end of my working day, both to wash off the sweat and grime and to soothe my aching muscles. On the second day after my shower Fugo said, 'Please can you only shower every third day, Margaret: we need to be careful with the water.' As their water came from the mains and there was no drought, I wondered at this. They also lived by the decree, 'If it's brown flush it down; if it's yellow let it mellow', which meant that the toilet smelt terrible. Fugo explained, 'It's a huge waste of drinking water to use it to flush the loo.' I agreed with this but, remembering how things were in New Zealand, I was astonished that they hadn't fixed up a rain water butt to flush their toilet with.

Tree Paul arrived a few days later after dark and finally surfaced late the next afternoon. Unusually, it was a rainy day and we were all sitting in the kitchen which was warm and cosy with the wood range burning brightly. He came in carrying a big bag of cherries, which he dumped on the table. 'Hi, folks! I come bearing cherries,' he announced in a strangely high feminine-sounding voice. I looked at him curiously. He was tall and slim, with long, thin, straight blonde hair and a finely-featured face. He immediately dominated the conversation with extravagant tales of his wanderings and I kept seeing him as a drag queen, with his elegant gestures and colourful hippyish clothes: a purplish-pink tie-dye T-shirt and a pair of baggy blue pantaloons. On his travels he resided in his large van, which he ran on used vegetable oil. He was a fascinating character and I enjoyed listening to his stories as we destoned the cherries, our fingers and lips scarlet with their sweetness. Fugo was going to make cherry jam, while the stones would be germinated and grown up to be cherry trees on the croft and elsewhere. Paul stayed for dinner, contributing a pizza which he'd found while skip diving, another intriguing activity which I'd never heard of, but which sounded like a great idea, especially when I drank and ate more of the goodies (including bottles of out-of-date beer) that he'd found. After dinner he said, 'I'm off to a ceilidh in Portmahomack tonight and I'll sleep there in my van.' And with that he was gone. *He's so wild and carefree,* I thought, wishing that I could live like that.

I told Fugo about Ian from Skyelarks idea of his WWOOFers leaving something more permanent on the croft. She responded by accompanying me to the beach to look for material with which to make a design. It was blazing hot but the sea was too shallow for swimming. We paddled, looking for interesting shells, stones, pieces of crab, broken crockery and glass. The beach was a veritable treasure trove and we arrived back at the croft with laden bags. We took them to the circular garden – a piece of grassy ground enclosed by a ridge of raised turf in a circle. Wild flower seeds had been scattered on the ridge and scarlet poppies, bright blue cornflowers, lacy-white cow parsley and other flowers bloomed in abundance. There was a wooden seat and Fugo suggested that I make a design in front of it. She cut away the turf and spread a thick layer of sand on the ground. 'Right, Margaret, I'll leave you to it,' she said, disappearing. I laid out the treasures on the grass and sat on the bench looking at them, waiting for inspiration. I knelt down in front of the sand and began carefully arranging the pieces in a design. The crab's empty shell and claws were pressed into the centre, above which I placed a glass bottle's brilliantly blue bottom; a helical design of colourful shells, stones, small pieces of crockery and differently coloured bits of glass surrounded it. I became totally engrossed until it was finished. I sat back admiring my handiwork and hoped that it would survive the elements.

On the last day, a Sunday, of my fortnight's stay I went with Fugo and Geoff to the Milton Community's Woodland Fair, near Invergordon. They had built a magnificent log cabin from large trees and also a huge log barn, both of which had turf roofs. I met Geoff's brother, Chris and his partner who gave storytelling sessions and puppet shows for the children. Another interesting character was a young man called Steve, who made a living conducting drum classes in schools. I joined in one of his drumming sessions and noticed that Tree Paul was also there, beating gustily on one of the African drums. He seemed to know everybody and was constantly circulating and chatting. He behaved like a youngster, but was probably more my age. There was a river meandering through the surrounding forest where boat and coracle rides were taking place. The air was filled with the sound of children's screams and laughter as they played in the water, some jumping into the deep pools in wetsuits.

It was a fine end to my stay. Fugo drove me to Tain the next morning where I took a bus to Inverness, then another to Edinburgh where I would stay for a week before returning to Chisholme.

*

'So you're back here again in September,' various people remarked, with knowing looks. The place was once again being prepared for the six-month course and we were encouraged to go to meditation sessions. I was too tired to rise for the morning ones but managed a few evenings. One evening as I was settling down on my cushion, slowing my breathing and attempting to empty my mind of thoughts, a strong man's voice pounded in my head, 'Do the course, do the course, do the course'. This command took me completely by surprise as I had no intention of doing the course. I became agitated and angry, arguing with the voice, 'I'm not going to do the course. I've got a month's holiday booked to Cuba in January and I'm going back to Anam Cara in October.' The voice was silent but my thoughts were not.

After dinner I went to visit David and Hiroko in their steading cottage. 'Of course you must obey the command,' David said, while Hiroko was less certain.

'Do what you feel inside,' was her advice. The trouble was that my feelings were in a state of confusion. The next day as I was working in the garden Hakim appeared to feed the bantams. 'May I speak with you?' I asked him and we sat down on a bench in the herb garden. I took a deep breath and told him about the voice. He didn't seem surprised.

'Did the voice say when you should do the course?'

'No, it didn't.'

'If you hear it again, ask who it is,' he advised. I never heard the voice again but I was relieved that I didn't feel I had to cancel all my plans and do the course that year. *I'll just wait and see how I feel next year,* I decided.

FORTY-FIVE

Cambo Snowdrops

It was difficult to find anywhere to WWOOF in the winter months, but there was a place in north-east Fife which had a snowdrop festival each February. The Cambo Estate was home to the National Snowdrop Collection and I was soon to discover the many different varieties of this herald of spring. I had arranged to stay for six weeks and was looking forward to this new experience.

I was met at St Andrews bus station by Carolina, one of the young Polish workers at Cambo, who chatted cheerfully in perfect English while she drove us through the fertile farmland of Fife, where lapwings were busily searching for worms in the ploughed fields. After about ten kilometres she turned into a driveway, where there was a lodge. It was a fine drive through mature woodland, where pearly-white clumps of snowdrops grew in abundance, until we came out of the trees and saw Cambo House, rising high from an expanse of lawn.

'Here we are,' announced Carolina.

'Wow! It's huge,' I said, taking in the massiveness of the three-storey, 19th-century building, with its many chimneys and distinctive clock tower at one end. I had thought that Chisholme was the most grandiose WWOOF residence that I would ever stay in (although my room had been in the Steading), but Cambo House was far more magnificent: and I would be dwelling inside it!

'Let me take your bag,' offered Carolina as she led the way through one of the entrances. I followed her down a long corridor, past many old paintings on the walls, a faded patterned carpet on the floor. She pushed open the door of the kitchen which led into another room with a splendid view of the garden through huge bay windows. Two female dogs – a black Labrador and a terrier, came to greet me, wagging their tails and barking.

'Down, girls!' commanded a man, who'd been sitting at a large wooden table, next to an Aga, which, along with the sun shining through the windows, made the room comfortably cosy. 'I'm Peter,' he said, shaking my hand firmly. *So this must be Sir Peter Erskine*, I thought. I'd never met a member of the aristocracy, but he seemed to fit my image of one, with his confident demeanour, his portly appearance and his tweed jacket. What didn't fit were his kind, grey eyes, blinking at me through his glasses, his bushy, crumb-spattered, greyish-white beard and his somewhat crumpled appearance.

Once our introductions were finished he ordered me to 'explore', which I duly did, after having been shown my room, which was near the kitchen, along another corridor. I needed to 'explore' – the place was a confusing maze of corridors and doors, some of which were open. The Erskines had five children, all of whom had left home, but who often returned for visits. One of their sons, who was a tree surgeon, was staying and I later discovered that he was cutting down an old yew tree: a useful occupation to have when your parents own a large estate. My small ground-floor room, with a view of the lawn and woods beyond, had been one of the children's. Like the others it was still stuffed with their old toys, belongings and pictures. As I wandered around, I found a huge room, again full of what looked like antiques: a grandfather clock, solemnly ticking; a stuffed red squirrel in a glass case; a stag's antlered head on the wall above the door, his glassy eyes glinting down on me. It was all a bit spooky and I gladly found a door into a conservatory, near the kitchen, which was full of exotic-looking flowering plants, then another exit to the garden.

There was much to explore outside too. The two-and-a-half-acre beautiful walled garden had a stream rushing through its centre, with greenhouses along one wall. It was all kept neat and tidy, as the whole estate was open to the public year round. I found a large garage at the front entrance, in which was a marquee, housing a café for the festival. Another Polish girl was working there, selling soup and filled rolls and snowdrop biscuits. Peter had told me to eat there, but usually we ate together in the room by the kitchen. Afterwards I walked through magical snowdrop woods by a rushing burn to the sea, where there were beaches on either side of the stream's mouth. The Fife Coastal Path passed through there, continuing alongside a golf course and then onwards to St Andrews.

Back in the house there was no sign of anyone, so I sat near the Aga reading the newspaper. Around 5pm, when the estate closed to the public, people re-appeared. Susan, a young WWOOFer from New Zealand and Struan, Peter and Catherine's son, plus his friend, Joe, all came in starving hungry and made themselves tea and toast. 'We're going for a curry in St Andrews,' Struan said, inviting Susan.

227

'Where's Catherine?' I asked, curious to meet my host.

'Oh, she'll be here soon. She's always working but you'll meet her later at dinner.'

Peter was out at a meeting so I had the opportunity to get to know Catherine over our meal. 'Is lasagne and fruit compote all right with you?' she queried, adding, 'I often ask the Polish girls to cook us something, especially when we're busy, like now with the festival on.'

'That's fine,' I said, taking in her short, straight grey hair, her bright eyes and her green sweatshirt and beige trousers. Her cultured accent marked her out as a 'Lady', which she had become on marrying Peter. We discovered similarities: she was the same age as me and had been born in the same place – Guildford, in Surrey; she also obviously shared my love of horticulture, although snowdrops were her passion. It felt strange to be sitting at a kitchen table chatting easily with 'The Lady of the Manor'. Peter and Catherine seemed to live very simply in their palatial abode, only occupying an en-suite bedroom near the kitchen. The other end of the house had been upgraded into luxurious bed and breakfast rooms, as well as self-catering accommodation. This, plus the running of the estate, the walled garden, gift shop, plant sales area, the snowdrop collection and festival, created a huge amount of work, which Catherine in particular did tirelessly – at least that was my impression during my short visit. She even had sufficient energy left to go Scottish folk dancing with Peter in the evening.

Although I wasn't actually told to work the same hours as the staff, the other WWOOFers did, which put pressure on me to do likewise, but I did get two days off in the middle of the week. The weekends were the busiest with over one thousand visitors per day if the weather was fine, which it was for most of my stay. The first day I was put to work in the outside plant sales area, under cover. It was cold and despite my warm clothes I suffered from a lot of back pain. Catherine was understanding and supplied me with a hot water bottle which I stuck down the back of my trousers to relieve the pain. I could sit down labelling plants and potting up endless pots of single and double snowdrops, placing a handful of moss around them for moisture retention. The time passed quickly joking and chatting with the other WWOOFers, Cambo's horticultural trainee and local women who were either part-time or full-time members of staff. I soon adjusted to the routine and enjoyed being part of a team. At the weekend I began to deal with customers, glad that I had some horticultural knowledge, but always called on Catherine or other staff members if I couldn't answer some tricky questions. Catherine also bought in other spring flowering plants, such as hellebores, polyanthus, daffodils and hyacinths and the display area needed to be constantly reorganised and replenished as the plants were sold.

On very cold days Catherine took pity on me and allowed me to work next to the Aga, folding up Cambo newsletters and maps, which visitors got when they paid their entrance money, as well as writing plant labels. A lovely young French WWOOFer called Samantha came and sometimes we worked together inside, giving me a chance to practise my French.

Before my day off I commented on the house's distance from the road, which would be difficult for me to walk in both directions. 'You may use our old Ford to drive to and from the gate – it's not taxed and shouldn't be a problem,' Catherine suggested. I was overcome by her kindness, especially as I hadn't driven for several years. However, it was not to be as they couldn't find the keys.

Susan was a competent driver and often ran errands for them. 'I'm going to St Andrews tomorrow so I can give you a lift,' she offered. Before we went I found time to visit the other attraction on the estate – the two enormous Tamworth pigs and their two-week-old adorable piglets. One lot were huddled inside their hut for warmth but the other group were out playing and foraging for food, while their mum watched protectively.

I had never been to St Andrews and explored the castle, cathedral and main street, with its historic buildings, breathing in the frosty air, glad of a work-free day. I managed the twenty-minute walk down the drive fairly easily. The next day Susan was on another errand, this time to the picturesque fishing village of Crail, in the opposite direction. Cambo was well placed on the coastal bus route and I visited most of the fishing towns and villages during my stay. In arty Pittenweem I found The Cocoa Tree, a shop and café with the yummiest hot chocolate I'd ever tasted, while in Anstruther I treated myself to fish and chips, the most delicious in the country. On my return from Crail I was given a lift in a butcher's van from the gate and after that I often managed to hitch rides with visitors.

An American woman arrived from the States to help with the festival. 'My name's June and I was Cambo's second horticultural trainee six years ago. I try to come at this time every year,' she told me. She was immediately likeable, in her forties with an easy-going charm, and we had some fun evenings together with Samantha, playing Scrabble and watching films.

When the festival finished the marquee café was taken down and the space used for another Cambo business – mailing snowdrops. Long wooden tables were set up and more workers appeared, including Czech lads who were also busy digging up snowdrops and bringing them in to be bunched up for the mail orders. The snowdrop plants were roughly counted into 25s, then 100s, 500s and 1000s, after which they were carefully wrapped up, mainly by Catherine, ready for the post. One afternoon seven of us worked on an order for 30,000 snowdrops!

One day Cambo hosted an event for Galanthophiles (snowdrop lovers and collectors: Galanthus is the Latin generic name) and we were invited to attend the snowdrop talks. There were three male speakers from different parts of Britain, and each one showed slides of different species of snowdrops. What Galanthophiles get most excited about are the marks on the petals. Normally there is a single U-shaped or V-shaped green mark at the open end of the inner petals, but sometimes other marks appear. At Cambo you can see many different varieties. There is a special children's snowdrop display, with 'Mr Grumpy' (two green 'eyes' and a down turned 'mouth') and 'Heffalump' (with two droopy petals, green 'eyes' and 'mouth'). There are single and double-petalled snowdrops and some have been bred to have distinctive green-patterned petals. Cambo also sells online in February and March, as do many other places. It can be a lucrative business, with a single specialist snowdrop bulb selling for £3-400. That afternoon we received some big sales from the Galanthophiles, which included expensive single specialist snowdrops. That evening we were again invited upstairs to a 'Snowdrop and Pig' poetry reading, accompanied by glasses of wine.

Catherine had a good idea during my stay, when she heard that I was an experienced EFL teacher. 'Would you like to teach some of our Eastern Europeans English, Margaret?' I hadn't taught for a while and welcomed the opportunity to get back into it.

'Yes, I would if it's possible to print and photocopy some materials,' I said.

'Of course you can. Just ask the office.'

I was given time off from the plants to prepare and teach the lessons, which happened in the early evening when they'd finished work. I used the guest dining room which had a long table and was even supplied with a flip chart. My first lesson was directly after Mother's Day so I cut out an article on it and made up some comprehension questions after which we discussed Mother's Day and how it was celebrated in our different countries. There were seven students: five Poles, one Czech and one Latvian and they were all motivated to learn and speak in English; it made a pleasant change from bundling up snowdrops. Later a young Japanese WWOOFer joined the group on her arrival.

After the snowdrop festival and the mail orders had been finished I stayed on for another three weeks to work in the delightful walled garden. The work was varied and included the usual weeding as well as seed sowing, potting up and planting out. Spring is always a busy time, as I knew from the Beshara School, and this public garden had to be kept especially tidy. I worked a full day, enjoying the banter in the tea breaks with the other gardeners. The only problem was the head gardener, who admitted that he found it difficult to relate to me. Someone had told him that I had MS and this made him nervous. He said some hurtful things to me – the first and only time that anyone I had been a WWOOFer for had criticised me. I was working extremely hard and doing my best so it was particularly upsetting. I told the assistant head gardener about it. He, by contrast, was an understanding, kind young man. 'Don't let him worry you, Margaret,' was his advice, but it wasn't easy and put me off returning there to work, which was a shame.

So, it was with mixed feelings that I said my goodbyes to everyone who had become close colleagues during my nine-week stay. I was off to another, very different WWOOF, also in Fife.

FORTY-SIX

Monimail Tower

Monimail Tower is all that remains of the once splendid Monimail Palace, residence of the Bishops of St Andrews, built in the fifteenth century. The tower, a category A listed building, was recently restored by the Monimail Tower Preservation Trust. The walled gardens around it are managed by a small, resident community, WWOOFers and local volunteers.

When I visited the residents lived in a Segal house, named after Walter Segal, an architect who had developed a simple system of self-build, timber frame housing. Adam, one of the residents, met me off the St Andrews bus at the village of Letham, with his mud-spattered car. He was an easy-going young man, tall, blonde and lean-looking. 'It's not far to our place,' he assured me. 'I usually cycle everywhere and only use the car when I have to. We try to live as sustainably as possible. We're vegans, is that all right with you?'

'Yes, that's fine. I'm mostly vegetarian but I don't mind being vegan,' I said.

'That's good. You might find that you feel healthier on our diet.'

'Do you grow most of your food?'

He grinned and shrugged his shoulders. 'We do our best but this time of year supplies are low. We're at the end of our stored root vegetables; onions and salads are only growing in the polytunnel. I'm glad you've come to sow and plant – it's a busy time of year.'

'Oh, I know from when I managed the walled garden at the Beshara School,' I said. Before I could continue we pulled into the parking area which was outside the garden walls, the three-storeyed tower rising in front of us, while on the other side was an old church and graveyard. I followed my new host through a gate in the stone wall and along a narrow path to the Segal house. He showed me to a comfortable room adjacent to the communal kitchen-cum-dining area.

'Our hot water comes from solar panels on the roof, so it's best to shower later on sunny days,' he explained. The kitchen was warm and full of tempting smells of freshly baked bread and home-made soup. A young woman with rosy cheeks was busily stirring a big pot of soup, while a baby girl sat in her high chair in the dining area playing with a plastic spoon.

'This is my wife, Louise,' said Adam.

'Hi, Margaret. Welcome to Monimail,' said Louise, smiling warmly. The child banged her spoon, wanting her lunch. 'That's Ruby making all that noise. We'll need to eat now.'

One-year-old Ruby watched delightedly as we gathered around the table. Adam began cutting slices of dark brown seeded bread. 'That looks tasty,' I commented, my mouth watering.

'Yes, it is. I make it myself,' he said.

'We take it in turns to cook,' added Louise, 'but Adam bakes most of the bread because he's so good at it.'

After lunch Adam showed me the garden which was about two acres, surrounded by woods and orchards. He gave me seeds to sow in trays as well as lettuces to plant out in the polytunnel. Afterwards I met the other community members: James, Elly and their four-month-old baby girl, Megan. They had just returned from visiting family in Lancashire. Elly had made a delicious vegan stir fry, with rice, beans and salad.

WWOOFers were only required to work four hours per day at Monimail but I often did more as there was so much to do. I spent a lot of time planting out a large area with red and white onions and shallots. Then there was more seed sowing and the constant weeding. Often Adam, Louise and Ruby would retire after dinner to their hut in the orchard where they would spend the night. The babies were both contented, fed on breast milk with real (not disposable) nappies. I tried to explore the tower but was unable to ascend the steep spiral stair. Some volunteers stayed there in warmer weather as although it had heating it was too expensive to heat up such a cold, damp environment.

One afternoon I went with Louise and Ruby in their car to another WWOOF place – The Pillars of Hercules near Falkland Palace, an intriguing name for a wonderful vegetarian café, shop and organic smallholding. Louise was meeting a friend, another young mum, in the café, so I went for a wander. It looked extremely well-organised with many polytunnels full of produce, as well as fields of brassicas and soft fruit. They had a large vegetable box delivery scheme and employed people in addition to volunteers, much like Mcleod Organics. I briefly met the owner, Bruce, who seemed quite a character.

Back at Monimail James had made spelt pancakes with vegetables in a peanut sauce – yummy. His parents were there for dinner, staying in a nearby B&B. I helped his mum with the dishes afterwards and managed to drop one of their big kettles, half full of boiling water on my foot. His mum acted fast, throwing cold water on my foot, then got me sitting with it in a bowl of cold water. Meanwhile James cut some leaves off of a large Aloe Vera plant growing on the kitchen window sill and placed them on the scalded area, which covered over half my foot. Everyone was most concerned but I slept well, having drunk two glasses of James's home-made blackcurrant wine at dinner.

In the morning there was a huge blister on my foot and everybody agreed that I should rest up for the day. I felt guilty about this but it would have been foolish to work as the blister could have burst. James, Elly and Megan went out for the day with his parents. In the afternoon Elly phoned – James had fallen and had broken his wrist, putting it out to save Megan, who was strapped to his front in a baby carrier. He was in Perth hospital and would be operated on the following day. There was no vegan food at the hospital so they all came back for some to take in to him.

The next day a lot of liquid had come out of the blister but the skin was still unbroken. I stayed in and cooked, steering clear of kettles and hot water. After two days I felt able to return to gardening with a waterproof dressing on my foot. James returned from hospital with plates in his wrist, looking worn and tired.

I had a day off and went on a tour of the Earthship: a self-sufficient house with grey water recycling and sewage treatment from the greenhouse's plants. It was fascinating and I hoped that one day in the not too distant future that most houses would be built like this.

After another day in the garden my foot began to feel very sore. In the morning Adam drove me to the doctor in Auchtermuchty. She examined it and said, 'It's slightly infected. I'll prescribe you antibiotics and a dry iodine spray.' I also bought proper burn plasters. My foot slowly healed with this treatment, although it left a scar.

Ten days after my arrival at Monimail I was off again, back to Edinburgh for a month's break from WWOOFing.

FORTY-SEVEN

Rosie's Garden

After some enjoyable island hopping to Gigha, then Islay and Jura, I sailed from Oban to Mull where I was to WWOOF for a fortnight. The ferry to Craignure on Mull took just forty-five minutes, sailing past the imposing Duart Castle, perched on a promontory, the mainland mountains a splendid backdrop. The bus to Fionnphort met the ferry and filled up with many tourists, mostly heading to the small isle of Iona, a short crossing from there. The twisting, single-track road had not been built for all the traffic and the bus had to stop continuously in the passing places, the driver cursing at the tourists' slow driving. The road wound its way through high mountains, where eagles soared and deer roamed, until it reached the flatness of the Ross of Mull, studded with lochs and sea inlets.

Nigel, my new WWOOF host, was waiting for me in the car park at Fionnphort. I was easy to spot, being the only person not heading towards the Iona ferry. He came towards me, extending his hand, his blue eyes smiling. Not for the first time I wondered at how many WWOOF hosts were good-looking, no doubt a result of healthy living. 'Hop in,' he said, flinging open the car door and taking my backpack. 'We live ten minutes back down the road near the small hamlet of Kintra,' he continued, asking me about my journey that day. He was a builder: it was his wife, Rosie, who mainly ran the croft and garden, although he often helped with the heavier tasks.

I'd arrived at teatime and was treated to a tasty meal. 'Everything's from our croft,' Rosie told me proudly as I praised the delicious vegetables, salad and omelette. She was a petite, attractive woman, reminding me of Barbara, in the *Good Life,* while tall, handsome Nigel made a great Tom. After I'd eaten she showed me my caravan which was behind the small shop opposite the house. It had fine views of the croft's craggy hills, where Jacob sheep grazed, with the Isle of Ulva visible in the distance, when it wasn't shrouded in mist. Rosie and Nigel's place was in a sheltered valley which seemed to be blessed with sunshine, while Ulva received the rain.

My favourite type of WWOOF was one where there was a good

balance of varied work, stimulating company, tasty food and interesting social outings and events: Rosie and Nigel's well run place offered all of these. Rosie was an astute person and on my second day asked, 'What's wrong with you, Margaret?' I suppose it was a give-away as I was lying on the grass doing back stretching exercises after a couple of hours work.

I don't like to mention my health problems but was forced to admit that I had multiple sclerosis and osteoarthritis. 'Is this a problem for you?' I asked, still feeling upset after my experience at Cambo with the Head Gardener.

'No, no. I was just interested, that's all,' she reassured me and regularly praised my work. I weeded, cut hedges, took side shoots and dead leaves off of the tomato plants in the polytunnel, tidied up the strawberries and processed them for eating and jam making, planted out leeks and other vegetables, picked peas, beans, blackcurrants and other soft fruit. There was also work to do in the shop, preparing mixed leaf salad and herb bags, punnets of strawberries and replenishing the supply of other fruit and vegetables.

Emma, their daughter, came to stay for a couple of days and told us about the deep sea diving course she was attending. A couple of young American girls came to WWOOF and we had a welcome meal with wine in the house. Whenever a new person came or left there was a communal dinner; the rest of the time we prepared our own meals in our caravans, using fresh produce from the croft and staples such as milk, bread and rice which Rosie supplied.

On my first day off I investigated their home-built meditation space, with large stones from the beach for walls and an upturned rowing boat for a roof. I had to bend low to get inside, where there was a small statue of the Buddha, candles and incense holders. It was a little too uncomfortable and damp for me to settle down and meditate; I preferred sitting on a grassy tussock, high above the sea which crashed on the rocks below. From the croft there were marvellous views of the small islands of Staffa, the Treshnish Isles, Lunga and the Dutchman's Cap, with the thin, grey line of Coll and Tiree in the distance, over which the sunset on clear evenings was a constantly changing shift of colourful hues.

Nigel had just finished building a super luxury self-catering cottage, which sleeps ten, at the croft entrance and he said that I could look around. It was beautiful, bathed in light from the large windows and economically warmed through heat exchange from the air. I explored the tiny hamlet of Kintra, its ten stone houses, only four of which were permanently occupied, clustered round a small, sandy bay, with a stony island offshore from the rugged coastline.

My hosts were both active in the community and one evening took us to a concert, part of the Mendelssohn on Mull week, an annual event which takes place at various venues on Mull, as well as a final concert in Oban. Mendelssohn's famous Hebrides Overture, inspired by a visit to Fingal's Cave on Staffa, is the reason for this festival. Rosie and Nigel were in the local Gaelic choir which were performing in Tobermory. The Americans and I worked in the morning then after lunch Nigel and Rosie, resplendent in tartan kilt and skirt respectively, drove us there. It was nearly a two-hour drive to the north of the island, along narrow, twisting roads, but it was a fine day and the summit of Ben More, the highest mountain on Mull, could be clearly seen. Tobermory was extremely busy as that morning Princess Anne had opened the harbour's new information centre. There was also a raft race to watch at the harbour, teams of children competing with various degrees of competence and hilarious results.

Suddenly, late in the afternoon, a violent storm blew up, and we sheltered underneath an awning outside the Arts Centre, eating Cornettoes, watching as the rain smashed down with heavy fury. After about an hour it eased and we went to the outside concert stage, which was set up by the harbour. It was deserted so we headed to the pub, where everyone was still sheltering, drinking, eating and socialising. We were about to order when we saw that the Gaelic Choir had assembled on the stage. We rushed out to listen, our hosts standing tall and proud with the group, who sang haunting melodies, ending with a more upbeat one, to get us in the mood for the headliners: The Red Hot Chilli Pipers. We managed to consume fish and chips, washed down by Tobermory beers, then returned to the stage, where the eight-piece pipers were busily tuning up their bagpipes, accompanied by drums and a piano. They were dramatically dressed in black kilts and tops, with maroon sporrans and pipe bags. The fabulous music, which had us all tapping our feet and dancing, was played in a spectacular atmosphere of coloured smoke and bright, flashing lights. We left at midnight, coming down from our highs, gazing at the shadowy mountains and silvery loch reflections in the twilight, while deer peacefully grazed and owls went about their nightly business.

The week after this outing it was the ceilidh in Bunessan's village hall, where there was a prize giving for the winners of the round Mull yacht race. Rosie was busy cooking vegetable curries, preparing mounds of salads and baking cakes for this occasion and we went along to help and join in the dancing and drinking. We just managed to get some of Rosie's food before it was devoured by all the hungry yachtsmen. A handsome one in his thirties began chatting to me near the end. 'I'm part of the winning yacht crew,' he told me. 'We race to Oban tomorrow at half past eight so we'll need to head for bed after the prize giving.' This was rather disappointing as I was hoping for a dance, but as he'd predicted the hall emptied directly after the prizes had been awarded and we were left with all the tidying up to do.

The following day, Sunday, was the Wimbledon tennis men's final and Nigel invited me to watch it on the self-catering cottage's large flat screen TV. It was an exciting match between Nadal and Federer, which went on for hours as rain kept stopping play, but eventually Nadal won.

My last day dawned hot and sunny and Rosie gave me the afternoon off to swim at the small cove down from the croft. The place was deserted and I skinny dipped, feeling the calm, warm sea water caressing my body with its smooth, silky touch. It was heavenly and as I floated looking up at the blue sky I wished that I could stay suspended like that for ever. Directly after swimming in the sea all my aches and pains disappeared, no doubt soothed by the salty water.

On my return I helped Rosie prepare vegetables for my farewell meal. I would miss this WWOOF but booked my stay for the same time the following year, to enjoy the Mendelssohn, the ceilidh and the sunshine, not to mention the strawberries.

Epilogue

I was back at Beshara on 1 October, 2008, ready to start the six-month course. The command, 'Do the course', had never been far from my thoughts the whole year and I had committed myself to do it several months earlier. There were eleven of us initially but then three dropped out, leaving a mixture of English, Scottish, Israeli, Turkish, German and Indonesian students, which made for some fascinating interactions and discussions. We soon settled into the routine of two study days followed by two work days, rising for meditation at 6.30. We did all the work: table laying and clearing away; dish washing and drying; helping the chefs with cooking and the housekeeper with housework. The garden had been neglected and I was regularly sent there to work, showing whoever was with me what to do. This was a challenge as its upkeep threatened to become more important to me than the course itself. Each of us faced our own demons as the months went by and we struggled to grasp the meaning behind the various study texts, which ranged from the twelfth century Sufi mystic Ibn 'Arabi's deep writings, to the Hindu's Bhagavad Gita, Rumi's mystical poetry, the Chinese philosophy of the Tao and Christian scriptures.

My experience of the Turkish trip as a component of the course was very different to when I simply had accompanied the students. We were in our own special bubble, moving as one entity from one place to another while simultaneously having our own private feelings at each holy tomb and historical site. When we saw the Whirling Dervishes in Konya we were right down in the front row, directly behind the journalists and photographers, who were there to also record President Tayyip Erdoğan's speech made prior to the ceremony. The dervishes were so close we could smell their scent and feel the heat emanating from their bodies as they twirled past us, their tall-hatted heads inclined, their hands raised and their feet moving closely in intricate circles. It was an incredible experience to be so near them, unlike on my first visit when I'd elected to stay at the top of the vast stadium's seats, afraid that I'd fall if I'd attempted to climb down the steep, rail-less steps between the rows. On the course my fear had evaporated and my fellow students supported me as I slowly descended.

On another occasion we were visiting some ruins where there was a huge Roman amphitheatre with worn, uneven, steep stone steps ascending up to a temple complex at the top. Unlike on my previous visit, when I'd stayed fearfully at the bottom, I suddenly heard a voice (*the* voice?) saying, '*Go on your hands'*. With that command all fear left me and I placed my hands on the warm stone step in front of me and easily passed up to the top, where the group hugged me, amazed at what had happened.

Near the end of the course we went through six weeks of saying 'Allah' after our evening Zikr. A member of the group would be chosen by our supervisors to lead the chanting, counting the number of times on a tesbih (prayer beads). The number of repetitions increased over the period: 1000 for week 1, then 3000, 5000, 10,000, 15,000 and 20,000, which took around two-and-a-half-hours, with us retiring to bed about one and still rising for meditation at 6.30. This procedure was supposed to energise us but I needed extra rest in the afternoons, which I was given because of my health. The group experienced all kinds of upheavals but we finished on a high, feeling united. Sometimes I felt that I was flying back to the Steading after saying His name so many times, the stars often bright in the frosty air, the moon a big, radiant ball. After the 20,000 there was one night of 21,000 chants, led by Hakim in the Mead Hall and attended by many members of the community. This was very special and I managed to sit up straight on my cushion without pain or cramps, feeling wonderful energy flowing through me with each 'Allah'.

There was a huge open buffet to mark the end of the course after which some of the group immediately departed for home. I had no desire to leave and stayed on to work in the garden for a few days before returning to my daughter's flat in Edinburgh. After two weeks I began to roam once more, going to the Rubh, then Iona followed by another two weeks at Rosie's on Mull, trips to the Isles of Tiree and Coll, more wee trees at Anam Cara then three weeks with my son in Canada. Finally, on 31 October, 2009, I went to live in my home in Edinburgh. My life as a WWOOFer was at an end: I could no longer cope physically with the work and began to adjust to a sedentary lifestyle, helped by an inner strength which the six-month course had provided. It was time to hang up my boots and pick up my pen.

Acknowledgements

This book could not have been written without the existence of the WWOOF organisation, both in New Zealand and in the United Kingdom. I would like to thank all my wonderful hosts for both their kindness and patience, as well as the other WWOOFers who I met. Lastly, many thanks to my sister for her assistance with editing.

CPSIA information can be obtained
at www.ICGtesting.com
Printed in the USA
LVOW05s2129030616

491128LV00029B/838/P